Retirement
Preparation

Retirement Preparation

**What Retirement Specialists
Need to Know**

Edited by
Helen Dennis
University of Southern California

LexingtonBooks
D.C. Heath and Company
Lexington, Massachusetts
Toronto

Library of Congress Cataloging in Publication Data

Main entry under title:
    Retirement preparation.

    1. Retirement—United States—Planning—Addresses, essays, lectures.
2. Retirement—Planning—Addresses, essays, lectures. I. Dennis, Helen.
HQ1064.U5R43   1984   646.7'9   83–48130
ISBN 0–669–06949–3

Published simultaneously in Canada

Printed in the United States of America on acid-free paper

International Standard Book Number: 0–669–06949–3

Library of Congress Catalog Card Number: 83–48130

*Dedicated to
my parents,
Hedy and Eric Gutman*

Contents

Tables

Preface

In recent years, preparing for retirement has gained attention among professionals involved in aging, retirement services, and the media. Many books and articles have been published for the preretiree—how to plan, save, invest, relocate, and stay healthy. However, little has been written for those providing planning, educational, or counseling services to the millions of Americans who are contemplating retirement.

The purpose of this book is to provide up-to-date information for professionals and students on subjects that are typically part of a preretirement-planning program and on topics that are less traditional—those reflecting economic and social changes in society that affect retirement decisions and experiences.

Although the current trend toward early retirement is still prevalent, there is speculation that employees may extend their work life. In an increasingly complex society, two recent developments stand out as having major impact on retirement decisions. The first is legislation. The U.S. Congress has enacted laws that have raised the mandatory retirement age to 70 years; have made age discrimination in employment, promotion, and termination illegal for 40- to 70-year-olds; and have increased the future age to collect full Social Security benefits. Consequently, workers have more choices and incentives to remain in the labor force. The second factor is the economy. Many preretirees and retirees express concern about their retirement incomes, particularly in an inflationary economy. Postponing retirement or working part time are options that retirees may consider to maintain or increase their income. Therefore, retirement specialists may have to take a broader view of the field. It is likely that they will no longer be dealing with a homogeneous group of preretirees that defines retirement as a permanent exit from the labor force.

Many topics for this book were selected in response to these changing social and economic conditions in U.S. society. Numerous inquiries from retirement planners and informal discussions with an advisory board provided additional guidance for the content development.

The impetus for this book originated when David Peterson, director of the Leonard Davis School of Gerontology, Ethel Percy Andrus Gerontology Center, University of Southern California, and I were developing a course on retirement planning for the school. After an exhaustive review of the literature, we concluded that no specific text was available for the course.

Consequently, I asked Andrus Center faculty and staff, and others from the broad academic and professional community, to write papers on selected subjects that would be useful to professionals and students in retirement planning. The first collection of papers was completed in 1981; a revised edition was completed in 1982. During this time, the collection, called a manual, was used as a text for retirement-planning classes at the school. After receiving several hundred requests, it occurred to me that the manual might have a broader professional appeal. Lexington Books agreed.

In 1983 new topics were added to the collection, and all papers have been revised and updated. The end result is *Retirement Preparation: What Retirement Specialists Need to Know*. It is my hope that this book will serve your professional interests.

Each chapter has been written especially for the practicing retirement specialist. Selected research findings and information have been tailored to the current and anticipated needs of retirement planners, particularly those who are designing, facilitating, and teaching retirement preparation programs.

Organization and Content

The chapters are organized into seven areas. The first provides a broad *background to aging.* Chapter 1 describes normal changes with age and the characteristics of older persons who are satisfied with life. Chapter 2 focuses on selected characteristics of the aging in the United States and includes current data and trends on health, life expectancy, income, employment, and marital status.

The second area emphasizes *selected content* for retirement preparation programs. Chapter 3 presents a proactive approach to health and wellness in the later years. Chapter 4 describes concepts and principles that are applicable to preretirees' financial plans and decisions. Sources of income of retired persons are described in chapter 5. The last chapter in this section, chapter 6, delineates various work schedules that middle-aged and older adults may choose as an alternative to full retirement.

The third area focuses on the *educational process.* Chapter 7 presents effective teaching styles for adult learners, while chapter 8 describes strategies to demonstrate program effectiveness.

The fourth area relates to the *psychological and social aspects of retirement.* An inventory designed to assist adults to assess and plan for later life is described in chapter 9. Chapter 10, on preretirement counseling, differentiates preretirement counseling from preretirement planning. Chapter 11 focuses on the purpose, process, and content of the leisure-counseling technique.

The fifth area is devoted to *special groups.* Chapters 12 and 13 describe the particular retirement issues for minorities and women respectively, with recommendations for programming and planning. Chapter 14, the last chapter in this section, summarizes the family response to retirement with a thorough review of the literature.

The sixth area describes *resources* available to those interested in the field. Chapter 15 recommends and describes audiovisuals for retirement programs. Chapter 16 presents an extensive annotated listing of books, organizations, and informal networks.

The last chapter, chapter 17, focuses on the *future* of the field, emphasizing needs and issues and the prospects of an expanded role for the retirement specialist.

The information in this book has multiple uses. It can be used by retirement specialists in the development, implementation, and evaluation of their programs and services. It also can be used by instructors as an auxiliary text for teaching preretirement to professionals and students. On a programmatic level, the book may serve as a basis for innovative program design and designation of emphasis areas and as a guide to the selection of resources. Finally, the contents may be useful to human-resource specialists to increase their awareness of new roles, techniques, and ideas regarding their middle-aged and older employees.

The retirement specialist will play an increasingly important role in the retirement plans and decisions of middle-aged persons. I hope that portions of this book will enhance the specialist's knowledge and skills, which will increase the availability and effectiveness of retirement services for adults confronting their future.

Acknowledgments

Appreciation is extended to Valerie Remnet, associate director of the Leonard Davis School, Andrus Gerontology Center, and David A. Peterson, director of the Leonard Davis School, for their support and encouragement in the development of this book.

A special thank-you goes to Eleanor Hudson for typing the manuscript, to Tally Mintie for her assistance in preparing the text, and to Barbara Strange.

Very little can be achieved without family support. Thank you, Lloyd, Laurie, and Susan.

Helen Dennis
Andrus Gerontology Center
University of Southern California
Los Angeles

1 The Aging Process

James E. Birren

Retirement and Aging

To gain the most from preretirement counseling, one must have a perspective on the processes of aging. As we move toward the end of this century, more mature adults are seeking ways to take best advantage of longer life and retirement. There are currently about as many retired persons in the United States as there are people in all of Canada. The fact of large numbers of older persons plus a much longer average life expectancy makes retirement one of the dominant issues of the twentieth century.

Prior to this century, retirement was rare. With the exception of a few wealthy persons, most persons did not retire. In 1900, the average life expectancy was only about 47 years, and the average family would dissolve if one of the spouses died before the last child left home. In the early part of this century, the average couple could expect to have no married life together after the last child left home. Today they may look foward to about fifteen years of life together after retirement because of the technological society of the twentieth century, which has resulted in longer life expectancies and, thus, the opportunity of retirement.

Of course, many older persons find themselves in unfortunate circumstances such as poor health, lack of money, inadequate housing, and few friends or family. Such persons are not the majority, and research and services are being organized to help them. This chapter is more oriented to those who are in a position to help themselves to direct their lives but for whom a poor image of aging may have developed.

Research indicates that it is not bad to grow old in the United States (Birren and Renner 1980). It is bad to be poor, to be lonely, and to be in poor health. Surveys (Guttmann et al. 1977; Harris and Associates 1975) show us that given modest or adequate money, reasonably good health, and the opportunities for contacts with other people, most persons in their later years enjoy life. In fact, most of them find it so good that they would not want to relive their earlier years.

The later years provide an opportunity for many persons to experiment with new things. Traditionally, we have regarded young adults as the experimenters with life. Now we find, in the last quarter of the twentieth century, a new group of experimenters with life. They have the opportunity of redefining their lives so they get maximum opportunity for doing things in which they are most interested and from which they take greater satisfaction.

1

Recent research of a large longitudinal project in Germany reports similar findings to those studies in the United States (Thomae 1976). The principal point is that with advanced age one's life satisfaction can continue to increase and be higher than it was at middle age or before retirement.

Health

The average life span in the United States has risen from 47 to about 74 years in the twentieth century. Much of this increase has been a result of the reduction in infectious diseases. Infections in early life may induce disabilities that last over many decades. There has been an extension of adult vigor far into what previously would have been regarded as old age. Disability and chronic disease now often are compressed into a short period of time near the end of the life (Fries 1980).

Various vital organ systems may change with age, which reduces their maximum functioning capacity. However, a gradual reduction in the functioning capacity of selected vital organs does not necessarily translate into a progressive loss of ability to exercise self-reliance and to function effectively. Thus, an accelerating mortality curve for the population cannot be translated into a direct consequence in terms of an individual's prospect of living effectively and enjoyably in the later years.

What is emerging is a concept of a natural death with declining function limited to a short period of time in the upper age range. That period of terminal decline is unrelated to the effectiveness of the individual in months and years prior. One man, for example, retired from a job at the age of 60 and then managed several farms until he was 102. His period of decline leading to a natural death occurred at 104. Similarly, a 102-year-old woman traveled about alone, often on curiosity excursions, using the public transportation system in Los Angeles. Her period of terminal decline was but a few months when she also died at 104.

The consequence of assuming that dwindling health is a necessary result of aging is that one expects less from life than it may offer and restricts the opportunities for effective living and enjoyment.

Intelligence

Along with health, one of the commonly assumed changes with age is a progressive decline in intelligence. Longitudinal research by Schaie et al. (1973) has clearly shown that there may be little or no change in intelligence in healthy adults over the usual working life and beyond. Particularly in verbal intelligence, the ability to store and use information seems not to be impaired with advancing age.

There is a tendency toward a slowing in processing information with advancing age. While the long-term storage of information may change little in the normal aged, the scanning of that information and utilizing it in new constructs may be slower but need not cause the individual to be less effective in daily living.

One of the interesting facets of the intellect that has been studied in relation to age has been creativity, the ability to form new concepts and to engage in divergent thinking. Convergent thinking reflects the desire to come up with only one solution to a problem as though every question had only one correct answer. Divergent thinking requires the individual to generate many alternatives. Studies of schoolteachers over the employed age range by Alpaugh and Birren (1977) suggest that while we do not lose intellectual functions as we age, we use those functions in a less creative way. One prospect is that the weight of years of experience causes us to be less playful in thought and less willing to consider alternatives. This, of course, is precisely the problem facing those about to retire. A divergent set of mind must be developed in which one generates and considers many alternatives.

Conformity

Previously we alluded to the notion that, with age, we may become less inclined to use our basic intellectual ability in a creative manner, to engage in divergent thinking. Another tendency is for mature adults to be more socially conforming. The research of Klein (1972), for example, indicated that older adults are more willing than young adults to conform to a group opinion even when that opinion is wrong. His research clearly showed that older adults could make the correct judgments when alone but that when presented with evidence that other people had voted to the contrary, they tended to conform to the group opinion. They did not trust their own judgment. Aside from this dynamic aspect of the tendency to become more conforming and to use one's creative abilities less, personality characteristics, for the most part, are shown to be remarkably stable over the life span.

Implications for Retirement Specialists

The facts show us that a large number of older persons exist whose current position in life in retirement is better than it had been at earlier ages. Furthermore, the research suggests that those who are getting most out of their living have enough but not necessarily a great deal of money, adequate but not luxurious housing, adequate but not necessarily excellent health, and comfortable familiar surroundings. It would thus appear that one needs enough of the necessities of life but that more does not bring about a greater life satisfaction.

One of the most distinguishing characteristics about older people with high life satisfaction is the fact that they have a future orientation. The new group of experimenting retired persons not only has plans but also is identified with other people in activities and has intimate friendships.

A study conducted by the American Institutes of Research (Flanagan 1978) surveyed a nationally representative sample of adults over the age of 70 in reference to how well basic needs of life—money, friends, recreation, health, housing, transportation, education, and creative expression—were being met. This survey yielded many interesting findings about older adults; perhaps the most startling is the fact that individuals over the age of 70 indicated that learning opportunities are the least frequently well-met need that would add to the quality of living. It would appear essential that the well-adapting older adult seeks out new learning opportunities.

Perhaps one should delineate three processes of aging. One of these, "senescing," refers to those processes that lead to biological vulnerability with the passage of time. "Eldering" is a process of progressive social role changes in which individuals behave differently as a function of expectations and opportunities in the society. Eldering should be a comfortable process in which persons may become more venerable. "Geronting," the third process, refers to actively growing old while trying to execute control. Geronting consists of modifying the environment so that it meets needs or, if not modifying it, so adapting that the environment works for, not against, aging individuals. Some people seem remarkably skilled at geronting, and when minor disabilities occur they manage the environment in a way that they are not handicapped. Perhaps, as mentioned earlier, the adaptive, or geronting, person can alternate between the divergent and convergent modes of thinking. By the use of divergent thinking, it is possible to come up with more alternatives for creating a satisfying way of life in retirement, partial retirement, or employment.

As preparation for a new look at life in retirement, writing an autobiography can be useful in planning next steps. One of the first experiences of individuals preparing an autobiography is the realization of how rich their life has been. Their self-esteem increases as they see how many things they have lived through. Relevance to the future lies in the fact that people do not really know where they are going in life unless they know where they have been.

References

Alpaugh, P.K., and Birren, J.E. "Variables Affecting Creative Contributions Across the Adult Life Span." *Human Development* 20 (1977): 240–48.

Birren, J.D. and Renner, V.J. "Concepts and Issues of Mental Health and Aging." In *Handbook of Mental Health and Aging*, edited by J.E. Birren and R.B. Sloane. New Jersey: Prentice-Hall, 1980.

Flanagan, J.C. "A Research Approach to Improving Our Quality of Life." *American Psychologist* 33 (1978):138–47.

Fries, J.A. "Aging, Natural Death, and the Compression of Morbidity." *New England Journal of Medicine* 303 (1980):130–35.

Guttmann, D., Sinnott, J.D., Carrigan, Z.H., Holahan, N.Z., Flynn, M.J. and Mullaney, J.W. *The Impact of Needs, Knowledge, Ability, and Living Arrangements on Decision Making of the Elderly*. Washington, D.C.: National Catholic School of Social Service, Catholic University of America, 1977.

Harris, L., and Associates. *The Myth and Reality of Aging in America*. Washington, D.C.: The National Council on the Aging, 1975.

Klein, R.L. "Age, Sex, and Task Difficulty as Predictors of Social Conformity." *Journal of Gerontology* 27 (1972):229–36.

Schaie, K.W.; Labouvie-Vief, G.; and Buech, B.U. "Generation and Cohort-Specific Differences in Adult Cognitive Functioning: A Fourteen Year Study of Independent Samples." *Developmental Psychology* 9 (1973):151–66.

Thomae, H., ed. *Patterns of Aging*. Contributions to Human Development, vol. 3. Basel, Switzerland: S. Karger, 1976.

Suggested Readings

Birren, J.E., and Sloane, R.B., eds. *Handbook of Mental Health and Aging*. Englewood Cliffs, N.J.: Prentice-Hall, 1980.

> Definitive chapters on the many facets of mental health and aging. Researchers in many disciplines from the United States and abroad have presented a comprehensive summary of what we know about some difficult problems.

Lieberman, M.A., and Tobin, S.S. *The Experience of Old Age*. New York: Basic Books, 1983.

> A book for those who want to dig more deeply into the personal struggles of coping with stress and surviving into old age. Insights are provided about how some survive well and others do not.

Woodruff, D.S., and Birren, J.E., eds. *Aging: Scientific Perspectives and Social Issues*. Monterey, Calif.: Brooks Cole, 1983.

> A multidisciplinary introduction to the processes and issues of aging. Nineteen chapters look at a broad range of topics, from age and political behavior to the biology of aging.

2

Selected Characteristics of the Aging in the United States

Ruth B. Weg

It is clear that careful examination of demographic variables is extremely important for policymakers today and in the future. . . . We must understand the present and future size, structure and location of our elderly population.
—Congressman Claude Pepper

Preretirement and retirement preparation programs are logically developed as a function of the nature, number, and needs of the middle aged and old. Today is part of an era in which, for the first time, there is not only a significant older population but also a substantial middle-aged group that can look forward to becoming old. The following selected demographic facts, trends, and projections present characteristics of the lives of these persons in the society now, as well as in the future. We explore a range of factors that provide the most recent data available (1978–1983), including number (age and distribution), life expectancy, mortality, health, health-care costs, education, income, employment, marital status, and probable future perspectives.[1]

Number

Every day, about 5,200 Americans become 65 years old, and approximately 3,600 people over 65 die—a net increase of almost 600,000 elderly people each year (U.S. House 1982). This older portion of the population has grown from 3.1 million at the turn of the century to 26.8 million in 1983; from 4.1 percent to about 11.5 percent of 232.1 million—the total number of resident Americans ("U.S. Growing More Elderly" 1983). This increase represents 6 million more elderly since the 1980 census count.

The older population has been expanding at a faster rate than the under-65 age group. Between 1900 and 1980, the over-65 age group increased more than eightfold as compared with the almost threefold growth of the total population. An accelerated growth has continued.

7

Age

In spite of this unprecedented phenomenon of an aging society, it is noteworthy that in 1980, 61 percent of older Americans were still under 75, over one-half were under 73, and 34.4 percent were under 70. The 1980 census counted 2.4 million persons over 85 (no doubt greater in number today); 32,000 persons were over 100 years of age, and 75 percent of them were women (U.S. House 1982; "U.S. Growing More Elderly" 1983). As a consequence of this burgeoning number of elders, the median age of the nation also continues to rise—from 22.9 years in 1900, to 30.3 in 1981, 30.6 in 1983.

Lower mortality has been thought of as the primary factor in a population's aging because the increased average age at death indicates more older persons living at any one time. However, lower mortality may not be the only important factor. Demographer Ansley Cole has suggested that the major cause of this aging is low fertility, which results in a lower proportion of young people and a relative increase in the proportion of old persons (van der Tak 1982). Today, death rates are so low among people under age 40 that further mortality reductions would tend to occur among older people (van der Tak 1982).

The low mortality rate for the under-40 age group relates to the fact that biomedical advances and practices since 1900 have diminished critically the morbidity (illness) of childbirth, childhood diseases, and other infectious disease. Immigration has resulted in a younger U.S. population than otherwise would have been predicted since young persons have been heavily represented among recent immigrant populations. However, the impact of this immigration on the age of the society has been minimal.

Distribution

Between 1975 and 1979, 18 percent of the total U.S. population changed residences, with significant numbers moving to the sunbelt states. Although the 65 + age group tends to distribute among the states in a pattern similar to the total population, there is a slightly higher concentration of elders in some of the larger states. The most rapid growth rates for the over-65 population occurred between 1970 and 1980 (table 2–1). Florida has the highest proportion of older persons (17.3 percent, and Alaska has the smallest number and proportion (2.9 percent).

Health

The health sciences in the United States have achieved significant victories in the cure and treatment of the acutely ill. Dr. Julius Richmond, a former

Table 2–1
Growth Rates of the Over-65 Population, 1970–1980

State	Percent
Nevada	112.9
Arizona	90.7
Hawaii	72.7
Alaska	71.4
Florida	71.1
New Mexico	51.1
South Carolina	51.1

Adapted from U.S. House. Select Committee on Aging. *Every Ninth American*, Comm. pub. no. 97-332. Prepared by H.B. Brotman. 97th Cong. 2nd sess. 1982, p. 2.

surgeon general, noted that Americans are healthier now than they have ever been (U.S. Dept. HEW 1979). There is little doubt that a number of factors have contributed to this reality: better nutrition, improved sanitation, success in combating childhood and other infectious diseases, less crowded housing, more employment opportunities, and greater access to education.

Deaths from coronary heart disease and cerebrovascular accidents (stroke) have dropped dramatically. These rates should continue to decline if the major identified risk factors are prevented and/or minimized. There is a growing positive response of government and the allied health professions to a preventive, holistic mode, emphasizing the efficacy of exercise, prudent diets, cessation of smoking, and stress management (Stamler 1981; Weg 1981).

However, during the 1970s, the incidence and mortality rates of most cancers have risen. Most experts believe that a majority of the cancers can be correlated with carcinogens in the environment as well as certain aspects of life-style such as nutrition, smoking, and stress. This suggests that with a commitment to health promotion, improved consumer education, a cleanup of the environment wherever possible, continued research, and improved therapies, cancer will also eventually respond with a fall in incidence and mortality.

Health can no longer be perceived as the absence of disease or infirmity; persons can no longer be thought of as sick or healthy. Instead, the idea of positive good health—or high-level wellness—may be more appropriate, characterized by continually working toward a fulfillment of whatever the individual potential is in the integration of physical, emotional, mental, and spiritual capacities.

Health Status

Although between 80 and 85 percent of older persons have at least one chronic disorder, most retain enough capacities to live full, independent lives (NCHS, 1980). The National Center for Health Statistics (NCHS) reports that fewer than one in six older persons could no longer participate in their normal activities because of the impact of chronic disease.

In spite of the various illnesses reported, a national survey of the over-60 age group indicated that many older persons perceived themselves fairly positively: more than 50 percent are highly optimistic. The survey found that happiness and optimism for the elderly are linked to good health, economic security, and a satisfying relationship with an equally healthy spouse (Soldo 1980, p. 18).

Mobility

Of those older persons living in the community, 14 percent have no identified chronic conditions, and about 55 percent have chronic disorders that do not interfere in any way with mobility. Therefore, approximately 69 percent of the elders in the community have no physical limitations on their mobility; 13 percent have some trouble getting around but do manage; 13 percent need the help of another person or a mechanical aid; and 5 percent are homebound. The majority of reported limitations does not take place until after 75 years of age (U.S. House 1982; Soldo 1980).

Hospital Stays

The average number of days in an accute-care hospital in 1980 for persons of all ages in 7.3 days; the average number of days for those 65 + is 10.7 days (U.S. House 1982). In comparison to those under 65, it appears that the 65 + group is twice as likely to have some disability, is likely to have four times as much limitation of activity, and is twice as likely to be hospitalized for about 50 percent more time.

Nursing-Home Stays

A 1976 study that included those persons with and without nursing-home stays indicated a rising trend in nursing home stays with age. Individuals between 55 and 64 years spent a fraction of a day in a nursing home; those 65 to 74 years spent 4.4 days; those 75 to 84 years spent 21.5 days; and persons 85 + spent 86.4 days (average days are reported). The nursing-home population is 74 percent female, 69 percent widowed, 14 percent single, 12 percent married, and 93 percent white (U.S. House 1982).

Physician and Dental Visits

On the average, persons over 65 have more physician visits per year (6.4 visits) than those under 65 (4.8 visits) (U.S. House 1982). Almost 44 percent of persons 65 and over have not seen a dentist in at least five or more years, compared with 13.6 percent of all ages. Health surveys reveal that about 60 percent of all older persons 65 to 74 years have dental problems that go untreated (U.S. House 1982).

Morbidity

People 45 and older report fewer acute conditions per person per year than all other age groups. There is a major shift from acute to chronic disorders as people grow older (Weg 1982). Men in this group report fewer problems than women, and this difference can be misleading. Sex-related illness/health behavior is regarded as primarily a function of early socialization and continuing societal expectations. Men have higher mortality at all ages, but women appear to experience higher morbidity with reported higher rates of disability and use of services (Verbrugge 1976; Waldron 1980).

   Three chronic disorders have been responsible for the major morbidity characteristics of the middle-aged and older populations and are still the primary contributors to mortality at any age—diseases of the heart, cancer, and hypertension (and related stroke). At present, many of these account for the necessity and significance of the continuum-of-care concept and practice (table 2–2).

Table 2–2
Most Frequently Reported Chronic Disorders of Noninstitutionalized Elders, 1979

Condition	Percent
Arthritis	44.3
Heart disease	27.4
Hypertension	39
Hearing impairments	28.2
Vision impairments	12
Arteriosclerosis	12
Diabetes	8

Source: U.S. House. Select Committee on Aging. *Every Ninth American*, Comm. pub. no. 97-332. Prepared by H.B. Brotman. 97th Cong. 2nd Sess. 1982, p. 12.

Cardiovascular Disease. Of the cardiovascular diseases, coronary heart disease is the most serious type. The risk factors associated with this disease include elevated serum cholesterol, high blood pressure, cigarette smoking, diabetes, lack of physical activity, and basic personality traits.

Ischemic heart disease (inadequate blood supply to the heart) accounts for 80 to 90 percent of all cardiac deaths (Lakatta and Gerstenblith 1982). Narrowing or total occlusion of the coronary arteries that bring blood to the heart leads to ischemia. Although these blood-vessel changes (arteriosclerosis, atherosclerosis) do increase with age, research suggests that dietary modification, regular exercise, cessation of smoking, and stress management can not only slow and/or reverse atherosclerosis but also may contribute to the prevention of fatal heart attacks. (Turner 1982; Barndt, Blankenhorn et al. 1977; and Blackburn 1977).

Cancer. Approximately 58 million persons now alive will have cancer at some point in their lifetime. If current rates persist, one in four will become a cancer patient, and this will affect two of three families. For 1983, it was estimated that about 855,000 people will have been diagnosed as having cancer (American Cancer Society 1982). It is estimated that up to one-half of those expected to die might have been saved by earlier diagnosis and prompt treatment. Cancer can occur at any age, but it develops more frequently with advanced age. The highest death rates for five leading cancer cites occur during the years between 55 and 74. Thus it would appear that age is a risk factor in cancer. The American Cancer Society (1982) reports that with the exception of lung cancer, the age-adjusted cancer deaths are leveling off for the major, more common cancers, even declining in some. About 38 percent of all people who developed cancer in 1983 will be alive at least five years after treatment. However, if normal life expectancy is considered (noting deaths from heart disease, accidents, and other diseases), 46 percent of cancer patients will survive for at least five years.

During 1981 and 1982, renewed emphasis on prevention as the best treatment has identified some substances in the environment and work place as carcinogenic and some nutrients as inhibitory to cancer. This approach holds promise and hope that changes in the work site, the polluted natural environment, and dietary intake will lead to significant reduction in cancer-related morbidity and mortality of the middle and later years.

Hypertension. Hypertension is a silent disease that causes no pain. It reveals itself most frequently when it has been left undetected for too long and is later associated with the occurrence of cardiac disease, stroke (cerebrovascular disease), or kidney failure. Thirty-eight percent of white men (55 to 74 years) knew they were hypertensive in 1977; the other 62 percent did not know. Sixty percent of the white women, 50 percent of black men, and 60 percent of black women in this group knew they were hypertensive.

In recent years, successful management of hypertension has been made possible by governmental screening programs, the development of effective drug therapy, and dietary and exercise changes.

Mortality

Taking all causes of death into consideration, female mortality rates are only 56 to 64 percent of male rates (Verbrugge 1976). It is significant that the diseases with a female excess are characterized by morbidity, whereas diseases with a male excess are heavily weighted in mortality. Although sex ratios in mortality continue to show relative improvement and advantages among women, sex differences are narrowing, suggesting relative improvement for men (Verbrugge 1976; 1980). There appears to be a growing consensus, though evidence is still limited, that sex-differentiated disease and mortality data have been more behaviorally rather than biologically based (Lewis and Lewis 1977). It is suggested that life-style factors such as smoking, alcohol consumption, and driving and other accidents have had a more adverse effect on men than on women and may account for men's higher mortality rate (Verbrugge 1976).

Mortality rates in the United States have been declining since 1950 for most age groups and both sexes, and the lowest age-adjusted death rate ever recorded was reached in 1981: 12 deaths per 1,000 births (Brandt 1981). Between 1965 and 1978, annual death rates for the 65 + age group dropped about 12 percent, from 6 per 100 to 4.3 per 100.

Age-specific death rates for 1980 suggest that the top five causes of death—diseases of the heart, cancer, cerebrovascular disease (hypertension, stroke) accidents, influenza, and pnemonia—accounted for 76 percent of all deaths, with the first-ranked cause—heart disease—responsible for 37.8 percent of mortality (NCHS 1983). Cancer is running a very strong second to death from diseases of the heart (and gaining), with cerebrovascular accidents a distant third.

Health-Care Costs

The cost for health-care delivery is growing faster than the cost of almost any other service or aspect of U.S. living and is well above general price levels as measured by the consumer's price index (CPI) for all items in the early 1980s. The cost of health care for older persons is a financial burden for them because their needs increase as their income diminishes with retirement. Rising prevalence of chronic conditions, other diseases, and impairments appears to increase the need for long-term care of some elders, which probably contributes to higher costs (Brandt 1981; U.S. House 1982).

Total personal health-care costs, consisting of expenditures such as hospital care, physicians' and dentists' services, drugs, and so forth, have increased more than sixfold from 1965 to 1980; from $35.8 billion to an estimated $217.9 billion. Per capita expenditures appear to have increased more than fivefold during that same period from $180.73 to $940.62.

In 1978, it is noteworthy that per capita, the cost for the over-65 person was 3.4 times greater than for the under-65 person. Of the total $49.4 billion for those over 65, 37 percent came from private funds and 63 percent from public programs. Eighty-six percent of public outlay was federal; 14 percent was from state and local programs. Three items led the list in health-care costs for the elderly: hospital care, 43 percent of total expenditures; nursing-home care, 26 percent of total health bill; and physicians' services, 18 percent of the total costs. Five other categories were less than 7 percent of the total. In four—dentists' services, other professional services, drugs and drug sundries, eyeglasses and appliances—private payments represented between 58 and 97 percent of the support. This reflects the fact that public programs do not usually provide these services.

Although Medicare has decreased the cost of hospital bills for older people, direct costs to the elderly are increasing. During 1978, direct out-of-pocket payments by elderly persons for so-called health care (currently, after-the-fact disease care) was an average of $608 per person, an increase of 15 percent over 1977 and $371 more than in 1966. Escalation of out-of-pocket costs will continue well into the 1980s since Medicare now requires beneficiaries to pay higher rates for hospital care and skilled nursing-home stays and monthly premiums for supplementary medical insurance.

The 1979 cost for nursing-home care was $12.6 billion, almost 26 percent of the total health-care bill for older persons and more than eight times the level in 1965. The two major reasons for this increase are the substitution of nursing-home care for hospital care and the extension in 1972 of Medicaid reimbursements for care in intermediate facilities.

Barriers still exist to impede rapid progress to effective, appropriate health care in the middle and later years, as follows:

Inappropriate level of care that leads to excessive institutionalization is often a result of incompetent or insensitive assessment of needs.

Financial bias toward institutionalization exists on the part of many health professionals since home health care is not always recognized adequately by private insurance or Medicare.

Few facilities such as day-care centers, day hospitals, and home-health agencies are under low-level financing.

Poor or no educational programs for caretaking personnel involved with elders have kept the quality of care low.

Inadequate respite programs for family caretakers of ill elderly exist.

There is a lack of major commitment to health education for the consuming public.

Poor coordination of services and agencies involved in programs for the older population results in economic waste and needless human suffering.

Lack of widespread preventive health-care programs and practices for any age group or at-risk populations defeats the goal for high functional health among elders.

Education of the major medical community is still based largely on the acute, catastrophic disease model—unrelated to the essentially chronic nature of disorders that accompany age.

The Medicare program has failed to meet elders' preventive health needs and care of chronic conditions. Medicare and Medicaid are still geared primarily in payment schedule and recognition to acute, after-the-fact disease care.

Since 1978, the National Institute on Aging (NIA) has undertaken an active program to stimulate and facilitate the development of geriatrics programs in medical schools. The Administration on Aging (AoA)–funded Geriatric Fellowship Program and an NIA-sponsored Geriatric Medicine Academic Award now exist for development of medical-school curricula in geriatrics. In the early 1980s, growing numbers of medical schools have mobilized to develop geriatric education. Increased numbers of journal articles, books, and symposiums reflect the now active concern and serious search of the allied health professionals and academic communities for improved health care in the later years. There may be some significant changes in attitude, philosophy, and practice of health care of the older population in the near future that not only will improve health care and the quality of life for elders, but also will decrease expenditures for premature custodial care.

Income

Older families typically have about one-half the income of younger families. As heads of household retire from the labor force, they experience a one-half to two-thirds cut in income. For the first time many families become part of a low, fixed-income group. It can be noted that there is post facto indexing of Social Security and some other benefit systems, but a number of money sources for elders remain nonindexed. In 1980, one-half of the 9.2 million families headed by those aged 65 and over had an income less than $12,881. Although the $12,881 represents a small increase over the 1979 figure of $11,316, there was a loss of purchasing power because of the significant rise in the Consumer Price Index and inflation.

Consumption Patterns at Lower, Intermediate, and Higher Budget Levels

The proportion of the retired couple's budget spent for consumption decreases as their budget level rises. The cost of consumption claimed 95.7 percent of the lower, 94 percent of the intermediate, and 92.5 percent of the higher budget levels, with the remainder going for gifts and contributions (table 2–3).

In 1978 and 1979, housing continued to be the major expense for a retired urban couple and continued to account for about one-third of each of the budgets. The cost of food ranked as the second highest expense. Housing and food combined accounted for more than 60 percent of the cost of each budget level.

Sources of Income

Most elderly persons rely on a mix of income sources: Social Security benefits; pensions (both public and private); wages; income from savings,

Table 2–3
Annual Expenditures for Retired Couples, 1979

| Component | Budget Level | | |
	Lower	Intermediate	Higher
Food	$1,882	$2,507	$ 3,149
Housing	1,996	2,862	4,481
Transportation	420	820	1,528
Clothing	225	378	581
Personal care	169	247	362
Medical care[a]	837	842	848
Other family consumption	234	390	770
Other items	259	515	950
Total budget	$6,023	$8,502	$12,664

Source: National Clearinghouse on Aging, *Statistical Notes*, no. 6, January 1981.
[a]Preliminary.

real estate, or investments; and familial support. Social Security is by far the most important, accounting alone for nearly $4 out of every $10 of money income among older persons. In July 1980, cash Social Security payments were sent to 35.1 million persons of all ages for a total of almost $10.5 billion. The average monthly Social Security benefit for retired workers was $338.69; spouses received an average of $170.66, and children received $137.03 (U.S. Senate 1980).

As of August 1980, approximately 11 percent of all those aged 65 + depended, in part, on public assistance programs, mostly Supplemental Security Income (SSI). These payments were made to a total of 2.2 million older persons in 1979. During that time, 3.6 million older persons lived in households with income below the poverty level.

Poverty

The most recent data indicate that poverty has increased among the elderly from 14.3 percent in 1978 to 15.1 percent in 1979. In 1980 3.9 million (15.7 percent), or more than one out of six older persons, were poor. Women and minorities are heavily overrepresented in this subgroup. The aged poor consist of 38 percent blacks, 31 percent Hispanics, and 14 percent whites (van der Tak 1982). These percentages and categories are based on the governmental definition of the poverty line: $4,954 for older coupled households and $3,941 for an older individual living alone. The income picture would be incomplete unless we noted that in addition to the high poverty rate for older families, approximately 14 percent of older families had incomes between $25,000 and $50,000, with approximately 3 percent having incomes over $50,000 (U.S. House 1982).

Employment

Labor Force

The percentage of older persons in the work force has declined in recent years (table 2-4). Between 1950 and 1980, among persons aged 55 to 64, there was a 10-percent drop in labor force participation for men and a leveling of women's participation. There was about the same number of over-65 persons in the labor force in 1980 as in 1950. However, since the size of the over-65 group has doubled, the percentage of elders in the labor force has fallen from 26.7 percent in 1950 to 12.6 percent in 1980. Although the number of older women in the labor force has "almost doubled in the 30-year span," the drop is primarily a function of fewer older men at work (*Aging and the Work Force* 1982, p. 8).

Table 2-4
Labor Force Participation Rates of Men and Women, Selected Years

	Percent			
	Women		*Men*	
Year	*55–64*	*65+*	*55–64*	*65+*
1947	24.3	8.1	89.6	47.8
1960	37.2	10.8	86.8	33.1
1970	43	9.7	83	26.8
1979	41.9	8.3	73	20
1982	41.8	7.9	70.3	17.8

Source: Adapted from *Handbook of Labor Statistics.* U.S. Department of Labor, Bureau of Labor Statistics. Washington, D.C.: Government Printing Office (1980), table 4, p. 13; and E. Crimmins, "Labor Force Participation" (paper in progress 1983).

Factors for Re-evaluation of Existing Employment Policies

The noted proportions still relate to traditional retirement policies that have removed the majority of older workers by age 65. A number of compelling facts have already alerted managerial/supervisory personnel to a careful re-examination of such policies. An information paper on aging and the work force to the U.S. Senate Special Committee on Aging (1981) stresses the need to develop age-free employment policies. Suggested reasons for a re-evaluation of existing, traditional employment policies in the report of the committee and in various gerontological articles include:

Increased numbers of available older workers: Demographic data continue to forecast significant social and financial impact on the work place, families, and communities. The fall in the birth rate will result in lower availability of younger workers; the older worker is more likely to be kept longer and retrained. There is a graying not only of the nation's population as a whole but also of the labor force.

Economic pressures of a troubled economy: It is conceivable that inflation and the falling buying power of the already fixed incomes of the retired (and about to be retired) will inhibit those who might have retired between the ages of 58 and 70. An assumption that current older workers will retire according to earlier expected patterns would appear to be mistaken. Changes in Social Security legislation now permit additional retirement income benefits for each month elders continue to work between 65 and 72 years of age.

Life expectancy tables: The increase in life expectancy of about 27 years since the turn of the century also finds workers now aged 40, 45, and 50 who can anticipate a greater number of years of work life with probable improved health and work capacities. They represent a generation that has completed more education and has achieved more political savvy than their counterparts earlier in the century.

Management role in retirement decisions: Unilateral decisions by management regarding what is normal retirement age and/or early retirement are less feasible today. Age discrimination is still practiced. However, it is becoming increasingly difficult to retire workers over age 40 on the basis of age alone.

There is recent heightened interest and activity on the part of management concerning retaining the older worker and/or retraining the soon-to-be-retired worker for other full-time or part-time work. Major corporations, faced with rising costs of retirement income/pensions and health care, have developed work site health maintenance and promotion programs. Evaluations of these programs indicate that benefits accrue not only to the individual participants but also to the involved companies in fewer absentee days, greater efficiency and productivity, improved sense of well-being, and a more positive corporate image.

Entry of women into the labor force: The increasing influx of women into the labor force has initiated more flexible work patterns, a probable boon to both older men and women.

Marital Status

Marriage among Age Subgroups

Data on marital status are available now for ten-year subgroups within the 45 to over-75 population. Since each ten-year period may be accompanied by important changes in mobility, work patterns, economic level, health, and family situations, it is useful to examine marriage data by age and sex (table 2–5).

Sex ratios (the number of women to men) of older persons are a result of differential health, age changes, life-style patterns, and genetics, with consequences for the quality and quantity of life. Women outnumber men in the total older population—148 women to 100 men. With increasing age, the ratio grows in favor of women. For this reason, gerontological literature refers to problems in aging as primarily concerns of older women.

In 1979 the marriage rate for older men was close to six times greater than for older women. Roughly 75 percent of older brides and grooms had been widowed. In 1982, 1.9 million persons of the opposite sex were sharing living quarters; 184,000 of these persons were over 65 (Brotman 1983). The financial penalties of marriage for older persons and the human need for af-

Table 2–5
Marital Status, by Sex and Age Group, 1980

	Percent Distribution			
Sex and Marital Status	45–54	55–64	65–74	75+
Men				
Total	100	100	100	100
Married	85.3	85.2	81.6	69.4
Not married	14.7	14.8	18.4	30.6
Single	6.4	5.7	5.5	4.4
Widowed	1.6	4	8.5	24
Divorced	6.8	5	4.4	2.2
Women				
Total	100	100	100	100
Married	79	69.9	50.1	23.4
Not married	21	30.1	49.9	76.6
Single	4.7	4.6	5.6	6.4
Widowed	7	18	40.3	67.9
Divorced	9.2	6.7	4	2.3

Adapted from U.S. House, Select Committee on Aging. *Every Ninth American*, Comm. pub. no. 97-332. Prepared by H.B. Brotman. 97th Cong. 2nd sess. 1982, p. 25.

ection and companionship would appear to account for this contemporary behavior.

Widowhood

Differential life expectancies between the two sexes is reflected, in part, in the fact that most older people are women and that 51 percent (7.1 million) of these women are widowed. In 1980, 78 percent (7.6 million) of older men were married, and 34 percent of them were married to women under 65. Factors that contribute to the differences include the larger number of older women—15.2 million women and 10.3 million men—and the fact that men over 65 often choose to marry younger women.

The probability of widowhood appears to increase with the age of the husband. If the husband is five years younger than the wife, the chances of widowhood are one out of two; if the husband and wife are the same age, the chances are two out of three; if the husband is five years older than the wife, the chances are three out of four.

Most older women are widows, with 5.3 times as many widows as widowers. The average age at widowhood for American women is now 56. It is noteworthy that in 1979, 66.4 percent of all widows over 65 lived alone. Among men over 75, only 24 percent were widowers. The marriage rate for over-65 widows is about 1.8 percent and 15.6 percent for widowers. In 1979, women were widowed at the following increasing rates with age: over 65, approximately 51 percent; 65 to 74, approximately 40 percent; and over 75, approximately 70 percent. The marital status, especially in the middle and later years, interacts with overall health and socioeconomic conditions and is therefore an important population attribute.

Education

Persons of any age use education to improve their potential for earnings and to remain in touch with the rapidly changing postindustrial society. For the late middle-aged and older person, education may be the retraining for necessary job or career shifts, the means to participate more in the mainstream of society. Continuing education is essential in adapting to the acceleration of automation and technology and in coping with societal devaluation of the human spirit and worth with age.

A 1978 Survey of Adult Education conducted by the Bureau of the Census (National Clearinghouse on Aging 1981) revealed that the increase in participation of older persons in adult education has been increasing steadily since 1969. The number of persons 55 and over attending adult education programs almost doubled from 1 million to 1.9 million, an annual growth rate of 6.7 percent compared with 2.9 percent for adult participants of all ages. Highlights of the survey information of subgroups in this over-55 population provide some specifics for the overview:

Women were more likely than men of same age to participate.

Older whites were more apt than minorities to attend programs.

Participants had a higher level of educational attainment than older populations in general.

Main reasons cited by 55-to-64-year-olds for taking courses were evenly divided between improvement or advancement in current job and personal or social reasons.

For the 65 + group, the majority of courses was taken for personal or social reasons.

Courses for the older population were given more frequently by private community organizations, public two-year colleges, and/or vocational/technical institutions.

Available data from 1979 indicate that almost one-half of the older population had not completed the tenth grade; among the 15-to-64-year-olds, high school graduation was the median. Approximately 9 percent of those over 65 were functionally illiterate—no schooling or fewer than five years—but 8 percent had completed college (U.S. House 1982; Soldo 1980).

Nevertheless, the trend continues to be toward more highly educated older persons and higher educational levels for all age groups, so a relative change may not be apparent. Each cohort has had, and will have, exposure to more formal education as well as increased informal learning opportunities. Those in their later years at the beginning of the twenty-first century then will most certainly be better prepared (educated) to take advantage of the automated technology that will surely characterize this society and the world.

Educational programs in high schools for adults in the community, in community colleges and universities, and at multiple sites where older adults come together now finally reflect the changing perceptions of older individuals by educators, and themselves, as people who can not only continue to grow and cope throughout their lives but also who can be expected to contribute to their peers and society at large (Peterson 1983).

Life Expectancy

At a meeting of the American Association for the Advancement of Science, predictions by the Census Bureau for human life expectancy were categorized as too low. Revisions were proposed to raise the predicted life expectancies in the year 2000 from 70 years for men and 78 years for women to 74.3 and 86.2 years respectively. The need to alter earlier predictions about the older population is, in part, a function of the unplanned for impact from biomedical advances with infectious disease and with disorders of the young and from the continuing fall in birth and death rates. These victories have meant more people live to adulthood and into their later years. Estimates of life expectancy for the past few years would appear to have been consistently conservative and have invariably fallen below the actual figures.

The 1980 census figures indicated that, for the population as a whole, life expectancy (at birth) averaged 75 years for whites and 68.2 years for nonwhites. In the white subgroup, life expectancy for women was 78.1 years and 70.5 years for men; the nonwhite subgroup had lower figures: 74 years for women and 64.3 for men. These numbers also reflect the continuing rise in life expectancy since the turn of the century.

Unpublished life expectancy data for FY 1982 from the Census Bureau have been collated by Crimmins (1983b) and demonstrate that the rise persists. In table 2–6 the information is separated by sex and race, with the inclusion of only selected age intervals from 50 years and over. The Social Security Administration (SSA) (1981) developed life expectancy tables that projected to the year 2050 (table 2–7).

Increases in life expectancies have had and will have consequences for a wide range of socioeconomic realities in society—for example, growing numbers of middle-aged and older persons, aging nature of the population, health behavior and status, health-care costs, work and retirement policies, income, education and preretirement planning, family relationships, marital patterns, and voting. These consequences have significance for the present as well as the future.

The Future: A Summary Conjecture

An unmistakable direction is indicated by the data—namely, the already substantial number of older persons will continue to grow. Whichever mortality projection is followed, the population over 65 will be older by the year 2000. The twenty-first century will have a longer-lived and larger aged population than predicted to date.

According to the Bureau of the Census (1983), there would be a significant increase in the older population (over 65) from 11.4 percent in 1981 to 13.1 percent (35 million) in 2000 to 21.7 percent (67 million) in 2050. "After 2000, the range of the projected number of older people widens; for 2020, the range is 48–56 million people; for 2050, it is 58–79 million" (p. 13, Crimmins 1983a). The number of those 85 and older would increase at an even faster rate, from 1 percent in 1981 to 1.9 percent (5.1 million) in 2000 to 5.2 percent (16 million) in 2050. A concomitant rise in the median age is predicted from the 30.3 years of 1981 to 36.3 in 2000 to 41.6 in 2050. A rapid growth of the older population is suggested from 2000 to 2025 as the postwar babies reach their later years, then a sharp drop in the rate of growth since the present low birth rates will produce a smaller cohort who will reach 65.

Table 2–6
Life Expectancy, Fiscal Year 1982, by Age, Sex, and Race

Age Interval	Average Number of Years Remaining at Beginning of Age Interval			
	Black Men	Nonblack Men	Black Women	Nonblack Women
50–51	22.45	25.73	28.48	31.52
60–61	16.38	18	21.04	22.98
65–66	13.85	14.64	17.83	19.04
75–76	9.18	9.28	11.78	12.07
79–80	7.71	7.57	9	9.70
85 +	6.10	5.82	7.86	6.84

Adapted from unpublished data from the U.S. Census Bureau for FY 1982, collated and calculated by E. Crimmins, "Labor Force Participation" (paper in progress July 1983).

Table 2-7
Expectation of Life at Birth and at Age 65, by Sex: Middle-Series
Projection of Mortality, 1920-2050

	Expectation at Birth		Expectation at 65	
Year	Men	Women	Men	Women
1980	69.8	77.7	14.3	18.7
2000	72.9	81.1	15.8	21.1
2050	75	83.6	17.3	23.2

Source: Adapted from Social Security Administration, *Social Security Area Population Projections, 1981*, SSA pub. no. 11-11532, Actuarial Study no. 85 (Washington, D.C., 1981), table 18.

What kind of older population may we expect? There will be a noticeable graying of the work place, schools, and families—a graying already in evidence. The 1980 census data suggest that by 1990, 32 million households will be headed by someone aged 55 +, 20 million by someone over 65. Though movement into nonmetropolitan areas and southern states will increase, most elders will continue to live in metropolitan areas. More persons will be living independently. A large proportion of elderly will remain homeowners, though home rentals, mobile homes, and multi-unit structures will increase; about 65 percent of those over 65 will be in their own homes or apartments (Information on Aging 1981).

Although some researchers still have concern with growth in numbers of the old old (85 years of age and older) and the heightened potential for illness and disability (Brody 1982), many gerontologists (and elders) perceive the health of older persons as good and becoming better (Fries and Crapo 1981). Elders will be increasingly active in the community as volunteers, workers, and advocates. The trend to return for adult education will expand as more elders seek retraining for jobs, careers, socializing, and enrichment. The mixture of young and old in classrooms across the country will contribute to the minimization of the negative stereotype of aging.

Government encouragement, inflation, and interest will bolster an emerging inclination of many older men and women to remain at work longer or to return to work. This opportunity (and/or necessity) will help to improve financial status, broaden social exposure, and enhance self-image. In turn, these positive changes will contribute to a heightened sense of well-being and better health status.

Planning and implementation of new strategies are essential for appropriate responses to the changing nature, needs, and demands of an aging society. It is apparent that the policies and actions of yesterday and today will not be useful mechanisms for either problem solving or success.

Implications for Retirement Specialists

Preretirement and retirement programs have the responsibility and opportunity to plan for the more than 12 percent older population in the year 2000 and an impressive 16 or more percent in 2020.

Human aging is multidimensional, and retirement specialists can use the information presented here to help the middle-aged and young old (as well as people of all ages) to understand the facts, context, and changing potential for the later years. The selected data and trends point to the increasingly positive realities and possibilities for recent and future cohorts of elders. Finally, this information can stimulate retirement program participants to maximize and control the direction and quality of their lives.

Note

1. Most numbers in this chapter have been rounded off to facilitate reading and remembering. More exact figures are available in referenced sources. Data from governmental sources for a current year are usually estimates and/or projections since real figures do not become available to the public and the research community for about two years following the projections.

Projections presented in this chapter are based on middle-series assumptions regarding middle levels of fertility, mortality, and immigration as discussed by the Bureau of Census (1982).

Fertility rates are assumed to be fairly steady but increasing slightly as follows:

1980: 1.83 births per woman,
2000: 1.96 births per woman,
2050: 1.90 births per woman.

Life expectancy is as follows:

Year	Women	Men
1981	78.3	70.7
2005	81.3	73.3
2050	83.6	75.1

Net immigration is assumed to be a constant 450,000 per year.

There is increased use of the kind of statistical methodology that enables the appropriate division (for some attributes) of persons over 45 into ten-year subgroups—45 to 54, 55 to 64, 75 +, and so on.

References

Aging and the Work Force: Human Resources Strategies. Prepared by Julia French for U.S. Senate, Special Committee on Aging. Washington, D.C.: U.S. Government Printing Office, 1982.

American Cancer Society. *Cancer Facts and Figures, 1983.* New York, 1982.

Barndt, R., Blankenhorn, D.H., Crawford, D.W., and Brooks, S.H. "Regression and Progression of Early Femoral Athenoderosis in Treated Hyperlipoprateinemic Patients." *Annals of Internal Medicine* 86 (1977):139–146.

Blackburn, H., "Coronary Disease Prevention: Controversy and Professional Attitudes." *Advances of Cardiology* 20 (1977):10–26.

Brandt, E.N. Reported in *Los Angeles Times*, December 4, 1981, part I, p. 1 (in column by Bruce Nelson).

Brody, J.A. "Life Expectancy and the Health of Older Persons." *Journal of American Geriatrics Society* 30 (1982):681–83.

Brotman, H.B. Personal communication, 1983.

Crimmins, E. "The Changing Pattern of American Mortality Decline, 1940–1977, and Its Implications for the Future." *Population and Development Review* 7 (1980):229.

_____ . "Recent and Prospective Trends in Old Age Mortality." Paper presented at the Annual Meeting of the American Associates for the Advancement of Science, Detroit, May 26–31, 1983a.

_____ . "Labor Force Participation." From a paper in progress, July 1983b.

Fries, J.F., and Crapo, L.W. *Vitality and Aging.* San Francisco: W.H. Freeman & Company, 1981.

Information on Aging, no. 29. Detroit: Institute of Gerontology, Wayne State University/University of Michigan, July 1981.

Lakatta, E.G., and Gerstenblith, G. "Cardiovascular System." In *Health and Disease in Old Age*, edited by J.W. Rowe and R.W. Besdine. Boston: Little, Brown & Co., 1982.

Lewis, C.E., and Lewis, M.A. "The Potential Impact of Sexual Equality on Health." *New England Journal of Medicine* 297 (1977):863–69.

National Centers for Disease Control. *Morbidity and Mortality Weekly Report* (annual summary) 24 (1980). DHHS pub. no. (CDC) 81–8241, Atlanta, Ga., 1981.

National Center for Health Statistics. DHHS (PHS) pub. no. 81–1120. *Monthly Vital Statistics Report*. Provisional statistics, annual summary for the U.S. Washington, D.C.: U.S. Government Printing Office, 1980.

National Center for Health Statistics. *Monthly Vital Statistics Report* 32 (supplement) (1983).

National Clearinghouse on Aging. *Statistical Notes #6*. Washington, D.C., June 1981.

Pepper, C. "Foreword." In *Every Ninth American*, U.S. House, Select Committee on Aging, prepared by H.B. Brotman. Comm. pub. no. 97-332. Washington, D.C.: U.S. Government Printing Office, 1982, p. iii.

Peterson, D.A. *Facilitating Education for Older Learners*. San Francisco: Jossey-Bass Publishers, 1983.

Social Security Administration. "Expectation of Life at Birth and at Age 65 by Sex: Middle Series Projection of Mortality 1980-2050." *Social Security: Area Population Projections*. SSA pub. no. 11-11532, Washington, D.C.: U.S. Government Printing Office, 1981.

Soldo, B.J. "America's Elderly in the 1980's." *Population Bulletin* 35 (1980):13-48.

Stamler, J. "Primary Prevention of Coronary Heart Disease: The Last 20 Years." *American Journal of Cardiology* 47 (1981):722-35.

Turner, R.W.D. "Diet and Epedemic Coronary Heart Disease." In *Nutrition and Killer Diseases: The Effects of Dietary Factors on Fatal Chronic Disease*, edited by J. Rose. Park Ridge, N.J.: Noyes Publications, 1982.

U.S. Bureau of Census. *Current Population Reports: Population Estimates and Projections 1982-2050* (Advance Report), Series P-25, no. 922 (Washington, D.C.: U.S. Government Printing Office, October 1982.

U.S. Bureau of Census. Unpublished data. 1983.

U.S. Bureau of Labor Statistics. *Employment and Earnings* (rev. annual averages) 29, March 1982, table 1.

U.S. Department of Health, Education, and Welfare (PHS). *Healthy People: The Surgeon General's Report on Health Promotion and Disease Prevention*. Pub. no. 79-55071. Washington, D.C., 1979.

"U.S. Growing More Elderly." June 6, 1983, part I, p. 2.

U.S. House, Select Committee on Aging. *Every Ninth American*, Comm. pub. no. 97332. Prepared by H.B. Brotman. 97th Cong. 2nd sess., 1982.

U.S. Senate, Special Committee on Aging. *Every Ninth American*, Sen. rep. no. 97-62, part 1. Prepared by H.B. Brotman. 97th Cong. 1st sess., 1981.

van der Tak, J., ed. "U.S. Population: Where We Are, Where We're Going." *Population Bulletin* 337 (1982):1-51.

Verbrugge, L.M. "Sex Differentials in Morbidity and Mortality." *Social Biology* 23 (1976):275-96.

Verbrugge, L.M. "Recent Trends in Sex Mortality Differentials in the United States." *Women and Health* 5 (1980):17-37.

Waldron, I. "Sex Differences in Longevity." In *Epidemiology of Aging*, edited by S.G. Haynes and M. Feinleib. Washington, D.C.: NIH, 1980.

Weg, R.B. *The Aged: Who, Where, How Well.* Los Angeles: Andrus Gerontology Center, University of Southern California, 1981.

Weg, R.B. "Selected Characteristics of the Aging in the United States." In *Retirement Preparation: An Update,* edited by H. Dennis. Los Angeles: Andrus Gerontology Center, University of Southern California, 1982.

3 Health Promotion

Robert M. Tager

Trends

Health promotion, health enhancement, wellness, prevention, and other similar terms describe an extremely important, positive, and growing movement in our society. Many health professionals and laypeople alike are realizing that it is possible to achieve higher levels of health or wellness than the mere absence of disease and that it is possible to take active measures to prevent disease and to maintain optimal health.

These trends are reflected in extensive professional and lay literatures, the popular press, and other media. There is growing interest in exercise, nutrition, and stress management and a significant growing trend in retirement planning to provide related programs. Unfortunately, there has also been some exploitation of this positive trend. Sound programs with high credibility are needed to improve awareness and to augment knowledge in retirement planning.

Risk Factors

Although I believe that, in the long run, individuals are responsible for their own health, most people need some help in achieving their potential. The major risk factors that may be the cause of poor health are smoking, excess use of alcohol and drugs, poor nutritional habits, lack of exercise, high blood pressure, and stress. It is important to realize that stress has its own effects and, in addition, tends to increase the other risks. There is much agreement on this list, and it closely matches some lists of national recommendations for health improvement. However, the mere listing of these factors does little or nothing toward changing health behaviors. Even direct warnings, such as the notice on cigarette packages and advertisements, do not seem to have the effect necessary to result in healthful changes in long-term habits. In addition to contributing to disability, these same half-dozen risk factors are major contributors to the ten leading causes of death in later life. These causes are heart disease; cancer; stroke; influenza and pneumonia; arteriosclerosis; diabetes mellitus; accidents (other than motor vehicle); bronchitis, emphysema, and asthma; cirrhosis of the liver; and motor-vehicle accidents.

Stress

Stress contributes, in varying degrees, to all of the leading causes of death listed. Also, the techniques for managing stress overlap partially or completely with the management of the other risk factors and are discussed here as a principal example of health promotion.

It is important to realize that stress, which is a response of the body to physical and emotional demands made upon it, is nonspecific and qualitatively the same for positive events as it is for negative occurrences. The total amount of stress from all sources results in health problems. It is also important to consider that some degree of stress is necessary to achieve peak productivity and that, within limits, an increasing amount of stress or arousal will heighten individual or group abilities and accomplishments. However, there is a limit to this phenomenon, and after the stress exceeds a certain ill-defined level, there will be a progressive drop off of efficiency and productivity. This is exemplified in the sports world where a baseball pitcher, who has been doing very well during the first phase of a game, eventually blows up as the pressures accumulate and experiences a drastic reduction in effectiveness.

Although stress can contribute to productivity, can be an enriching factor in living, and can be lifesaving in a danger situation, it can have the opposite effects when the stress response is prolonged, frequent, or extremely intense. Thus, it becomes valuable and necessary to understand the nature of the response and to recognize its occurrence and some of the early symptoms that are clues that one's stress needs to be better managed.

The parts of the stress response that can be felt or readily measured are a focusing of attention on the stimulating event, tightening of muscles throughout the body, elevation of blood pressure, increase in pulse and breathing rates, a feeling of tightness in the abdomen, cold and clammy hands, and a flushed feeling in the forehead and face. When the events are negative in nature, there may be emotional responses of frustration, anxiety, fear, and under certain circumstances, depression. Some hidden responses such as the production of adrenalin and cortisone can have profound effects. Other signs of stress may be noticeable to friends and family as well as to the individual. These include chronic irritability, worry about situations for which worry is no help, difficulty concentrating, and inability to relax. Considering the broad spectrum of these parameters, it is not surprising that the importance of managing stress and other health risk factors is becoming increasingly evident in our society from both personal and organizational perspectives. There is no doubt that health-related problems generate a formidable cost to both governmental and private sectors of our society.

The management of stress and other health-related risk factors involves both organizational and personal strategies. In addition, it is evident that positive health behaviors not only can decrease the risk of disease, illness, and injury but also can help people to achieve higher degrees of health and well-being that add a further protective buffer against health risks and promote higher levels of creativity and accomplishment.

Management of Risk Factors

The management of stress and other risk factors includes the four far-reaching areas of communication, exercise, nutrition, and deep relaxation.

Communication

An open line of communication with spouse, friends, relatives, co-workers, or others is very valuable in modifying the stress response. Expressing one's feelings about stress-producing events helps to temper the stress response and to clarify the issues that are easily clouded by emotions. The other person need not solve the problems but only needs to be a good listener and someone who will hold offered information in confidence.

Exercise

Individuals in our society tend to be underexercised, a condition that contributes to health risks. An effective exercise program—definitely after medical clearance in the retirement age group—not only can have some positive effect on health risks but also is an important element in managing the stress response. The effects of appropriate exercise may include a lowering of blood pressure, of pulse and breathing rates, and of muscle tension.

Nutrition

Malnutrition is usually not a problem in the active working population, but nutritional excesses are. The four most common excesses are calories, salt, fat, and refined carbohydrates such as sugars and refined flour. Proper adjustment of caloric intake can, of course, lead to achievement or approximation of ideal body weight, which aids in the control of blood pressure and strain on the musculoskeletal system. Lowering salt intake is a major step in controlling high blood pressure, which is the major risk factor for heart attack and stroke. Lowering fat intake, especially that of saturated fats and cholesterol, is a positive step in the control of arteriosclerosis. Finally, decreasing the intake of sugars and refined flour in favor of an increased amount of complex carbohydrates is helpful in managing obesity, arteriosclerosis, and various gastrointestinal problems.

Deep Relaxation

Deep relaxation, which differs from recreation, leisure activities, and sleep, is a major element in managing the stress response. Deep relaxation is a wakeful state in which there is a clearing of both mental and physical tension. Techniques for such relaxation include meditation, progressive relaxation, autogenics, biofeedback, yoga, guided imagery, and others. Just as with exercise, these techniques must be learned and practiced in order to gain a positive effect.

One of the most important things to remember about stress management and other risk factor management techniques is that they take time to learn and even more time to make the necessary health behavior changes. Changing behaviors that may have been developed over a lifetime, or over many years, is not easy and must be approached with care and respect.

Implications for Retirement Specialists

Professionals working in the area of retirement planning should be aware of the health risks facing the groups with which they are working and the elements of health promotion that can modify these risks and improve health. It is never too soon to start improving one's health, but the preretirement period is far preferable to further delaying such attention until one is retired. Retirement, even with preparation, is stressful to varying degrees, and such stresses can be handled much more effectively by the person who has incorporated a personal stress management and health promotion program. Even without the element of retirement, people of retirement age are entering a stage of life when many illnesses tend to occur and when chronic diseases present a particular problem. Appropriate health planning can help to prevent or at least modify the adverse effects of such illnesses and to assist in promoting higher levels of health.

A number of considerations arise for retirement specialists in arranging the health portion of their programs. First of all is the question as to who is the best person to do the health presentation, and is it necessary that that person be a physician? If specialists are to provide their own information and materials, they should, of course, be very knowledgeable in their field and experienced in doing group presentations. If, however, very high-quality instructional materials with guided presentation are used, the knowledge of the presenter is much less important. With respect to questions and answers, there is no substitute for knowledge and experience. It is not necessary that the person be a physician though, in some situations, this might be preferable. Credibility is important as well as an assurance of accurate information. Health educators are specially trained in the field (there are a number of master's degree programs in health education) and can provide both knowledge and credibility. Nurses and other health-care providers may be good candidates as presenters, depending on their knowledge and experience.

It is important to realize that the words of even the most knowledgeable and authoritative person will fall on deaf ears if the material is not presented in a palatable and interesting manner. This, again, brings up the possibility of a relatively inexperienced person using high-quality instructional materials designed for presentation by a trainer. Such programs can be quite successful or can fail completely. The success depends largely on how personalized the program is to the participants and how well the trainer is trained in the art of presenting that particular program.

In arranging health components for a preretirement program, retirement specialists have a responsibility to select appropriately both authoritative content and a credible, enjoyable presentation. The former often can be derived from review of content outlines and by checking credentials. The latter is more difficult. The philosophy and orientation of presenters can be as important as their knowledge. Strong knowledge of the group to which the presentation will be given is a significant aid. Some groups may want a more traditional medical approach, but the majority of the groups to whom I have presented in recent years prefer a broader approach that relates health to all aspects of their lives and discusses health in a broad sense that includes quality-of-life issues.

Suggested Readings

Benson, H. *The Relaxation Response.* New York: Avon, 1976.

> Describes relaxation as it relates to stress management and gives a readable description of meditation in Western terms.

Cooper, K.H. *The New Aerobics.* New York: Bantam, 1970.

> A well-written and quantitative book on exercise and how to develop a personal exercise program.

Farquhar, J.W. *The American Way of Life Need Not Be Hazardous to Your Health.* New York: Norton, 1978.

> An authoritative book about stress and risk factors with suggestions on how to effect change.

Selye, H. *Stress without Distress.* New York: Signet, 1975.

> A lucid description of stress and the stress response by the person who coined the word *stress* and did much of the early work leading to our present knowledge of the subject.

Tager, R.M. "Physical Health Realities—A Medical View." In *Prospects and Issues,* 3rd ed., edited by R.H. Davis. Lexington, Mass.: Lexington Books, D.C. Heath and Co., 1981.

> An organized approach toward looking at major factors regarding health and independent living in the later years.

U.S. Department of Health, Education, and Welfare (PHS). *Healthy People: The Surgeon General's Report on Health Promotion and Disease Prevention.* Pub. no. 79-55071. Washington, D.C., 1979.

> An excellent overview of health problems and national goals for people in the United States.

4 Financial Planning

Gordon P. Ramsey

The Role of Financial Planning

The two words *financial planning* have as many different definitions as the number of individuals reading or hearing them. It is quite clear that the one common denominator is the wide disparity of those definitions from one person to another. It is also clear that the subject ranks either first or second in a list of priorities and major concerns of middle-aged and older persons.

Every survey of retirees, or those about to retire, gives empirical evidence supporting the importance of financial planning. Indeed, to many, financial planning is both the beginning and the end of retirement planning. Practitioners in retirement planning should recognize that this may very well be the case and deal realistically with that possibility. Failing to do so may very well block all other discussions, regardless of the topics. In most cases, it is a completely reasonable hypothesis that financial adequacy in retirement is a direct result of financial planning during most of the individual's working life or at least during the latter portion. It is also axiomatic that, without some perception of a reasonably adequate income level, the whole issue of retirement planning may be moot.

Educational Concepts

Several educational concepts exist that are useful in contemplating the financial-planning portion of a retirement-planning program. The role of the instructor is an extremely important consideration. According to Peterson (1982), "instructors are too frequently perceived to be a fount of knowledge from whom the answers will flow if the student has sufficient patience" (p. 48). This perception of the instructor is counterproductive in financial planning. In fact, exact and specific advice should be avoided at all cost. First, there is simply not enough time in the typical retirement-planning program to get into the specific details on a particular investment, merits of one to another, or historic performance. Second, it is extremely difficult, if not impossible, to generate any broadly applicable advice items. Giving specific advice may be a disservice rather than a help because of the uniqueness of each participant's financial issues.

As contrasted to advice giving, a substantially more effective and efficient teaching approach deals with the instruction of basic concepts and principles that are relevant to each discrete case. Of course, the application of that principle or technique will vary from one case to another.

Another important concept to consider is that "learning is increased when the learner is able to relate it to existing knowledge, experience, or need" (p. 48, Peterson 1982). The thrust of the program should be building on information that all attendees know in one order of magnitude or another. Then, present the material in such a manner that individuals will relate to the concept being developed and apply it to their own case. The tenor of the program should facilitate an interchange of ideas, both between the instructor and the attendees and even from attendee to attendee, leading to a very specific and concrete course of action for that individual, which may or may not be articulated during the program. The following concepts demonstrate generic principles that can be applied to individual cases of financial planning.

Figuring Spendable Income in Retirement

Without going into the numerics, the basic premise propounds that one does not need the same total dollar cash flow in retirement as needed while actively employed in order to sustain the same standard of living. The exercise takes the group through the analysis of where their cash is going now—for example, federal and state income tax, Social Security tax, work-related expenses, and savings. Next, the group reaches conclusions as to what current cash flow items will not be required in retirement. A reasonable conclusion for most salary levels is that income in retirement that is 60 to 70 percent of preretirement income will indeed sustain the same standard of living as before retirement.

Understanding Tax Facts

Since income taxes are typically the largest single expense item for an individual while actively employed, it is extremely valuable in financial planning for the individual to understand basic tax facts. For example, it is important to know that the income tax rate is progressive. The tax rate on the last dollar earned is higher than the tax rate on the first dollar earned. Tax planning involves reducing taxable income that will be taxed at the highest marginal rate which, in turn, will result in tax savings.

It is important for sound financial planning to understand that the estate/gift tax is also progressive. There are substantial exclusions and exemptions that might, through basic estate-planning steps, entirely exempt a given estate from federal tax. Finally, retirees must recognize the importance of the need for estate planning to encompass both the first and the second death (in the typical husband and wife circumstance). Basic steps here, as in the income tax section of a program, capture the law's intrinsic savings through knowledge and implementation of some relatively uncomplicated planning steps. Representative course content, which will vary according to time constraints and course objectives, are described in the following section.

Content for Financial, Income Tax, and Estate Planning

Financial Planning

Objective. This section sets the stage and prepares individuals for the program's content and process. As mentioned, the program should not contain specific advice with respect to a particular investment. It should not in any way suggest that there is a cure-all for the financial-planning problems that we all encounter. However, the thrust of the program should deal with the basic tools and concepts that individuals can apply to their specific circumstance that obviously will vary widely from one attendee to another. The underlying theme is that hard work pays handsome profits and that no one is going to do it for you.

Risk Analysis. Taking a risk analysis concept from business management, every individual is exposed to the economic risks of retirement, death, disability, medical expense, termination of employment, and loss of capital. All financial planning should be directed toward responding to one or more of those hazards. The spendable income concept discussed previously is essential in the planning process. For example, few individuals can provide 100 percent of their preretirement income as a retiree. Human nature tends to mitigate against any planning activity if the individual is convinced that it is impossible to achieve the desired goal. Thus, preretirees must inventory those assets that would be available to respond to that economic hazard. Certainly, Social Security would loom important in that analysis as well as company benefits and personal assets. It is interesting that another resource is emerging in current planning: employment in retirement, either full or part time, which is often quite different from the prior employment.

Inflation. Inflation is probably the first concern in the minds of most individuals making their retirement financial plans. Preoccupation with it, however, can be disastrous to good planning. The purpose of this section of a program should be to illustrate how a wide variety of assets and planning ideas can respond to the inflation risk—for example, the recent excellent history of real estate investment in keeping up with inflation and the use of leverage along with the basic knowledge of the income tax law.

Life Insurance. Since life insurance represents a relatively large expenditure for most family units, the purpose of this section is to remove some of the mystery of the various kinds available. Discuss the risk analysis concept with respect to deductibles versus insurance premium size. Make a lazy asset (cash value life insurance) increase its after-tax return by over 100 percent by borrowing out the cash value and investing it in an alternative asset.

Social Security. Social Security presents somewhat of a dilemma. Currently, it represents a very large asset in most personal resources against the financial risk of retiring, while at the same time there is a broad-based concern and apprehension about the ability of Social Security to meet its future liabilities. It is recommended that discussion of Social Security not center on its mechanics, such as quarters of coverage or calculation of benefits, but on more broad-based planning issues. Examples include: What are the postretirement restrictions on earned income, and how do they work? What are the implications of retirement before age 65 (the so-called penalty of commencing benefits at 62)? How can one check on whether or not Social Security has the proper record of earnings credited to one's account? What is the income tax liability of receipt of benefits?

Income Tax

Objective. The purpose of this section is to help individuals to increase their understanding of the basics of the tax law. Most invidiuals have never had the occasion or reason to comprehend the federal income tax law. Information regarding the progressive nature of the tax law is rarely understood. Facts regarding the progressive tax include the following: some income has no tax, some has a tax of 11 percent, some at 14 percent, and under current law, the federal government cannot take more than 50 percent of any of your taxable income. Unfortuantely, this progressive tax rate is structured so that the more we earn the higher the percentage on the last dollar of income the federal government can tax. However, a little tax planning can reap large dividends since that planning occurs at the highest marginal rate of taxable income.

Intra-Family Shifting of Income. One of the most productive and basic of tax-planning ideas is to remove income from the relatively high tax bracket of, for example, the parents and to shift that income to the relatively lower marginal income tax brackets of, for example, a child or grandchild. The use of the ten-year short-term trust and/or interest-free loans presents an excellent planning device for most individuals.

Tax Shelters. It is axiomatic that most individuals already have one of the best tax shelters under the law—their principal residence. A discussion of what makes tax shelters work can be very helpful in removing some of the mystery while at the same time assisting individuals in the decision whether or not they should be interested in the first place.

Estate/Wills

Objective. The objective of this section is to recommend strongly that the primary purpose of estate planning is not the saving of taxes. The primary purpose should be, in all cases, to distribute the decedent's assets to those individuals the decedent has elected. The secondary purpose is to minimize taxes within the framework of the primary purpose.

Administration. The purpose of this section is to remove some of the mystery of the function of the will and to clarify the meaning of *trust*, the duties of an executor, and activities in probate proceedings.

Taxable versus Probate Estate. Probably one of the least understood facts by individuals is that the taxable estate, in most cases, is substantially larger than the probate estate. For example, life insurance in most cases is includable for federal estate tax purposes but is not part of a probate estate. Also, everything is taxed at fair market value on the date of death. What was paid for the asset is not relevant for estate tax purposes.

Gift and Federal Estate Taxes. Emphasis here should be on the fact that the United States now has a transfer tax. The rules are substantially the same whether you transfer your assets during your lifetime or distribute those assets on death through the vehicle of your will. Everyone has a lifetime credit against the tax otherwise due. How and when to use that credit can be very productive toward reducing the total tax bill.

Selecting an Attorney and an Executor. A discussion is recommended with respect to what an attorney and an executor do under the terms of the will and state law. A thoughtful analysis of who should serve in each of the capacities and an awareness of the expenses concomitant with the performance of these services is recommended in this section.

Implications for Retirement Specialists

The designers of the financial-planning section of the retirement-planning program have several instructional alternatives available to them. They may provide:

Individual counseling on the employer's benefit plan package only;

Group meetings on the benefit plan package only;

Group meetings that include discussion of the benefit plan package and outside speakers/experts on selected subjects;

Print material only, like magazines mailed to the home, and home study courses;

Group meetings and print materials;

Group meetings combining custom-designed print materials or a combination of packaged and custom-designed materials;

Group meetings featuring outside speakers on financial-planning subjects integrated with general program content or inside speakers specifically trained on financial subjects;

Interactive and group participation models with the leader serving as a facilitator rather than a speaker.

As a broad-based overview, it seems clear that the first and foremost decision to be made is to determine the employer's objective in sponsoring such a program. Is there a commitment to the necessary time and money to design, initiate, implement, and sustain a worthwhile program? Having commenced a program, is the employer prepared to make the follow-up expenditure of time and money to respond to what is almost a certainty— interest in and desire for the programs at all locations of the business on a continuing basis? The answers to these questions will largely dictate the content emphasis and style of the program.

With respect to the financial-planning portion of the total program, it is suggested that the individual responsible for the retirement-planning program be knowledgeable of, at least, the rudiments of possible program content. It would be extremely difficult to assume responsibility for the presentation of a program without having knowledge of the financial program objectives and the content that should be included. Such responsibility should be assumed, however, since attendees are likely to ascribe a certain element of approbation to the sponsor of the program. Further, the purpose of the financial-planning section is not to provide a vehicle for outside speakers to display products and services they desire to sell. Thus, the retirement planner should have continuing interest in the course content and how well that content is achieving the program's objectives.

References

Peterson, D.A. "Instruction in Retirement Preparation Programs." In *Retirement Preparation: An Update*, edited by H. Dennis. Los Angeles: University of Southern California, 1982.

Suggested Readings

The subject of financial planning does not lend itself well to hardcover text and research data; general and financial contemporary magazines and newspapers provide the most timely and relevant information on the subject. Notwithstanding, the following suggested reading list may prove helpful. Examples of popular press articles are "Tax Free Ways to Save for Retirement," *U.S. News and World Report*, August 31, 1982; and "The Coming IRA Bonanza," *Newsweek*, December 1, 1982.

House and Garden regularly features an article entitled "Money." Furthermore, nearly all local newspapers feature a business or commerce section that contains information helpful to personal financial planning. A regular feature in the "Money and Banking" section of *Business Week* displays "Investment Figures of the Week." Finally, the *Wall Street Journal* discusses personal financial planning matters in a periodic feature article, "Your Money Matters." A daily presentation of current returns on a broad range of investments is entitled "Money Rates."

Harris, L., and Associates. *1979 Study of American Attitudes toward Pensions and Retirement*. New York: Louis Harris and Associates, 1979.

> Survey of a national cross section of 1,699 current and retired employees from 212 companies. Special attention is devoted to the issues of financial independence in retirement.

Internal Revenue Service. *Your Federal Income Tax*. Pub. no. 17.

> A layman's language approach to federal income tax that is updated in the fall of every year.

Weinstein, G.W. *Retire Tomorrow—Plan Today*. New York: Dale Publishing Company, 1976.

> Financial planning and a twenty-five-year planning guide are described. Advantages and disadvantges of various income sources and investment strategies are presented as well as practical hints and sources of additional information.

5

The Three-Legged Stool of Retirement Income

Phoebe S. Liebig

Retirement Income Planning

Retirement income is one of the most important topics covered in preretirement planning, counseling, and training programs. Indeed, for many persons, financial planning is preretirement planning. Although finances are hardly the only issues, they certainly constitute a major portion of each individual's concerns about and strategies for retirement. The amount and types of financial resources available to individuals obviously have great impact on the quality of their lives in the postretirement period. The several types of income are often designated as the legs of a retirement income stool.

Although employment after retirement and intrafamily transfers of cash and other resources from younger to older members might be designated as legs of this retirement income stool, many retirees do not have these resources and are unlikely to have them. After retirement from a particular job, postretirement employment opportunities are not often readily available, and postretirement earnings are likely to be restricted by pension policies. This situation may be unchanged even after the new, higher age for Social Security eligibility (age 67) goes into effect in the year 2027. Similarly, many younger family members may have obligations that make it difficult, if not impossible, to provide cash resources for retired family members.

The majority of individuals, however, is almost sure to have one or more of the three basic sources of retirement income: Social Security, an employer/union pension plan, and private savings for retirement, so-called self-pensioning. In assisting individuals to plan for a relatively secure retirement, it is vital for preretirement educators and trainers not only to be knowledgeable about specific aspects of each of these three legs of the retirement income stool but also to comprehend relevant factors that affect the overall retirement income picture. Thus, preretirement specialists need to be aware that situations such as sustained inflation and the consequent reduction of purchasing power of those on relatively fixed incomes are important considerations in any rational retirement-planning program.

Additional decision-making factors include the prospect of a longer life span and the likelihood of an extended period of retirement for an ever-growing number of older persons; changing family circumstances, often multigenerational in nature; and the probability of failing health and some functional losses for most persons in their upper seventies and beyond. Still other important factors in retirement income planning include changes in the tax laws and additional amendments to the Social Security program as have occurred in the past several years and that are likely to continue.

Sources of Retirement Income

To comprehend the three major sources of retirement income, it is important to realize the wide variations in philosophy, coverage and benefits, financing and funding, and government regulation/policy constraints that determine the relative role played by each of them in providing income for the retirement years.

Social Security

Social Security, first introduced in 1935 during the New Deal years, is the largest and best known source of retirement income; more than 90 percent of all retirees receive some Social Security benefits. Designed to be both an insurance and income maintenance program, Social Security is a major means by which individuals can be sheltered from adverse economic circumstances over which they have little or no control—specifically, loss of income due to disability, ill health, or retirement. The system now includes three major programs: (1) Old Age, Survivors and Disability Insurance (OASDI) programs; (2) the retirement income/survivor benefits program; and (3) hospital insurance for persons 65 and over (Medicare). OASDI provides a guaranteed floor of retirement income and benefits based on each individual's wage history and thus is based on concepts of adequacy and equity.

Since its initial passage, Social Security coverage and benefits have been extended. Although less than half of all private sector employees originally were covered, 93 percent of the labor force currently participates. Until recently, notable exceptions included the federal civil service, as well as many employees of nonprofit organizations and state and local governments. The 1983 amendments, however, now require new federal employees to participate in the Social Security system, bar state and local governments from exercising their former right of withdrawal, and require coverage of nonprofit organization employees, thereby insuring virtually universal coverage within the next several years. More than 160 million people have Social Security earnings credits, and that number will grow steadily over the next decade.

Benefits have also been extended since 1939 to cover the entire family unit against the loss of income stemming from retirement and disability. Monthly benefits, which are skewed toward lower-income workers, have been increased markedly in recent years and are indexed annually for inflation according to the Consumer Price Index (CPI) to insure that retirees' purchasing power is not severely eroded. Payments that are increased for costs-of-living adjustments are called COLAs.

Benefits are not subject to the income tax except for older individuals or couples whose combined sources of postretirement income exceed base amounts legislated in 1983, which include all outside income plus half of Social Security benefits. Although 65 is the normal retirement age currently at which individuals are eligible for full benefits, they may opt for early retirement at age 62. After retirement, however, if individuals earn wages beyond a certain limit, they lose some Social Security benefits. They must work a minimum of covered quarters to be eligible for a benefit, and each individual's benefit is calculated according to a formula based on average monthly earnings. In 1976, Social Security paid out 54 percent of all retirement disability and survivor benefits in the United States. In 1980, in excess of $137 billion was paid to 35 million recipients, and recently that sum had escalated to more than $150 billion.

Social Security is financed by a compulsory payroll tax paid by employers and employees, as well as by self-employed persons. Funding is on a *pay-as-you-go* basis; no trust funds are invested on a long-term basis. Thus, benefits to current retirees are paid from the taxes of current workers. This retirement income program is administered by the Social Security Administration (SSA) of the federal government. The SSA has branch offices across the nation and will provide, upon request, information concerning covered earnings and prospective benefits.

Employer/Union Pensions

Employer/union pensions are plans established and maintained by an employer (whether private or public), a group of employers, or a union primarily to provide for the payment of benefits to participants after retirement. These pension plans include 68 federal employee and 6,630 state and local government employee plans, with 23 percent of the U.S. work force covered by public plans. There are 1.1 million private plans that cover more than half of all private industry workers. As one might expect, public and private employer/union plans differ significantly.

Public Plans

Federal. The Federal Civil Service pension plan, established in 1920, is the largest federal plan. Based on the philosophy of a reward for long-term services, it is an *advance-funding* system (see the glossary for an explanation of this and other pension terminology) and is financed by employer (the federal government) and employee contributions. In addition, general revenues are appropriated to cover the interest on the plan's *unfunded liability.* Coverage is virtually 100 percent. Eligibility for full benefits can occur at age 55 with thirty years of service, at age 60 with twenty years of service, or at age 62 with five years of service. The maximum pension benefit is 80 percent of preretirement salary after forty-two years of service, and benefits are automatically indexed twice a year according to the CPI. Survivor pensions for widows/widowers of retirees are part of the benefit package. In 1978, $10.7 billion was paid out to 1.6 million recipients, and more recently over $12 billion was paid out, including COLAs.

Other federal plans include the Railroad Retirement system, begun in 1937, which covers 550,000 active workers who match contributions with their employers to finance the fund and which paid out $4.1 billion to nearly 1.2 million retirees, dependents, and survivors in 1978; the military pension system, established after the Revolutionary War, which is a noncontributory, pay-as-you-go plan, financed by congressional appropriations as part of the defense budget and which pays out automatically indexed benefits semi-annually based on twenty- and thirty-years-of-service formulas; and miscellaneous plans for Congress, the Foreign Service, the Federal Reserve System, civilian employees of the military services, and other uniformed services. Because of a high level of *vesting,* 89 percent of the federal work force is either receiving or expects to receive federal pension benefits. Although 55 percent of employees in all current federal plans are excluded from Social Security, many have established or will establish eligibility for at least the minimim number of covered quarters. As noted earlier, new employees of the Federal Civil Service are now required to join the Social Security system. Thus, the percentage of excluded federal workers will decrease over the next several decades.

State and Local Governments. These highly diverse pension plans were first established in 1857 for municipal police. The first teachers' plan began in 1893, and the first state employee plan began in 1911. Two basic philosophies obtain: (1) deferred compensation and (2) rewards for long-term service. For fire and police and other public safety employees, compensation for hazardous duty is also included.

Most plans are *defined benefit plans* and are financed by employer and employee contributions, plus investment earnings. Larger state-administered plans are usually *actuarially funded;* however, a few state plans are funded on a pay-as-you-go basis, as is true of many smaller and local plans. There is a strong continuing trend for many smaller and local plans to be merged with larger state plans and/or to be more highly regulated and monitored by state governments. Ninety percent of all full-time employees are covered, and many state plans also cover employees who work at least half-time. Vesting occurs within five to ten years.

The typical employee, after thirty years of service, can retire at age 60 on a pension of 50 percent of his or her average pay for the last five years. Because 72 percent of all state and local employees are also covered by Social Security, at age 65 pension income is increased to about 80 percent of final pay and sometimes more, if the plans are not integrated. Automatic COLAs are common but usually have a ceiling, or cap, of 3 percent. Benefits are normally not subject to state income taxes, but portions are subject to federal tax. Postretirement survivor benefits are not automatic; they must be selected, usually resulting in lower monthly payments to compensate for the longer payout period of benefits to retirees and surviving spouses. Early retirement benefits are also an option, with a similar actuarial reduction. Postretirement employment by the same employer or any employer participating in a given pension system is usually very restricted, resulting in benefit loss. Some larger plans also continue certain benefits, such as life and health insurance, into the postretirement period. The benefits paid out have increased from $9.6 billion to 2.2 million retirees, survivors, and dependents in 1978 to more than $13 billion in 1982.

Private Plans

Corporate and Union. The first corporate pension plan was established in 1875; the first union plan was begun in 1905. Corporate pension philosophy, then as now, is to reward long-term service to a particular company. For unions, the impetus has been to reward a lifetime (typically thirty years) of hard work, particularly if no company or industry plan existed and, not incidentally, to insure that jobs would be available for younger workers. When first established, corporate plans tended to be financed jointly by employer-employee contributions; however, they are now financed almost entirely by employers and investment earnings. Financing of union plans has been based on members' dues and investment earnings.

Private plans are regulated by the federal government under the provisions of the Employee Retirement Income Security Act (ERISA). Federal standards for actuarial funding, vesting, reporting, disclosure of information to participants, and investment procedures are enforced. Approximately 40 million workers, or 62 percent of all private sector workers, are covered and are vested after ten years. However, nearly 36 million, usually nonunionized workers, are not covered by a pension plan, nearly 60 percent of whom work in firms with fewer than 100 workers.

Benefits are based on one of two formulas: defined benefit or *defined contribution.* The employer portion of the benefit is taxed in the postretirement period. As a general rule, survivor benefits in the postretirement period do not occur automatically and must be selected. Benefit amounts, which on average are not very large, are not indexed automatically, may or may not be integrated with Social Security, and are subject to the overall economic health of the company. Under the provisions of ERISA, however, benefits are insured against loss through payment by employers of insurance premiums to the Pension Benefit Guaranty Corporation, a federal agency. Early retirement, often at ages less than the age of the Social Security early retirement option (62), is available to and often chosen by workers. Union benefits are often used to supplement the corporate plan until the retiree is eligible for Social Security benefits.

Similar to public plans, private plans put heavy restrictions on post-retirement employment, not only with the same employer but also often with any employer in the same industry. Unlike most public plans, private plans do not offer postretirement benefits like health insurance, but during the working years many companies provide *tax-deferred compensation* plans like employee stock option plans (ESOPs), which can be used to supplement the regular pension plan or for other purposes.

Self-Pensioning

In addition to investments and home equity, eligible individuals can establish retirement savings plans. Until recently, eligibility was restricted to self-employed and employed persons who were not active participants in a qualified retirement or pension plan. As individuals, they could create IRAs. As self-employed or small business owners, they could choose Keoghs. Eligibility for tax-deferred IRAs has now been broadened so that virtually anyone who can afford to do so may create this self-financed source of retirement income. Benefits, which are not indexed, can begin between the ages of 59½ and 70½. If withdrawn earlier, IRA benefits are subject to heavier tax penalties. They can be paid out in a lump sum or in periodic payments upon retirement and are taxable. Benefits for nonworking spouses can be elected but are not automatic. These plans/accounts are usually held by insurance companies, banks, savings and loans, or mutual funds.

Implications for Retirement Specialists

It is important for retirement planners, educators, and counselors to be aware of these several sources of retirement income, not only for general knowledge in order to lead discussions on financial planning but also to provide a basis for examination of the vital issues of adequacy.

A major concern of all retirees is Will my postretirement income be adequate? Faced with inflation and other uncertainties, as well as with the general expectations for a fairly comfortable period of retirement, it is becoming abundantly clear that most retirees will have an adequate income only if they have two or more sources. This is especially true for retirees in the last part of this century and in the next whose Social Security benefits will be proportionately less than those of today's retirees. It is mandatory, therefore, that preretirement courses explore the three legs of the retirement income stool and not just company/union plans, as is often the case. Prospective retirees should be very clear on the differing types of coverage, eligibility, vesting, and spousal/dependents benefits offered by the several kinds of retirement income plans, as well as the tax status of retirement benefits.

In addition, the changing circumstances of the American family must be taken into account when retirement income strategies are being planned. With the higher incidence of two-worker/two-career families, retirement income planning must include the pension assets of both earners, as well as the timing of retirement. Similarly, with the prevalence of divorce in the later years, the property rights inherent in vested pension benefits deserve consideration. In sum, by cultivation of broad knowledge about the major retirement income sources, retirement counselors and educators can stress the need for their clients and trainees to develop a pension mix plus savings to insure adequate income for the retirement years.

Glossary

Actuarial funding Advance funding that relies on mathematical predictions based on factors such as participant demographics, past experience of a particular plan, and economic projections such as rate of inflation and return on the investment of the assets of the specific pension fund. Used to determine rate of the employer's contribution.

Advance funding A method by which both current and projected obligations of a pension fund are covered by current and future assets and by current and projected contributions to the fund to insure that benefits will be paid to eligible participants. The opposite of pay-as-you-go funding and required of all private pension plans.

Defined benefit plan A pension plan in which participant's benefits are based on a predetermined formula directly related to the salary and service of the retiring employee.

Defined contribution plan A pension plan in which a participant's benefits are based solely on fixed-rate amounts contributed to his or her individual account with any income earned thereon.

Pay-as-you-go funding A method of funding like the Social Security method by which contributions of active plan participants are used to pay the benefits of retired workers. The opposite of advance funding.

Tax-deferred compensation Arrangements by which compensation to employees for past or current service is postponed to some future date. The income tax on that compensation is postponed, often to the postretirement period, when presumably, income tax liabilities are less.

Unfunded liability Pension liabilities for which there are as yet no assets. These unfunded costs can be a product of past services credited for employees prior to the initiation of a plan, of increased benefits for which contributions are inadequate, or incorrect actuarial assumptions/projections.

Vesting After a specified number of years of pension coverage, often ten years, an employee has earned a legal right of ownership in that pension to be paid out at retirement, whether or not the employee remains working for the employer under whom the pension has been earned.

Suggested Readings

American Council of Life Insurance. *Pension Facts.*

> An annual publication with facts about the several kinds of retirement income programs: Social Security, employer pensions, and IRAs and Keoghs.

Ball, R. *Social Security: Today and Tomorrow.* New York: Columbia University Press, 1978.

> A classic book on the Social Security system, written in a conversational manner by one of the early architects of the system, containing a lot of basic information.

Employee Benefit Plan Review

> A monthly periodical that focuses on all fringe benefits and all sources of retirement income. Easy-to-read, short articles are designed for employee benefit specialists.

Employee Benefit Research Institute Publications

> A think tank that explores fringe benefits and produces numerous publications, often technical in nature, that explore current policy issues in all areas of retirement income. Designed for the sophisticated reader.

Greenough, W.C., and King, F.P. *Pension Plans and Public Policy.* New York: Columbia University Press, 1976.

> A classic book that focuses on the ways in which public policy has shaped the creation of pension plans and Social Security.

Pension World

A monthly, somewhat tecnnical magazine that focuses on various trends in pension plans and changes in public and private pension policy.

Summary Plan Descriptions (SPD)

Private pension plans, as mandated by ERISA, must provide information via an SPD concerning retirement plan benefits and eligibility for those benefits. Reading this kind of document, which is usually provided by large public plans as well, is instructive, and participants should take the time to read theirs in some detail.

Tilove, R. *Public Employee Pension Funds*. New York: Columbia University Press, 1976.

A classic book on the characteristics of public employee pension systems—easily comprehended despite its technical presentation.

U.S. Social Security Administration. *Your Social Security.*

A folder put out by Social Security that sets forth basic information about benefits. It is part of a series on the several programs of Social Security. In addition to these suggested readings, information on Individual Retirement Accounts (IRAs) and Keoghs can be obtained from banks and/or savings and loan companies and mutual funds.

6

Alternative Work Options

Dorothy Fleisher

Role of Work Options

Retirement specialists should be familiar with alternative work options because such options offer the promise of meeting the needs of the middle-aged and older individual as well as providing benefits to the organization. Older persons may wish to delay retirement or to return to work after retirement for the intrinsic reward derived from the work role or to supplement their incomes in the face of inflation. In either case, they may prefer a job with lesser responsibilities, flexible scheduling, or reduced hours. Faced with escalating pension costs and labor force shortages, organizations may implement alternative work options as part of a policy to retain older workers. Work options may also be developed to create additional jobs while simultaneously providing older persons with a gradual transition to retirement.

Definitions, Trends, and Usage of Work Options

This section defines various alternative work options and notes trends in their usage. In addition, it highlights advantages and disadvantages and reports the degree of interest among older workers.

Flexitime

Individuals have the freedom to choose the hours they will start and stop working within certain constraints. For example, they must be present during a core time each day and work an agreed upon number of hours within a specified period (that is, day, week, or month).

Several types of flexitime have emerged that vary in the degree of flexibility permitted. Flexitour, the least flexible type, requires that starting and stopping times remain constant once selected by the employees. Gliding time permits variation in starting and stopping times on a daily basis but requires employees to work a standard eight-hour day. Variable day, the most flexible type, moves away from the standard eight-hour day, requiring that employees work a given number of hours by the end of a week or a month (New Work Schedules for a Changing Society 1981).

In 1980, approximately 7.6 million full-time workers or 11.9 percent of those holding nonfarm, wage and salary jobs were on flexitime. Flexitime scheduling is widespread among sales personnel, managers and officials, professional workers, and transportation equipment operators. In addition, flexible scheduling is growing among clerical and service workers. The sector of the economy most frequently using flexitime is the federal government, followed by service industries such as insurance and finance. Manufacturing industries report the lowest use (U.S. Bureau of Labor Statistics 1981).

The advantages of flexitime for employees include increased morale and job satisfaction, easier commuting, and a better fit between work schedules and family routines. For employers, flexitime results in decreased absenteeism, tardiness, and turnover; increased productivity; and reduced overtime costs (Nollen 1979). Obstacles center around the nature of the work. For example, some jobs are interdependent, requiring workers to be present at the same time (McConnell et al. 1980). Similarly, when shift work is involved, employees cannot have the freedom to come and go as they wish. Providing supervisory coverage over a longer day poses other problems. Front line supervisors initially report difficulty in communication, scheduling production, and assuring adequate coverage (Nollen 1982). Still another obstacle is the fact that anything but a standard eight-hour day may interfere with negotiated overtime policies.

Older workers' preferences for flexitime are largely unknown. It would appear that the ability to control their work schedule would be appealing. Support for this assertion is provided by a study of employees nearing retirement in the Los Angeles city government and the Lockheed California Company. Ten percent of those surveyed ($N = 333$) chose full-time work with flexible scheduling as their first choice among a range of work options presented to them (McConnell et al. 1980).

Compressed Work Week

In a compressed work week, individuals work the usual number of hours required for full-time positions but in fewer than five days. In 1980, 2.7 percent of the wage and salaried labor force worked a compressed week of 4½ days or less. Employees on compressed schedules tend to be service workers, transportation equipment operators, and factory operators. The greatest users of the compressed work week are public agencies, especially police and fire departments, and small manufacturing firms (U.S. Bureau of Labor Statistics 1981).

A compressed work week provides employees with several advantages: they have longer blocks of free time, spend less time commuting, and can use their day off to attend to personal matters. The organization can benefit because extended work days reduce the down-time cost in operating expensive equipment. Problems in utilizing this alternative involve scheduling to ensure that workers whose tasks interface are present at the same time, provision of adequate supervisory coverage, and reduction in productivity due to fatigue. In addition, compressed work weeks, like flexitime, may conflict with labor contracts that require overtime pay for working more than eight hours per day (Nollen 1982).

Relatively little is known about the appeal of this option to older workers. On the one hand, some evidence suggests that they may be more likely to object to a compressed work week than younger workers and that their job performance may be adversely affected because of their susceptibility to fatigue. On the other hand, the availability of increased free time to pursue other interests may make this option especially attractive to older workers (Copperman and Keast 1980; Nollen 1979).

Part-Time Work

Individuals work a reduced number of hours, on a permanent or temporary basis, in part-time work. Many patterns are possible, including part-day, part-week, part-year, alternating weeks, and alternating months. Several variations of part-time employment have emerged in response to differing needs of management.

Job Sharing. Job sharing is one such variation in which two individuals share responsibility for one full-time position on a permanent basis. In some organizations, employees have taken the initiative in convincing management of the desirability of this alternative, finding their own partners, and arranging their work schedules. In other settings, personnel analysts have identified positions that may be amenable to job sharing and have surveyed employees to learn of their interest. Job sharing has been successful for unskilled workers in manufacturing plants as well as for those in managerial and professional positions. For this option to be effective, top management must be committed to it, and job sharers must carefully plan the allocation of tasks based on complementary skills and must maintain open and ongoing communication (McCarthy and Rosenberg 1981; Nollen 1982).

Phased Retirement. Another variation of part-time work is phased retirement. Individuals gradually reduce the number of hours they work until they retire completely. The phase-in period varies with different plans and may range from one to five years prior to a worker's retirement. Similarly, the time reduction permitted differs. Work days may be shortened (for example, from eight to four hours); work weeks may be reduced (for example, from four days to three or two days); or extended leaves may be granted (for example, from one to three months). This option allows workers time to explore other interests, thus easing their transition to retirement. Management benefits because replacements can be trained and the work force can be reduced voluntarily (McCarthy and Rosenberg 1981; Swank 1982).

Returning Retirees. Still another variation of part-time employment involves the rehiring of retirees on an as-needed basis for temporary assignments. Some organizations maintain annuitant pools for this purpose (Jacobson 1980). Other organizations utilize job shops that allow former employees to be rehired without a reduction in their pension benefits (McConnell et al. 1980).

In 1979, 14 percent of the labor force was voluntarily employed in permanent part-time jobs. Most part-time positions are in sales, clerical, and laboring occupations and in the trade and service industries. Very few part-time positions are found in managerial and skilled blue-collar occupations or in mining and manufacturing industries (Nollen 1979).

Part-time employment provides management with the flexibility to match "the size of the job with the size of the staff" (New Work Schedules for a Changing Society, p. 19, 1981). For example, part-time workers can be used when the job requires more than an eight-hour day, to meet cyclical or peak work load demands, or to provide vacation relief. As a result, overtime costs are reduced, idle time is eliminated, and performance is improved, especially in jobs that are stressful. The major difficulties encountered are scheduling problems, additional paperwork, increased costs of providing fringe benefits, and resistance by unions who believe that part-time workers reduce the number of jobs available to full-time workers.

The evidence suggests that many older workers prefer part-time work to retirement. The major obstacles are the Social Security retirement test that limits earnings and pension policies that prevent employers from paying pension benefits to their own employees. In 1977, nearly half (48 percent) of the men aged 65 and over who were employed worked part time. A nationwide Harris poll conducted in 1978 revealed that 24 percent of those currently working preferred part-time work to retirement (Copperman and Keast 1980).

Similarly, a study of municipal government employees and aerospace workers found that one-half of those surveyed would extend their work lives if alternative work options were available and that part-time options were the most desirable. Those who were interested in part-time options preferred to work a reduced number of days per week, whether part-year or full-year (McConnell et al. 1980).

Job Redesign

With job redesign, individuals can be given responsibility for a larger or smaller part of the total product; stressful tasks associated with jobs can be eliminated; or the work environment can be changed. While the extent to which job redesign has been formally implemented by organizations is not well known, it is acknowledged that jobs are frequently modified on an informal basis to accommodate to individuals' differing capacities. Job redesign may be necessary to implement flexitime, the compressed work week, and part-time options.

Job redesign may result in improved morale and increased productivity. Modifications to accommodate workers with physical limitations reduce disability payment costs by enabling valued employees to continue working. Obstacles include both the difficulty of reassigning tasks to someone else and the possibility that the modified job will be reclassified at a lower grade level with a corresponding reduction in pay.

Relatively little is known about older workers' interest in job redesign as an alternative to retirement. One study indicated that 12 percent of those workers nearing retirement preferred job modifications to retirement on the condition that the change did not involve a reduction in pay (McConnell et al. 1980).

Job Transfers

Individuals are reassigned to different jobs, either with comparable responsibilities, status, and pay (lateral transfers) or with lesser responsiblities, status, and pay (demotion) in job transfers. For the most part, personnel policies provide employees with the option of transferring jobs. However, programs that involve voluntary demotions are not yet widespread.

Job transfers can accommodate workers' needs that stem from medical problems, job-related stress, or burnout. They can also provide an alternative to termination for employees who are not performing adequately in their current positions. Obstacles associated with job transfers include a reduction in pay and future pension benefits, the loss of status and power, and resistance by front line supervisors concerned with the productivity of their units.

Older workers' interest in job transfers, and particularly demotions, is not well established. Only 5 percent of preretirees in one study selected this option as their first choice (McConnell et al. 1980). Demotions may be more acceptable to European workers. A 1978 survey of Danish managers representing 154 large corporations found that when the choice was between demotion or early retirement, 70 percent of those 55 and over indicated a preference for a down-graded job involving fewer responsibilities and lower status (Copperman and Keast 1980).

Implications for Retirement Specialists

Retirement specialists should include information about alternative work options, especially part-time work, in their career-planning sessions with employees. The discussions should highlight the advantages and disadvantages of selecting one or another alternative. This requires retirement specialists to be conversant with the financial impact of various alternatives, which may necessitate consultation with benefits and compensation specialists within the organization. For example, they must know the extent to which a particular work option will influence the individual's wages, pension, and Social Security payments; eligibility for company-sponsored benefits such as medical, life, and disability insurance; and accumulation of vacation and sick leave. It may be that by making employees aware of available alternatives, the demand for work options will increase.

In addition, retirement specialists may need to work with human resource and planning specialists to explore the feasibility of implementing particular work options within their own corporations or agencies. This would necessitate an analysis of the organization's labor force needs and production demands as well as an assessment of employees' interest in each of the alternatives. It should be noted that unions have bargained for alternative work options when their workers have asked for them (Nollen 1982). However, union and professional association leaders are often unaware of employees' interest in such options (McConnell et al. 1980). To date, firms that have implemented work options have done so in response to labor shortages, demands made by employees, and a desire to retain valued older workers.

References

Copperman, L., and Keast, F. *The Last Few Years Are Free*. Portland, Oreg.: Institute on Aging, Portland State University, 1980.

Jacobson, B. *Young Programs for Older Workers*. Work in America Institute Series. New York: Van Nostrand Reinhold, 1980.

McCarthy, M.E., and Rosenberg, G.D. *Work Sharing: Case Studies*. Kalamazoo, Mich.: W.E. Upjohn Institute for Employment Research, 1981.

McConnell, S.R.; Fleisher, D.; Kaplan, B.H.; and Usher, C.E. *Alternative Work Options for Older Workers: A Feasibility Study*. Los Angeles: Andrus Gerontology Center, University of Southern California, 1980.

New Work Schedules for a Changing Society. Scarsdale, N.Y.: Work in America Institute, 1981.

Nollen, S. *New Patterns of Work*. Scarsdale, N.Y.: Work in America Institute, 1979.

Nollen, S. *New Work Schedules in Practice*. New York: Van Nostrand Reinhold Company, 1982.

Swank, C. *Phased Retirement: The European Experience*. Washington, D.C.: National Council for Alternative Work Patterns, 1982.

U.S. Bureau of Labor Statistics. News release, February 24, 1981.

Suggested Readings

Jacobson, B. *Young Programs for Older Workers*. Work in America Institute Series, 1980.

> A compilation of case studies which describe innovative personnel policies for older workers that focus on new work arrangements, re-entry workers, secondary organizations, redeployment, the new hires, and assessing and advising.

McCarthy, M.E., and Rosenberg, G.D. *Work Sharing: Case Studies*. Kalamazoo, Mich.: W.E. Upjohn Institute for Employment Research, 1981.

> Presents 36 case studies that illustrate three major types of work-sharing approaches: a temporary reduction in work hours, a permanent reduction in work hours, and flexible work-life options including phased retirement and voluntary time–income trade-offs. These approaches were designed to meet needs such as avoiding layoffs, preventing burnout, adjusting to shortages of workers with particular skills, and retaining valued employees.

McConnell, S.R., Fleisher, D., Kaplan, B.H., and Usher, C.E. *Alternative Work Options for Older Workers: A Feasibility Study*. Los Angeles: The Andrus Gerontology Center, University of Southern California, 1980.

> Summarizes a research project undertaken to examine the feasibility of alternative work options for preretirees in two organizations: the Los Angeles City Government and the Lockheed California Company. Perceptions of employees, managers, and union leaders are presented.

New Work Schedules for a Changing Society. Scarsdale: Work in America Institute, 1981.

> The executive summary of a report describing an eighteen-month study of alternative work schedule projects. Fifty recommendations are presented to guide labor unions, employers, and government in determining when and how to best implement alternative work schedules.

Nollen, S. *New Work Schedules in Practice.* New York: Van Nostrand
Reinhold Company, 1982.

   Detailed case descriptions representing a variety of settings to help
   employers manage alternative work patterns and overcome "sticky"
   problems associated with their implementation.

7

Instruction in Retirement Preparation Programs

David A. Peterson

Retirement Specialists as Educators

Effective retirement preparation programs have been offered by numerous organizations and individuals. These use a variety of methods and techniques to present information, help people plan, and attempt to improve perceptions and attitudes toward retirement. One issue that continually confronts leaders of these programs is the role they should play and the function they should perform. Comprehensive retirement preparation programs that include content on leisure, employment, services, housing, and attitudes in addition to finances provide an outstanding opportunity for leaders to play the role of the adult educator and to guide the learning of middle-aged and older adults in an effective manner.

Since retirement planning, in many instances, was developed from company benefits offices, the emphasis was on the pension and insurance privileges of retirement. However, the comprehensive retirement preparation program is much broader and requires the skills of an educator or facilitator to design an instructional experience in which the participants acquire new information and skills that will lead to changes in behavior or attitude.

For this to occur in the most effective way, the leader must become a facilitator and utilize the insights that have been generated from teaching and learning in middle age and later life. This information provides an understanding of differences between the adult learner and the child and suggests a series of behaviors on the part of the facilitator that will optimize learning and change.

The Older Learner

Although stereotypes prevalent in contemporary society suggest that intelligence declines with advancing years, in reality, people of any age are able to learn effectively. What we often fail to note, however, is that adults and other learners may be limited in the techniques they use to learn and in their belief regarding their potential in academic areas.

Most studies of learning performance have been conducted in a laboratory setting, but extrapolation to the classroom provides a number of insights into actions the facilitator can take to increase the learning of older students. It has been found that older learners have a difficult time concentrating on two things at once (Arenberg and Robertson n.d.). Therefore, interference occurs when extraneous noise is present or when people try to learn two items at the same time. The facilitator should try to be sure that one concept or fact is learned before a second one is addressed.

Laboratory studies have shown that older people perform less well when the learning task must be completed under the pressure of time (Canestrari 1968). Thus, facilitators should move slowly through the content and allow people to learn at their own pace whenever possible.

Older people also do more poorly than young learners in organizing material for future retrieval (Hultsch 1969). They tend to rely on rote memorization rather than organizing the material spontaneously in a way that will help it make sense and be remembered. When investigators in laboratory studies encouraged older people to categorize words to be learned, scores improved. This was especially true of older persons with poor verbal skills. The facilitator can improve learning by providing ways to organize the materials. This can be done by presenting it in clear categories, identifying relationships with current knowledge, and preparing outlines so the older learner can see where the lecture or discussion is leading.

We are all aware that acuity of vision and hearing decline with age. Studies have shown that older people benefit from using two senses when learning rather than one (Arenberg 1968). The implication is that if people see and here the same content, they learn more efficiently. Thus, if an outline or listing is put on the chalkboard, it should be very similar to what has been said verbally, or older people will have to concentrate on two different things at the same time and learning will be decreased.

A final consideration from laboratory studies is the effect of anxiety on learning performance. Older people tend to find learning difficult and to become concerned about their potential and performance. Studies have shown that when older learners are given supportive instructions and are expected to succeed, they do (Ross 1968). The opposite is also true; when the instructor does not expect them to do well and communicates that to them, they do poorly. The attitude and belief of the facilitator thus becomes crucial to success in learning.

There are many opportunities for the instructor to manipulate the environment and the instructional process to improve learning. Most of the instructional methods are familiar to leaders of retirement preparation who consider themselves to be teachers. What may be less familiar is the importance of using these methods in overt ways to make the participant sensitive to their preferences and skills in learning. In one instructional setting, for example, I asked a class of older people to describe my role as the teacher and their role as the students. They were unanimous that I was to present material and they were to write it down and raise questions if they did not understand. This was almost diametrically opposed to my view of how learning is facilitated, so we spent a portion of the time exploring our roles and relationships. Several points emerged from that session. Since they are relevant to instruction in retirement preparation, I use them here to identify a few areas for consideration.

Facilitating Learning of Older Adults

First, learning as adults is most effective when it is self-directed. This means that the participants are most likely to accept new material and to continue to explore the topic outside the class setting when they are actively involved in the decision and planning process. Time spent during the first session to determine content emphases, to set goals, and to determine format usually pays off in increased commitment and improved participation. This is not always the way that middle-aged and older adults expect to learn. They may be more comfortable in a setting in which the facilitator makes all of the decisions. However, by failing to involve them in the planning, it is difficult to obtain their commitment; failure to do so will greatly reduce the likelihood that they will put into practice the desired behaviors.

Second, more learning happens outside the group setting than inside. When the instruction is dominated by the facilitator, the students are not encouraged to design their own learning and proceed with it in their own way. The best learning may come in quiet reflection, in reviewing materials, in individual reading, in discussion with family or friends, or in another public forum. For the learning to be effective, the individual needs to become committed to it. The ideal is for members of a class to agree to do some activity outside class that will lead to learning—for example, to read an article, to design a plan, to try out an idea, or to refine a skill. Consequently, participants must become active learners in class and outside.

Third, learning is increased when the learner is able to relate it to existing knowledge, experience, or need. In teaching children, we are able to tell them that whatever they learn may be useful in the future. Older people are less likely to accept this rationalization. They want to see the relevance to their lives and to compare the learning with their previous understandings. By ignoring their experience and previous knowledge, we depreciate it and lose some portion of their commitment to build on what they know. We too often expect them to start with a clear slate, which is unrealistic because their lifetime of experience comprises their self.

Fourth, material is useful when it is needed. If the teacher determines what content is most valuable, the result is likely to be only mediocre success. People may not know what they want to learn, but they know what their concerns and problems are. The instructor must give them the chance to verbalize these needs and to identify the information that will be most helpful to them. This process of exploring what adult learners need and what is available is a helpful one that results in commitment and provides a way of determining the value to various content areas.

Fifth, specific and concrete results are likely to be better received than are those that are general and nebulous. It is so much easier to provide some general overviews of information on the various topics included in retirement preparation. These are useful in providing some understanding of the whole, but participants are seeking some relatively specific information. In the process of providing specifics, it may be appropriate to offer some insight into the larger context to help them see what additional knowledge would be helpful to them.

Sixth, "instructors are too frequently perceived to be a fount of knowledge from whom the answers will flow if the student has sufficient patience" (Peterson 1982, p. 48). This may occur on occasion, but for the most part, the knowledge, skill, or attitude the individual is seeking will be found through individual search, not through patience. In working with adults, the facilitator's role is to encourage this search and to help the individual find the most effective means of problem solving. This is different from the teacher's role with children in which the model of a learned person is displayed. Most adults do not want to become like the teacher, but most do want the help that can be provided through individual efforts. Thus, modeling knowledge is not enough; active support is necessary.

Finally, when a facilitator works with a group of adults or older people, a regular time needs to be set aside for feedback. This should allow the learners to display what they have learned, to compare it to their previous learning, and to explore further relationships. In addition, there needs to be a time to compare the expectations of the students and the facilitator, to criticize if that is needed, to ask for help when a lack has been detected, and to seek to understand how others are feeling about the learning situation. Too often, we do not confront the possibility of unhappiness, dissatisfaction, or frustration in the learning situation. These are exactly the points at which learning is likely to take place. When the learner and the teacher jointly examine the process and the content, people begin to learn about themselves and how they can learn and grow better.

Implication for Retirement Specialists

The coming cohort of middle-aged individuals has much more education than the present cohort of older people. The coming cohort will desire more variety in learning/teaching strategies and will expect greater control of the learning situation. They are likely to demand what the present group hesitantly accepts. Facilitators need to be aware of this change and to prepare for the modifications that are ahead. The younger learners will be less conservative, less awed by the position of the teacher, and less constrained by convention. They will be more likely to know what they want and to accept nothing less.

The implications for current retirement-planning facilitators are several. First, facilitators and planners may find it necessary to increase the amount of time devoted to assessing participant wants and planning the programs with them.

Second, facilitators may find it helpful to discuss with the participants their perceptions of the role of the learner and of the teacher so that there will be agreement on what each of them is expected to do.

Third, facilitators may find it necessary to plan several approaches to a session or program in order to accommodate the wishes of the participants.

Fourth, a program component that primarily involves one-way information giving is likely to be less effective than one that involves much participant involvement.

Fifth, when using outside content experts, it is important for the facilitator to insure that the expert uses instructional methods best suited to the needs and wishes of the group.

Sixth, continuous feedback to the facilitator from the group is imperative if individualized retirement planning is to be done. This likely will occur in the informal interactions outside the regular sessions and in group planning for outside activities.

Finally, the facilitator should keep in mind that although teaching may be impossible, learning is not. The role of the facilitator is to help people learn, and this involves knowing what the participants want to learn and how facilitators can best go about it.

References

Arenberg, D. "Concept Problem Solving in Young and Old Adults." *Journal of Gerontology* 23 (1968):279–82.

Arenberg, D., and Robertson, E.A. "The Older Individual as a Learner." In *Education for the Aging,* edited by S.M. Grabowski and W.D. Mason. Syracuse, N.Y.: ERIC Clearinghouse on Adult Education, n.d.

Canestrari, R.E. Jr. "Age Changes in Acquisition." In *Human Aging and Behavior,* edited by G.A. Talland. New York: Academic Press, 1968.

Hultsch, D. "Adult Age Differences in the Organization of Free Recall." *Developmental Psychology* 1 (1969):673–78.

Peterson, D.A. "Instruction in Retirement Preparation Programs." In
Retirement Preparation: An Update, edited by H. Dennis. Los
Angeles: University of Southern California, 1982.

Ross, E. "Effect of Challenging and Supportive Instructions in Verbal
Learning in Older Persons." *Journal of Educational Psychology* 59
(1968):97–106.

Suggested Readings

Knowles, M.S. *The Modern Practice of Adult Education.* Chicago: Fol-
lett Publishing Co., 1970.

> This is a classic book on the design and operation of adult education.
> Chapters 3 and 11 are especially relevant to the conduct of classroom
> instruction for middle-aged and older workers.

Knox, A.B. *Adult Development and Learning.* San Francisco: Jossey-
Bass, 1978.

> This book provides a good overview of the development of the adult
> and the relationship of this development to learning needs. Chapter 7
> is a good overview of how adults learn and how facilitators can use this
> knowledge.

Peterson, D.A. *Facilitating Education for Older Learners.* San Francisco:
Jossey-Bass, 1983.

> This publication summarizes current research and practice on the in-
> struction of older persons. A long chapter deals with preretirement
> planning, and a second chapter describes programs in retaining older
> persons for employment.

Sherron, R.H., and Lumsden, D.B. eds. *Introduction to Educational Gerontology.* Washington, D.C.: Hemisphere Publishing, 1978.

> This is one of the few books on the instruction of older people.
> Chapter 13 deals with the preparation of facilitators for retirement
> preparation.

8 Program Evaluation

Mary Jackson

Purpose of Program Evaluation

As funding for program development and implementation becomes increasingly scarce, the demand for accountability for funds that are awarded is more prevalent than ever. As noted by Suchman (1967), "all social institutions are required to provide 'proof' of their legitimacy and effectiveness in order to justify society's continued support" (p. 2). This applies to funding from a government agency or a budget allocation for retirement planning from a corporation. Program evaluation provides the means for demonstrating legitimacy and effectiveness by substantiating the attainment of program goals.

Program evaluation is an emerging field. While evaluation draws on the research methodologies developed in the social sciences, the unique nature of performing research in the setting of an ongoing program requires the development of models and methodologies specific to program evaluation. Program evaluation is a relatively young field, and many models (and their accompanying jargon) have been suggested and implemented with varying degrees of success.

Goal-Oriented Model

One model that has proved successful, particularly in the evaluation of services or educational programs, is the goal-oriented model. As the name implies, the basis for evaluating a program is the extent to which stated goals are attained. This model has appeal in the area of program development because it forces the program developers to state the goals of a program specifically at the outset. This often serves to clarify previously vague issues and to forestall potential problems before they occur. It also makes the criteria for a successful program reasonably succinct.

It must be noted here that the success of using a goal-oriented model is largely contingent on the clear and focused definition of the goals and objectives. The definition of the goal(s) should proceed from a general but clear statement of intent of the program. The objectives, which should proceed from the stated goals, need to be focused and specific statements. While the goals state the theoretical concepts to be addressed, the objectives state the measurable entities representing those theoretical ones. For example, a theoretical concept presented in a goal statement might be life satisfaction. This concept can be translated into a measurable entity, the objective, by the score one receives on a life satisfaction scale.

The goal-oriented model functions on what can be called the funnel approach; that is, conceptually, it begins at the broadest level and gradually focuses on the more specific. At the broadest level exists the need for the program in question. In response to that need, goals are defined. The theoretical statement expressed by the goal is made operational in the formulation of *objectives*. Finally, program elements, or action steps, are designed to meet the stated objectives specifically. With this type of evaluation model, the evaluation component of a program develops concurrent with the program. It is not an after-the-fact addition, which is so often the case with less structured approaches to program evaluation. As such, the evaluation component becomes as integral a part of program development as any other.

Where the goal-oriented model develops conceptually from the broad to the specific, implementation works in reverse order; that is, implementation of the evaluation component begins with the program elements, which in turn should substantiate the objectives, thereby supporting the attainment of the goals and the meeting of the stated need(s).

The specific program elements that are chosen for an evaluation component are closely tied to the types of objectives set for the program. In educational programs specifically, objectives typically fall into three broad categories: (1) attitudinal change, (2) acquisition of knowledge and/or skills, and (3) behavioral change (on the individual or organizational level). The methodologies chosen for a given evaluation component should be selected on the basis of the type of objective one is trying to substantiate.

Methods for Data Collection

Pencil and Paper Inquiry

Four basic methodologies are used most often for the collection of data in evaluation strategies. The first, which is decidedly the most common, is the pencil and paper inquiry. In this method, program participants are asked to respond, in writing, to a variety of questions presented to them. This method of data collection is quite appropriate for objectives focused on knowledge acquisition. It is often also used for attitudinal objectives, although self-report of feelings and emotions in the confined context of a pencil and paper questionnaire is often difficult. Such strategies are sometimes used for the assessment of a behavioral change, even though the self-reporting of behaviors is notoriously unreliable. Individuals often are not cognizant of their behavioral changes, and therefore, such reports are difficult, if not impossible, to make. Pencil and paper inquiries have the advantage of being easy to administer and requiring relatively little expense in time and money.

Interviews

Interviews are another important method for data collection. While less appropriate for objectives aimed at knowledge acquisition, they are useful for gathering information regarding attitudes and, in some instances, behaviors. While the paper and pencil inquiry often confines the respondent to very succinct and predetermined responses to questions, an interview allows the respondent to elucidate more fully on the issues presented. Thus, an interview is often useful in instances where issues are complex and cannot be expressed by responding to a multiple-choice-type questionnaire. The main disadvantage of interviews is in the expense of resources. Interviewing is usually a very time-consuming and expensive undertaking and necessarily limits the number of respondents from which data can be gathered.

Observation

A third method of data collection is observation. Observation techniques are often beneficial in assessing objectives aimed at behavioral change. Observing, rather than asking an individual how he or she is behaving in a particular setting, utilizes firsthand experience. For the sake of objectivity, a trained third party should be employed as the observer. This technique is especially useful when the stated objective is for behavior change within an organizational structure, which may be difficult to assess using other techniques. Included under the overall guise of observation techniques is examination of existing records. Personnel records, for example, are often of great benefit when the program objective is to change the structure of personnel within an organization. An example of an objective requiring observational techniques is to increase the proportion of older workers.

Simulation

Finally, a little used, but sometimes effective method of data collection is simulations. Unlike observation techniques that are used in naturally occurring situations, simulations are contrived situations into which an individual or group of individuals is placed and for which responses to the situation are recorded. These simulations could be used to see how knowledge

acquired is implemented, how attitudes manifest themselves, or what behaviors are utilized in a given situation. Although simulations are by far the
most elaborate of the methodologies outlined here, they are applicable in
some instances.

Timing of Data Collection

Pretesting

Once appropriate strategies for the collection of data have been established,
the next issue is when these steps are to be taken. Since most objectives are
intended to make some change, it is necessary to have some idea of what
state existed before the program began. More specifically, if one objective
of the program is to increase knowledge about a given area, then it would be
necessary to have some measure of initial levels of knowledge in order to be
able to demonstrate a change. As such, it would be necessary to make an
assessment of knowledge levels before the program began and again at its
conclusion.

Given these measures, classical statistical techniques could be employed
to test empirically where preprogram knowledge levels differed significantly
from postprogram levels. Similar baseline or initial measures and corresponding postprogram measures would need to be taken for objectives
aimed at attitudinal or behavioral changes. Thus, it becomes evident that in
some instances the evaluation process must begin before the program.

Posttesting

The timing of postprogram evaluation is also an issue. Many evaluation
assessments are made immediately after the program is concluded. Evaluation of program structure, quality of materials presented, and program
length and timing are issues that are addressed appropriately at the immediate conclusion of the program when they are still fresh in the participants'
minds. The kinds of objectives that focus specifically on program impact or
outcomes present a more complex question. If, for example, a program objective is to change participants' attitudes toward older workers, is the
primary interest to determine whether participants felt more positively
toward older workers at the immediate conclusion of a program or whether
that positive change still existed six months or a year after the program had
terminated? The answer to this question may suggest a need for a follow-up
assessment at some specified time after the program concludes to see
whether the program has had lasting effects.

A follow-up evaluation may be essential for objectives aimed at behavioral change where it would naturally take some time for the behaviors to manifest themselves. Such would be the case in a program that seeks to make some change in an existing organizational structure. Therefore, while it has been noted that the evaluation process may need to begin before the program, it may also need to continue for some time after the program has formally concluded. Program evaluation needs to be viewed as a continuum that evolves concurrently with the program.

The data collection stage of program evaluation is by far the most time consuming and demanding. However, once the data have been collected in appropriate manners and at appropriate times within the context of the program, they must be analyzed to determine empirically whether program objectives have been met. As mentioned previously, program evaluation draws on the methodological and statistical theories found in the social sciences. The intent of evaluation models is to follow the requirements for using classical statistical methods of analyses, recognizing the necessary constraints imposed by doing research in an applied setting. It is felt that, in most cases, a program developer would be involved with the conceptual decision making previously outlined and that the technical issues of statistical anlayses would be left to one specifically trained in that field; thus, these are omitted from this discussion. Connelly (1975) gives a good explanation of some of these issues and some suggestions for dealing with them within the context of program evaluation.

Implications for Retirement Specialists

Program evaluation provides the means for objectively assessing the success of a program. Obviously, being able to demonstrate such success is important for validating the program and use of funds to the funding agency. Beyond that, for those involved in developing, teaching, or directing retirement preparation programs, this information could be very valuable. For the developer, the results of the evelation would highlight successful strategies and those that need rethinking for future programs. If the program consists of a series of short sessions, the evaluations of earlier sessions could suggest some redirection of those to follow. For teachers and facilitators, evaluation results could indicate which subject materials and methods of presentation were most successful and avenues of improvement in others.

Importance of Defining Terms

Several issues regarding the design of evaluation components have been discussed. I address a few again here with specific reference to several concepts that are particularly relevant to retirement preparation programs. One issue that cannot be emphasized enough is the definition of concepts. For example, the phrase *adjustment to retirement* is often a part of the goals of a preretirement program. However, before the concept of adjustment can be measured, it must be defined specifically. Whether or not the goal of increasing or improving adjustment in retirement is met depends largely upon how it is defined. For example, adjustment to retirement may be defined as the retiree's state of mind: how happy is the person? It may be defined as financial stability and the ability to live on a fixed income or as the development or continuance of hobbies or outside activities. The list of possibilities is almost endless. It becomes quickly apparent that although these elements are likely to fall under the guise of adjustment to retirement, they suggest different kinds of measurements and evaluation strategies. There is no one right answer to the problem. The point is that the definition of concepts is a critical element in designing an evaluation component and should be addressed with great care and foresight. One suggestion to solving the problem of defining a concept as broad as adjustment to retirement is simply to avoid using such broad terms. If the interest is in the development of outside activities, then state the goal and objectives in those terms.

The example given highlights another important issue in designing evaluation strategies. Not only the definition of *adjustment* but also the time constraints of the term *in retirement* need to be addressed. As has been noted, the timing of data collection is an important aspect of an evaluation component. In this case, the determination of what constitutes the in-retirement state would dictate when postprogram measurements would be made. Most likely a criterion of a fixed number of years past the date of termination of full-time work would define the boundaries. This would mean that the time of data collection would vary from one program participant to the next on the basis of their chronological age and the date of their retirement. This could extend the data collection process over many years. Since the goals of many retirement preparation programs are intended to affect the lives of individuals several years after the program has been completed, this problem is especially relevant.

The discussion here of the problems associated with the development and implementation of evaluation components is intended not to overwhelm or to discourage their use but to note that an effective evaluation strategy takes a substantial amount of careful consideration and time. It is also intended to highlight some issues that should receive consideration and that might otherwise be overlooked. Developers should realize that it is often necessary to make compromises between the ideal evaluation and the realities imposed by available resources. However, a well-conceived and implemented evaluation can add immeasurably to the success of current and future programs.

Examples of Retirement Strategies

To illustrate how the concepts outlined could be integrated into an evaluation component of a retirement preparation program, this section provides some examples. Each example consists of a goal and objective that might be relevant to a retirement preparation program and a suggested strategy for the evaluation. It is important to note that these are only suggested strategies for the purpose of illustration and are by no means the only acceptable solution.

Example 1

Goal. Preretirees are prepared for financial issues in retirement.

Objective. Preretirees will make a financial plan for retirement.

Evaluation Strategy. To validate the successful meeting of this objective, the evaluation strategy would need to measure the number of preretirees who prepare a financial plan for retirement. The program developer would need to decide what criteria (probably a percentage of those who complete the task) would constitute meeting the objective. For example, the objective might be determined to have been met successfully if 80 percent of the program participants made a financial plan. Note that this objective does not make any reference to the quality or success of the financial plan but only to whether or not one is made. In addition, the concept of a financial plan would need to be defined clearly. Once defined, a count could be made of program participants who have made a financial plan.

The determination of when the measurement should be taken could vary from a very short time after the program to several years later. If, for example, one retirement-planning assignment was to construct a financial plan, the measurement could be made immediately. In contrast, if constructing such a plan was not a specific requirement of the program, it would be necessary to wait a reasonable period of time after the program ended to measure the impact of the program on an individual's behavior. Note that this objective only calls for a postprogram measurement. As such, there would be no way of determining if participants had made financial plans prior to the program. Thus, it becomes difficult to support the notion that the program resulted in a given percentage of the participants making a financial plan. It only serves to demonstrate that a given percentage of participants did complete the task, regardless of what prompted them to do so.

Example 2

Goal. Preretirees will have a more positive attitude toward retirement.

Objective. Preretirees will have a higher (more positive) score on a scale of attitudes toward retirement after attending the preretirement program.

Evaluation Strategy. This objective involves assessing a change in attitude. Thus, attitudes toward retirement will be measured by having program participants respond to a series of questions designed to assess a variety of issues related to retirement. The sum of responses to these items will constitute an overall scale score that is used to summarize an individual's attitudes toward retirement. This information would be acquired most probably by a paper and pencil questionnaire. Since the objective is to assess a change over time, it would be necessary to administer the questionnaire before and after the program so a comparison could be made. A significant increase from preprogram to postprogram attitude scale scores would indicate a successful meeting of the objective. Whereas the evaluation strategy for the first example given could only measure whether the task had been completed, measurements made before and after the program in this example provide more evidence that any significant change in attitude was, in fact, due to the program.

Example 3

Goal. Increase the use of older workers in the work force.

Objective. Increase the proportion of workers over the age of 65 employed by Organization A.

Evaluation Strategy. The desired outcome here is a behavioral change in the organization that will allow or encourage persons over the age of 65 to continue working. An appropriate method of data collection would be observation, most likely using personnel records as the source of information. Records could be examined before the program begins to determine the proportion of persons over the age of 65 currently employed by the organization. A similar measure could be made at six months and one year after the program to determine if the proportions have changed from the preprogram assessment. A statistical test applied to these data could determine whether a significant difference in proportions existed pre- and postprogram. This evaluation could be supplemented by selected interviews with members of the organization to determine if policy changes had been made or if incentives were offered to older workers to remain in the work force.

References

Connelly, J.R. "A Model for Organization and Evaluation of Short-term Training." *The Gerontologist* 15 (1975):442–47.

Suchman, E.A. *Evaluative Research.* New York: Russell Sage Foundation, 1967.

Suggested Readings

Davis, H. "Four Ways to Goal Attainment." *Evaluation* 1 (1973):23–28.

> This article focuses on a goal-oriented model for program evaluation. It suggests specific methods for attaining goals set for program development and implementation.

Rossi, P.H., and Williams, W., eds. *Evaluating Social Programs*. New York: Seminar Press, 1972.

> This book consists of a series of articles by various authors that focus on problems and strategies for evaluating social programs. The majority of articles are divided into two major sections; one emphasizes theory and the other emphasizes practice.

9 Self-Inventory for Planning

Margaret E. Hartford

Psychological Factors in Retirement Planning

Most preretirement planning focuses on the very important material aspects of the transition from full-time employment into retirement; less attention has been given to the psychosocial factors that are of increasing importance in the later years. As people move from the usual highly organized and demanding work day to retirement, they may find themselves having to take more personal responsibility for planning their daily living and ongoing relationships. Many retirees feel a temporary sense of relief of not having to meet a regular schedule and not having to maintain some of the relationships necessary in jobs and community. However, they usually have a reaction within the first year or two to the lack of roles, goals, and directions. Many people have been outside directed throughout their lives by their choice of work, family, community, or organizational responsibilities that kept them involved and connected at an almost treadmill pace. They may not have had much time or opportunity to direct their own lives for most of their adult years. Many people who have been employed for many decades must learn for the first time to make their own plans and schedules, to enjoy their own company, to make new connections, to form new relationships, and to be accepted for who they are as an individual rather than by title or place in an organization.

Even though they anticipate retirement as a new sense of freedom, most people have some feelings of regret or loss they cannot define as they retire. They search for direction and for new anchors. They seek new relationships with different and interesting people who are not working or involved in office politics, the demands of the community, or the pressures of time. People also may have been so busy meeting responsibilities of their jobs and social activities that they have not taken time or responsibility for cultivating and maintaining family relationships.

Spouses, friends, and close relatives, including adult children, may also experience life changes as someone close to them retires. Demands on their time and attention—for example, rearrangement of schedules to accommodate the newly retired person who expects others to be free for activities—may cause major adjustments in households, families, and friendships.

The Self-Inventory

The purpose of the self-inventory exercise for planning to maximize potentials is to help people look at past and current dimensions of their lives that add quality and meaning and, from that perspective, to plan their future. People must examine those qualities and types of experiences and relationships throughout life that have evolved into a life-style of customs, habits, beliefs, and ways of doing things of which they may not be aware.

This reflection on the past and present is based on the assumption that people are products of their life experiences; awareness of these experiences and ways of dealing with the social and personal dimensions can enhance their quality of life and sense of control over the present and future. Current research (Fiske 1979) on aging suggests that people can and do make dramatic changes in their lives in the later years. Evidence indicates that people who make plans and set goals they may or may not be able to implement appear to be happier, better adjusted, and more satisfied with their lives in the later years than those who do not (Kastenbaum 1979). By examining social and personal dimensions of life, people may become sensitized to those actions that can improve their well-being and enable them to have a sense of mastery and control over their lives in retirement (Hartford 1982).

Working with Preretirees

As preretirees work on developing their profiles, the retirement specialist or counselor should remember that while there is in each person a thrust toward health, strength, mastery, survival, independence, and perhaps, even optimism, there is also the potential for illness, weakness, defeat, dependence, and depression. This constant ambivalence in each person continues as a struggle throughout life; however, at some periods where there are major life transitions, the struggle is more apparent. For example, the crisis of retirement, the major change in life roles, bodily changes that may occur more dramatically during this period of life, and the impact of the social changes may be particularly stressful as one leaves late middle age and enters early old age. The transition may be facilitated by utilizing the approaches and adaptations one has employed throughout life.

The retirement specialist should be prepared to suggest resources for support and opportunities for engagement and involvement. If the exercise is used with a group, some group members may be eager to share their own experiences of what resources work for them, and this may stimulate others to do the same. As in any group discussion, the leader must use skill in engaging widespread participation so that the discussion does not become a dialogue between one or two participants and the leader, turning the rest of the group into observers.

It is important to keep the group from getting bogged down with grief, loss, depression, self-pity, anger, and resentment of the system. These feelings are real and should not be ignored or denied; however, it is extremely important to channel or guide those people with serious problems to the appropriate sources of support. While group discussion may be used for support and encouragement to help people take some individual responsibility for their future, a self-inventory helps them focus on the concerns and perspectives of life-styles of which they have not necessarily been aware.

The following statements should be made to participants about the purpose of the inventories: The inventories are for personal benefit and use. Participants will not hand their inventories in for judgment. If they wish to share their experiences with others, that is their choice. Couples have found it useful, once they have completed their inventories, to talk them over with each other.

An important part of the exercise, after the completion of the self-inventory, is for each participant to develop a contract with him- or herself, for future action in the ten dimensions of the inventory (listed in the following section). This can be done in the group, which may provide incentive to complete the exercise, or at home after the group session.

In order to set the mood for working on the inventory, make a few introductory statements about aging, retirement, and change. After most of the people have completed the inventory, usually about thirty to fifty minutes, ask them to stop, and indicate that you suspect some of them were reminded of things they had not thought of for some time. Such life review can be useful in planning for the future.

Self-Inventory Questions

The following is the *Self-Inventory for Planning to Maximize Your Potential in Later Life.* [1] Questions for the self-inventory are organized into ten areas.

Instructions for leader: Read the questions under each topic to the group or to the individual, and allow approximately five minutes for each answer. Ask participants to think about the question and write down the words or phrases that first come to mind. Tell them not to dwell very long on answering a single question.

1. Happiness and Humor

Think of the most humorous or happiest events or experiences in your lifetime, and note one or two examples.
State why these experiences were happy or humorous.
Note what events in your present life or in your plans for your future could contain some of these same feelings of happiness or humor.

2. Grief, Sadness, and Loss

Think of the saddest, most difficult, or stressful times in your life, and note these experiences.
How did you cope with these experiences?
What can you do now to prepare for difficult transitions and losses?

3. Activities

List the most rewarding activities throughout your life.
Which activities did you wish to do more?
How can you pursue these activities or variations of them in the future?

4. Health

How would you assess the state of your health throughout your lifetime?
Indicate areas about which you need to be concerned.
List preventive or sustaining actions you can take to maintain your health and secure your future.

5. Relationships

Think of the relationships that have had the most meaning throughout your life: family, friends, associates, lovers, and pets, and list three of the most important.
What are you doing now to preserve or renew old relationships or to begin new relationships appropriate for your future life?

6. Living Arrangements

Think over the kinds of housing arrangements you have had over your lifetime, and note the following things about them: arrangement of space—openness or closed protectedness; one- or two-story single unit or part of an apartment complex; location in city, suburban, small town, rural or wilderness area; remote from or near to cultural, political, recreational and service resources, and neighbors.
Which arrangements and locations were the most pleasant, satisfying, and comfortable to you?
What environment will be most satisfying and comfortable in your future living arrangement?

7. Time Arrangement

As you review the way your time has been arranged throughout your life on a daily, weekly, monthly, and yearly basis, have you been used

to an organized schedule for work, meals, recreation, and family activities, or have you followed an unorganized, casual time schedule?
Do you manage your own schedule or is it set by your work and other activities to which you merely respond in a routine fashion?
As you plan for your future time, how will you arrange your time so that it will be regularly scheduled or casual according to what is most comfortable to you?

8. Self-Management and Leadership Roles

Do you like to take responsibility for planning and managing your life—your activities, work, recreation, and social life—or do you prefer to have someone direct it for you?
In general, do you tend to be an initiator and/or manager or a participant and follower?
Thinking about your future, how can you make realistic opportunities for you to manage or to be managed?

9. Risk and Security

Throughout your life, have you tended to take a secure and predictable course of action, or have you taken a fair amount of risks and chances? Indicate the risks you have taken or the activity you have undertaken to avoid risks.
Depending on how you feel about taking risks, what plans can you make for the future to permit some risk taking or to avoid risks?

10. Ambitions, Goals, and Unfulfilled Hopes

List the major ambitions, desires, and goals you have had throughout life.
Underline those that have not been fulfilled or only partially fulfilled. How could you pursue these hopes in the future? List two or three goals for your years ahead.

Discussion of the Topics

Retirement specialists can use the following information in leading the discussion for each topical area.

Happiness and Humor

A leading geropyschiatrist has suggested that keeping happy is one of the major requirements for successful aging. However, happiness, good humor, and laughter have to be sought out and developed deliberately by people who are facing a certain amount of decrements and losses. Therefore, people may need to think about what has made them happy in the past and try to infuse such experiences in their lives. Happiness and humor have proven to have great healing power. Different things bring happiness to different people; therefore, you may wish to review these differences.

People may prefer any one or combination of the following: being in solitude and quiet or being in social groups; working or being unattached, uninvolved, and free of obligations; achieving and being recognized or going unnoticed and being annonymous; acquiring material possessions or being free of the responsibility of ownership; being involved in romance, belonging, and sexual expression with exhilaration or being free of involvements; being in control or letting someone else take responsibility; watching something humorous such as a movie or play or creating humor by telling jokes or funny stories. Encourage people to seek out those experiences today that have given them a good feeling in the past.

Grief, Sadness, and Loss

The longer people live, the more they will find they have to face losses and sadness. Some people tend to deny their losses and grief and to hold them inside themselves. Current research on coping suggests that the human body and spirit are psychologically stronger if individuals recognize their griefs and work on them (Uris 1981). This means acknowledging the feelings, talking about them, and then moving on. Saddest times may include losing a job, a friend, a possession, or a pet; the death of someone important and close; or the ending of a school year or vacation. Additional losses may include leaving your children or helping them to leave you; moving away from a familiar place; giving up a car; giving up independent living; being subject to crime, accident, or injury; experiencing or observing the breakup of a relationship of close relatives or friends; and failure. People mellow as they cope with trauma and distress and as they face and deal with grief and sorrow. If they do not deal with their sorrows, they may become angry, embittered, and disillusioned. If they permit themselves to grieve and ritualize endings, they free themselves to move on to new experiences.

Activities

When people think about those activities that have given them the greatest satisfaction, they also should be encouraged to think about why they got such pleasure from these activities. Activities they list may include work, recreation, associations, leadership or followership roles, creative ventures, caring for others, intellectual pursuits, manual activities, and physical activity. People should be encouraged to consider ways in which they could engage in similar activities today. Studies of satisfaction in retirement show that being busy is not enough. People need not only undemanding recreation but also some activity in which they feel they are making a contribution as well as activities that make a demand on them.

Health

Today, life expectancy is approximately 74 years, but it can be increased or decreased by health habits, nutrition, exercise, relaxation, and stress reduction (Woodruff 1977). Most people over 60 have some type of chronic disease. However, good preventive health habits and health care make most chronic conditions manageable. There is also a very close association between a sense of well-being, attitude, and self-concept and immunity from disease (Michaels 1983). Participants should be encouraged to have regular health checkups and to become as knowledgeable as possible about their health conditions.

Relationships

The creation and maintenance of relationships with friends, family, lovers, and/or pets is crucial for successful aging (Fiske 1979). Patterns of relationships throughout life, maintenance of old friends, cultivation of family ties, and reaching out to new attachments to fill losses should be considered. Young friends and family members become increasingly important as one's peers die, move away, or become less able to contribute to a relationship. Extending oneself to people who are different in background, ethnicity, beliefs, and interests may be an enriching experience. Research indicates that the gathering of family, including distant relatives, can be a supportive and healing phenomenon in crises or in sustaining people (Yates 1979). In addition, the renewal of old friendships may bring rewards. Fiske (1979) has shown that people need at least one close confidante; research indicates that those who own pets have a strong survival thrust (Friedman et al. 1980). People with pets, friends, relatives, and lovers have a strong sense of being needed and wanted.

Living Arrangements

People tend to gravitate to a particular style of housing throughout their lives. Sometimes in retirement they select an environment that is very different and do not realize why they are uncomfortable. By looking at previous living arrangements, people can see a pattern. People may prefer open or closed, protected spaces; they may enjoy high rises or single-level houses. They may feel hemmed in without a garden or patio or too exposed with a yard and open spaces. Some people build their territory inside the walls that surround them, while others ignore their surroundings but need an open view. People should be encouraged to examine their last few residences and then to think of future living arrangements accordingly. This is particularly important for people who anticipate moving to reduced living quarters or a retirement community. Not only the physical plant but also location in a city, small town, rural or wilderness area, or an isolated or crowded surrounding should be considered. Available social and health resources should also be considered in any retirement move.

Time Arrangement

By the time people reach middle age or retirement, they have usually established a pattern for the use of time. Some have lived by a highly organized schedule for work, recreation, sleeping, and other activities, and these people may feel lost without a regular schedule. Others have responded to whatever demands have emerged. Some people have paced themselves to work intensively for short periods of time, followed by unscheduled time. By becoming aware of life patterns of time scheduling, people can make plans for their use of time in later years, either to phase in to changes or to structure similar patterns through new activities. Many people, upon their retirement, become so anxious about the possibility of not being busy that they overschedule their activities and become disconcerted by the pressures. However, by planning in accordance with old habits, they can avoid this stress and use time productively and within their energy level.

Self-Management and Leadership Roles

Many people like to be free spirits, taking responsibility for their activities and decisions. Others would rather have their lives planned externally by someone else or by some structure. The former group will resent traveling with a tour group or living in a structured and organized community, resisting organization by others such as friends, relatives, and spouses. The latter group flounders and feels uncomfortable trying to make decisions and chart courses. They are more comfortable in an organized community or on a tour, following the leadership and planning of others. Their security is based on having a well-patterned plan. People need to become aware of their natural tendencies for self-initiation and freedom or followership and secure patterns.

Risk and Security

For some people, security is based on eliminating risks and chances as much as possible by having specific plans. For instance, in planning a trip, some people want to secure all reservations in advance, to know when and where they will be at all times. Others want the excitement and freedom of taking chances on what may come. While all people seem to live more successfully if they have a plan, these plans can be more or less specific. Plans should be according to the way people have lived and their feelings about security and risk. In getting people to think about this dimension, they may want to consider many aspects regarding making plans, including setting agendas and being assured of outcomes in investing time, money, and energy.

Ambitions, Goals, and Unfulfilled Hopes

Throughout life people have hopes, ambitions, and dreams of what may be. Frequently, life circumstances prevent the achievement of these ambitions or at least delay their fulfillment. People should be encouraged to think about ways they might fulfill such hopes, either directly or vicariously, through second careers, avocational interests, recreation, relationships, or volunteer activities.

Ambitions may include being creative, assuming a different occupation or type of job, getting married and having a family (which may be adopted), traveling, getting more education, acquiring economic comfort, belonging to a particular type of group, being in charge of something, mastering a new skill, or doing something for public recognition. People should be encouraged to think about their ambitions and about how they could achieve them today.

After the participants have covered all the items in the self-inventory, the retirement specialist may begin the group discussion by asking if someone would share with the group his or her responses to the happiest event or experience. When someone has volunteered, ask that person if he or she could plan any events that would catch the same feeling today. Make some suggestions if none is forthcoming. Then ask for another example that covers a different area. Do not let any one person monopolize the discussion or the following responders to cover the same areas.

Follow the same procedure for all the dimensions. Do not let the discussion of any one item go on too long because you will want to cover all the items in the inventory. Summarize each with some generalized knowledge about the category of human development.

Contract for the Future

When all dimensions of the self-inventory have been discussed, encourage participants to make contracts with themselves for their future. Suggest that they refer to their responses in the inventory in making their contracts. Suggest that they may want to discuss their inventories and contracts with family, spouse, and friends. Advise them to look at their contracts from time to time over the years to determine how well they are doing in making the best of the rest of their lives. The following is a sample of such a contract:

1. I will deliberately seek happiness and humor in my life in the following ways:

2. I will anticipate and prepare to face losses and grief by:

3. I will make plans to undertake the following activities in my future years and will do the following now to prepare:

4. For the good of my present and future health I will continue or begin the following actions in nutrition, exercise, stress reduction, and modified health habits:

5. I will renew or sustain the following old relationships and begin plans to develop the following new relationships:

6. In consideration of my most satisfying living arrangement, I will plan my future housing as follows:

7. I will take into consideration my comfort in time arrangements by:

8. Considering my way of initiating or following, I will attempt to include in my future life plans the following:

9. Because of the way I feel about risk taking, I will plan my future activities as follows:

10. I will set the following goals to reach my ambitions and unfulfilled hopes so that my retirement can be a time of fulfillment:

This is my contract with myself to maximize my full potential during the rest of my life.

Signed _____

Date   _____

Note

1. This material is taken from *Making the Best of the Rest of Your Life,* copyright by the author, Margaret E. Hartford, Ph.D., and published by Personal Strengths Publishers, P.O. Box 397, Pacific Palisades, CA 90272-0397. Single and multiple copies may be obtained by writing the publishers. Do not reproduce.

References

Fiske, M. *Middle Age: The Prime of Life.* New York: Harper & Row, 1979.

Friedman, E., Katcher A., Lynch, J., and Thomas S. "Animal Companions and One Year Survival of Patients after Discharge from a Coronary Care Unit." *Public Health Reports* 95 (1980):307–12.

Hartford, M.E. *Making the Best of the Rest of Your Life: A Workbook for Self-Assessment.* Pacific Palisades, Calif.: Personal Strengths Publishing, 1982.

Kastenbaum, R. *Growing Old: Years Fulfillment.* New York: Harper & Row, 1979.

Michaels, J. *Prime of Your Life: A Practical Guide to Your Mature Years.* Boston: Little, Brown & Company, 1983.

Uris, A. *Over 50—The Definitive Guide to Retirement.* New York: Bantam Books, 1981.

Woodruff, D. *Can You Live to Be 100?* New York: Signet Press, 1977.

Yates, J. "The Ties That Bind Can also Heal." *Prevention* 31 (1979):44.

Suggested Readings

Dienstfrey, H., and Lederer, J. *What Do You Want to Be When You Grow Old?* New York: Bantam Books, 1979.

> In the authors' words, this book was written to let people know "there are more and better choices than you think." The authors, two journalists, prepared this small paperback book to show people how to take advantage of the later years to enjoy a new old age. It is written for laypeople and covers topics such as finances; the findings of research on aging and longevity; resources for recreation, health, and education; and retirement options. It includes a number of short vignettes about people who have aged successfully.

Harris, L. *The Myths and Realities of Aging in America.* Washington, D.C.: National Council on the Aging, 1975.

Of particular help to retirement specialists, this carefully calculated study with a selected sample of young and old people produced widely quoted evidence on some of the reactions to aging. Materials acquired in the study refuted some of the widely held myths about aging in the United States.

10 Preretirement Counseling

James A. Peterson

Approaches

As far as I have been able to determine by perusal of the literature, no one has made an adequate attempt to distinguish preretirement education from preretirement counseling. In this chapter I distinguish these two approaches to preretirement and then describe the characteristics of preretirement counseling. Of course, when dealing with the interaction of the person who intervenes with others in attempting to help the client make a better adjustment in retirement years, these two approaches overlap. However, a significant difference still exists in both the substantive content and the methodology used to differentiate the two distinctive approaches.

Preretirement Education

Preretirement education may be defined as the effort to share with a group of individuals or a single person those objective facts that will influence them when they retire. The subjects of that attempt are already well defined in a dozen manuals for preretirement educational programs. Topics considered important by clients of preretirement education include the wise investment of funds; problems inherent in both public and private pension plans; various insurance approaches to health care; subtleties of Medicare, Medicaid, and companionate insurance plans; coping with inflation; new full-time or part-time employment; the value of volunteer work; and reduced expectations regarding the purchase of clothing, transportation, food, recreation, and other essential life items. Most of the published programs for preretirement education outline ways to approach these subjects.

Preretirement Counseling

Preretirement counseling may be defined as helping preretirees deal with the emotional responses they often have toward retirement. The sessions conducted by a preretirement counselor will certainly deal with the subjects previously mentioned as constituting the curriculum of preretirement education but with one significant difference. While the facts about inflation or pension plans will be carefully presented, the focus of the preretirement counselor will be upon the anxieties or other emotional responses of the clients to those presentations. The preretirement counselor feels that unless these anxieties are confronted, worked through, and ventilated, the presentation of objective facts will have a minimum value because the anxiety or denial of the client will not permit him or her to utilize constructively that information. Furthermore, the preretirement counselor feels that the really critical aspects of adjustment after retirement do not lie in mechanical new ways of budgeting but in creative ways of handling feelings.

Methodologies

The methodologies of these two approaches also differ. The educator's concern is to obtain the most accurate and dynamic presentation of the facts of retirement. The educator will enlist the best in the way of Social Security experts, investment counselors, recreational consultants, and others to give an accurate picture of retirement. Many of the presentations may involve the media because some very good visual aids have been prepared by most programs in preretirement education.

The preretirement counselor, in contrast, is less concerned with such presentations and more concerned with devising ways in which the anxieties of preretirees can surface and be assimilated. The counselor will devote much more time to discussion of issues; he or she will divide a large group into much smaller groups where feelings can emerge and will choose audiovisual aids in a way that promotes basic confrontation of fears and traumas as a person looks foward to a new period in the life cycle. The preretirement counselor must be skillful and may enlist assistants who are skillful in group dynamics and individual counseling. The counselor is, after all, focusing on a much more-difficult task using this approach. The counselor is saying that retirement is a most significant period of life change. As such, it may be one of the most traumatic and fearful periods for people. The counselor consequently expects to deal in depth with psychological reactions. Obviously, this requires an entirely different kind of expertise than that of presenting factual information and discussing it.

Objectives

Maintaining Status and Identity

Let us now define much more clearly the objectives of preretirement counseling. The first objective is to deal with the loss of status and identity of the retiree. The retiree will go through a major period of individual and social amputation. Assuming that the retiree is a man, he will be cut off from the most meaningful preoccupation of forty years of his life—his work. The biblical phrase said, "Establish thou the work of my hands" (Psalm 90, verse 17, p. 842). When I visit many groups of intelligent, healthy, and bewildered persons in retirement communities and speak to them of the responsibilities they have in their new community for new social interactions and meaningful hobbies, one persistent question always comes up: What is the meaning of my life? What they are really saying to me is that there is no more work for their hands and they thus think they have no way of articulating their basic desire to contribute through their occupation to society. What makes this thought worse is that others geared to an achievement-oriented society have given retirees many indications that because they do not work they are now useless and unworthy of attention.

Avoiding Social Loss

A second objective is to deal with social losses. Retirees will be cut off from basic friendships that have been associated with life during employment years. For a college professor, for example, this means that he or she will not enjoy the departmental debates about the future of academic programs in the university. What it means for the factory worker is that those lunch hours when he or she could comment, complain, or interact with fellow workers about the company are gone. The retiree no longer is invited to participate in the company bowling team or committees that will meet with management regarding any variety of working conditions. The retiree may try to keep those friendships but will find that very difficult because he or she is no longer current with contemporary problems of the factory or shop. Basically, the retiree no longer has any power to influence decisions; the worker status is gone.

I remember a conversation at a midnight show in Las Vegas with the man who sat next to me. It turned out that he was the president of a large manufacturing firm in New England. His factory was located close to half a dozen others. He was concerned with his retirees so he built a social and recreational building for them next to the administrative offices of his company. He told his ex-employees that, within limits, his door would always be open to them. They should come in fellowship, drink coffee, visit their old friends in departments, and remain a part of company life. What saddened him was the complete denunciation he received from the presidents of other corporations close to him. They told him that he was setting a very bad example—that when a person retired, the company has no further obligations and that his program was pampering individuals who had already been well served by their companies. I did my best to reassure him that his efforts were meritorious and that he represented the future. Of that I am sure because more and more companies are not only instituting preretirement programs but also a continued interest in their retirees.

A second example comes from retirees at the University of Southern California. The faculty of the university requested me to conduct an indepth study of the conditions of our retired faculty. The study took one year, and as a result, I could report to the faculty and the president of the university that one-half of our retired faculty were content, had high life satisfaction, and were in no great need of intervention. However, another one-half had all kinds of difficulties. When I used multiple regression analysis on the results, I found that the one major complaint was their sense of having been amputated from the university. They had communication neither from their former colleagues nor from the university as a whole. One sad retiree said, "I would be happy even if I just had a Christmas card from the university." Of course, he was not primarily interested in a Christmas card; he was concerned that an institution to which he had given most of his life in selfless devotion was completely abandoning him.

The result of the study was a sudden and happy response from the university. They established an Emeriti Center whose purpose was to enrich the lives of the retirees and to promote their communication with the university. On further research I found that this condition occurred at many other institutions of higher learning. Since then, the university has regularized the kinds of benefits given to both retired faculty and staff, instituted programs of preretirement counseling, and made it possible for retired persons to find new methods of associating with the university. As the life expectancy of retirees is constantly increasing, the ways in which the company, group, or university continues to express an interest is a salient factor in the retiree's morale during the later years.

We now have 23 million persons over age 65. This number will grow in two or three decades to 40 million, and much of their life satisfaction will depend on the establishment of permanent bonds to that place where they worked most of their lives. Preretirement counseling is basically concerned with that bonding and learning how the work place and the individual can benefit by close relationships.

Retirement Considerations

Marriage and the Family

When Casey Stengel, the legendary figure in baseball history, had been retired for several years, his wife, Ethel, was reputed to have said, "I married him for dinner but not for lunch." This encapsulates one of the profound problems in terms of the relationships of husband and wife during retirement. Retirement introduces a totally new time dimension in marriage.

Sometimes problems arise because the husband is eager to help and he tries to impose his managerial excellence on a home routine that has been running smoothly for forty years before his retirement. Sometimes the opposite is true; the wife expects the husband to pick up part of the household routine with which he is unfamiliar and to which he is resistant. Sometimes the wife may regard his continued presence as being underfoot as she tries to continue a long-learned regime. Whatever the specific situation, new patterns of mutuality have to be learned. Preretirement counseling suggests, almost demands, the presence of both husband and wife in the consultations if these problems are to be foreclosed.

The relationships between husband and wife are but a small aspect of family relationships during retirement. The man may feel that he now has time to devote to his children and grandchildren. He may wish to cultivate relationships with them that have been long neglected. However, his children have their own lives to live and their own problems to solve. One of the discoveries of my research regarding intergenerational relationships was that grandparents often imposed too much on their children's families, and conversely, the children demanded too much from their parents and grandparents.

These problems are amenable to solutions, providing there is opportunity for discussion and honest confrontation. We like to have both husband and wife participate in every session of our preretirement-counseling sessions, and this often leads to later family consultations in which their children and often grandchildren can be a part of planning sessions.

Preparing Wives for Widowhood

The title of a book produced by the magazine *U.S. News and World Report* is *Teach Your Wife to Be a Widow*. The editors of the magazine had so many questions and letters from their subscribers that they felt it was necessary to help their clients prepare for the time when death came and the wife would be left alone to handle the estate and her life. Unfortunately, there is such a differential in terms of mortality between husband and wife that it is essential that the wife learn both financial and social consequences of the death of her husband, on the average, seven years before herself.

The issue is larger than simply writing wills and teaching a wife who has not previously done so to handle financial affairs. The basic issue has to do with facing death. Very few of our preretirement educational programs confront preparation for death either by an individual or by a couple. Our society has not been accustomed to thinking constructively about facing death. However, death will come to all of us, and it is no good to avoid honest planning for it. Only one-half of the families in this country have wills, and fewer than that have talked about the kinds of rituals that should follow a death. Thus, too often the natural grief of a widow or a widower is confounded and exaggerated by the confusions that occur when there has been no planning for the settlement of the estate or the disposal of the body.

When I lecture about this, some older and middle-aged persons regard such discussion as morbid and question why we have to consider such topics; but discussions of death are only morbid when there is denial of the inevitability of its occurrence or when the subject is treated as perverse. Still, death is a taboo subject for many persons. They cannot deal adequately with the thought of their own death or deal with the impact of the death of their loved ones.

The confrontation of death begins in middle age. This is a time when individuals look at a lifetime not as so many years from birth but as so many years remaining for living. It is an overriding consideration that causes much anxiety in a great many persons. Unless it is confronted, thought through, and resolved, thoughts of death may blight and shadow the remaining years of the older person. Not to include a discussion of death (and almost nobody does) in the agenda of retirement counseling is to leave unresolved a major issue of aging for the retiree.

Implications for Retirement Specialists

It should be obvious from the discussion in this chapter that there is a wide diversity in terms of both subject matter and methodology in dealing with the future for those who come for preretirement help. On the one hand, there is the safe course of dealing only with subjects that can be handled objectively: issues such as pension plans, Social Security, recreational possibilities, and hobby development. On the other hand, more major life issues such as family relationships, fears of loss of the meaning of life, anxiety over loss of status, and the constant and dreaded anticipation of death are at a much more dangerous and profound level of confrontation.

Both approaches have value. There is little question that dealing adequately with the technical means of staving off the effects of inflation can ease the anxiety of individuals over such problems. If the client is worried about returns from a pension fund or Social Security, some factual information may tend to quiet those fears. Evidence that a person's spending habits can be modified in retirement may ease some trauma over a reduced income. Information about diet and exercise can make retirement healthier; it may lead many persons to a better life-style in terms of prolonging and enjoying life. We applaud these efforts, but they do not tackle the psychological and social issues of either aging or retirement.

These issues are what worry older persons. They include the loss of meaning of life when one no longer contributes work; losses of friendship networks involved in the work society; coming to grips with family history, marital conflicts, and use of time; and ultimately finding a meaning for life with which to face the termination of life. If we are to deal with persons on a level of basic reality, we must deal with these issues.

Of course, not every personnel director has the psychological training to deal with these issues and at the profound level on which they must be confronted. That does not mean the director's other contributions may not be valuable. What it means is that he or she should be aware of his or her limitations and that when individuals exhibit anxieties about any issue, they should be referred to a company psychologist or an outside consultant who can constructively explore the meaning of those anxieties. There should be no fear that referring a troubled person to another individual with another skill is demeaning.

Preretirement education contributes much but on a different level of intervention from that of preretirement counseling. As this chapter has demonstrated, both the focus and the methodology differ between the two. They both have much to contribute; they overlap in many ways. However, they should not be confused by those who arrange programs for the future of retirees. In addition, those who arrange such programs should be aware of what they are expecting from program leaders. Only when program directives are vague and expectations unreasonable do problems emerge.

References

Newman, J. *Teach Your Wife to be a Widow*. Washington, D.C.: U.S. News and World Report, 1973.

"Psalms," *The Holy Scriptures*. Philadelphia: The Jewish Publication Society of America, 1954.

Suggested Readings

Greenem, M.R. *Retirement Counseling*. Eugene: University of Oregon Press, 1969.

> The University of Oregon has brought retirement counseling into focus. Their discussion of group dynamics, issues, and outcomes is superb.

Hunter, W. *Trends in Pre-Retirement Education.* Ann Arbor: University of Michigan Press, 1962.

> Woodrow Hunter is one of the most alert pioneers in preretirement education. This book summarizes growth in the field.

McCluskey, H. "Pre-retirement Education: Background and Issues." Background paper on preretirement for the Second White House Conference on Aging. Washington, D.C.: U.S. Government Printing Office, 1971.

> Harold McCluskey is a pioneer in the field of education for the aging and a seminal thinker about preretirement education. This paper summarizes current issues in the field.

11 Leisure Counseling

Patsy B. Edwards

Definition of Leisure Counseling

It is well known that the use and misuse of leisure time can be a problem in our society. What is less well known is that something can be done about it. In the late 1960s, a method evolved in the helping professions to assist individuals in using their leisure time for greater satisfaction, not only for themselves but also for their communities. This method was called *leisure counseling.*

Leisure counseling is a process in which a trained counselor helps adults, either singly or in groups, determine their present leisure interests, attitudes, needs, and limitations. The leisure counselor assists them in choosing and following leisure pursuits that are practical, satisfying, enjoyable, available, and not harmful. Techniques and materials exist to augment this process.

Planning leisure time should play as large a part in retirement preparation as any other subject. Although not usually an acute problem, leisure use can become a persistent problem because once the immediate planning for retirement is completed and executed, the increase in leisure time becomes evident and continues indefinitely.

Although different formulas, techniques, and materials have been developed for the process of leisure counseling, they all have a common goal—to increase the counselees' leisure awareness, self-awareness, self-confidence, and decision-making ability. The development of these attributes is likely to lead to more satisfying and socially acceptable leisure behavior and thus to happier, more fulfilled lives.

Misuse of Leisure Time

Leisure time activities are chosen for pleasure. Unfortunately, a less obvious side to the leisure picture must be taken into consideration when discussing leisure counseling: we may choose and enjoy an off-work activity, but that activity may be harmful to us or to someone else. Examples of this misuse of leisure are criminal activity, excessive gambling, and overuse of alcohol, drugs, or food. Most of these actions take place during off-work hours.

Leisure counselors are interested in promoting beneficial activities and helping counselees find acceptable ways to spend their leisure time.

Counselors who work with serious leisure abusers must be trained to deal with their particular abuse. Since only a minority of the population seriously misuses its leisure time, most leisure-counseling programs can concentrate on helping increase the leisure time enjoyment of the general public.

Barriers to Satisfying Leisure

Many people want more satisfaction from their leisure time. Ongoing informal surveys by the author indicate that approximately 35 percent of the population is content with its current leisure life, leaving 65 percent who are not wholly satisfied. It is hard for most people with leisure problems to think logically about their leisure without becoming involved with the barriers they have allowed to arise between themselves and what they would really like to do. Mothers, for example, have trouble distinguishing between what they like to do and what they enjoy doing because it gives pleasure to some members of the family. Health-conscious people have difficulty separating what they feel they must do for good health from what they enjoy. People who like their work find sometimes that they are over doing it and are so busy they no longer enjoy pure play. Sometimes the people one lives with dislike and interfere with one's leisure choices. At other times an individual may find that every easily accessible leisure activity seems a bore.

Leisure counselors cannot automatically relieve all unsatisfactory situations, but they can lead counselees to recognize the existence of barriers, to find more time for leisure, to isolate their personal interests from other considerations, to exchange new interests for old, and to discover new ways of following old favorites. Furthermore, in instances where a person's life seems static and unfulfilling, a change in leisure activity can offer new directions and satisfactions.

Facts about Leisure Counseling

Before summarizing the leisure-counseling process, we should be aware of four points. The first point concerns the currently popular practice of overall wellness and "holistic" life planning. Leisure is as important as any other part of life, and leisure counseling helps make overall life planning efficient and resourceful. The second point concerns the well known stress and burn-out problem. Effective leisure counseling can prevent stress from occurring and should be included in the treatment of stress that has already occurred, but few stress specialists utilize leisure counseling sufficiently.

Third, it is important to note that we change as long as we live and that our interests change with us. There is nothing wrong in stopping a leisure activity when it palls. Leisure is one's choice, and unlike work, it can be changed at will. We do not have to continue leisure pursuits that demand dependability, consistency, decision making, or brain power unless we want to. We can be dull, or we can be creative. We can say no when it suits us. Leisure counseling motivates people to be their true selves during leisure time. Counselors emphasize that there are not do's or do not's for leisure. The fourth point is, if a person is content and not harming anyone, there is no need for leisure counseling or any advice giving.

Leisure Counseling versus Therapy

This chapter focuses on leisure counseling for the general public, not for special populations or for people needing therapy. Counselors for the latter are in the field of therapeutic recreation and require more in-depth training and experience than those who deal with enriching the average person's leisure behavior. However, both types need education and training in counseling to enable them to bring out the counselees' needs and feelings and to allow counselors to express their own.

The nontherapeutic process recommended for retirement preparation uses an approach, usually credited to vocational counseling, which relates a person's interests to work opportunities. This approach can be applied to leisure by relating leisure self-awareness to awareness of existing leisure opportunities and understanding the relationship between the two. Leisure counseling adds a third dimension—counselor assistance in finding and initiating the chosen leisure activities.

The Leisure-Counseling Process for Individuals

Leisure counseling amplifies this approach by the following interlocking steps: interview, assessment, analysis, and referral. These steps may be followed with individuals or with a family of four or fewer. A counselor working with a family needs an assistant to help with the interviewing and other processes. A group of more than four people requires a workshop format, which is explained in a later section.

The length of time devoted to individual leisure counseling will depend upon the amount of time allocated to the subject by a preretirement program. The process may be handled in one or two sessions. A single session can range from one hour to three or four hours. Two-session counseling may run two hours or more for each session.

The main counseling steps are described briefly. The purpose of the activities within each step is to motivate clients to order their leisure lives in such a way that they will be more satisfied and aware of their leisure selves than when they began the counseling process.

Interview

The interview in individual counseling is the most important part of the counseling process because it establishes the relationship between the counselee and the counselor. A person's leisure choices should be made freely and with pleasure, and the counseling relationship should reflect this feeling. This quality of enjoyment and pleasurable anticipation is a distinguishing feature of leisure counseling. A feeling of counselor acceptance continues throughout the leisure-counseling process with both individuals and groups.

The interview reveals the counselee's demographic and biographical data. This information is usually recorded by the counselor on an interview form. The data include past and present leisure activities and work history; current leisure preferences; future goals; practical limitations such as health, age, finances, education, and transportation; transferable work and leisure skills; and reasons for a counselee's dissatisfaction with his or her use of leisure time.

The informal, friendly working relationship established during the interview will help clients clarify attitudes toward leisure, feelings about leisure experiences, and expectations of the leisure-counseling process. Each person has a leisure life-style that can be identified and examined for the needs it fulfils and the satisfaction it gives. Counseling affords counselees an opportunity to recognize their feelings about the people with whom they share their leisure and the situations to which their leisure has led them. It also allows a counselor to observe how a counselee interacts with another person. These opportunities give valuable insights into the individual's leisure disposition and help point toward the most satisfying choice of activities.

Assessment

At the time of the interview, activity surveys, standardized interest inventories, and/or open-ended questionnaires may be administered. Although the interview supplies much information, assessment instruments supplement these data with a more detailed examination of interests and activities that broadens the perspectives of both counselor and counselee, thus stimulating further ideas about leisure possibilities.

The amount of assessment will depend upon the complexity of the counseling service. Single session counseling will necessarily limit the time given to assessment instruments. In addition, it limits the amount of self-exploration and the number of leisure options to be explored, but it can still increase a counselee's awareness of leisure choices. Most retirement preparation programs are of the less complex type and prefer a single survey or questionnaire. Multiple session counseling usually utilizes several instruments that stimulate more deeply a counselee's leisure awareness between sessions.

A number of standardized interest tests are summarized in the Mental Measurements Yearbook (Buros 1978). Please refer to the following authors listed in the suggested readings for additional assessment instruments: Bolles, Edwards, Gault, Loesch and Wheeler, McDowell, and Overs et al.

Leisure counselors frequently develop assessment tools to fit their particular needs. They all consider assessment results as only one of many factors in activity selection. Some counselors do not use assessment instruments because they believe tests restrict reflection. Consequently, they rely solely on the counseling relationship or use other self-awareness techniques such as role playing, fantasy, and journal writing.

Analysis

In individual counseling, the analysis refers to the activity of the counselor, beginning with the initial contact with a client and ending with the final contact. Analysis is a continuing process that overlaps the other steps and that occurs whether the session is single or multiple. With multiple session counseling, analysis by the counselor takes place primarily between sessions. For single session, less complex counseling, the counselor keeps the analysis in mind throughout the process and is ready to look up referrals at the end of the session.

The analysis process by itself may be conceptualized into four parts that may occur in any sequence or simultaneously:

1. The counselor scores the assessment instruments and then studies and integrates results from the interview, the assessment instruments, and his or her subjective impression of the client. The counselor looks for patterns of client likes and dislikes, needs, values, attitudes, and interests that suggest practical leisure activities.

2. The counselor calculates the interests the client prefers, using the information from interviews, instruments, and impressions. The characteristics of the more feasible interests are examined to determine what needs they can fulfill for the counselee. Common needs are for beauty, solitude, companionship, physical exercise, recognition, leadership, knowledge, or helping others. Through a combination of training,

experience, and intuition, leisure counselors become aware of the various activities that can satisfy client needs and preferences.

3. The counselor selects practical activities to discuss with the client, based on the client's interests and needs. For activity selection, leisure counselors utilize community activity resource materials and national, state, county, and local sources of leisure information. If an activity seems to fulfill a client's interests but conflicts with client limitations that cannot be overcome, the counselor analyzes the need-fulfilling qualities of the activity and looks for a practical substitute.

4. The counselor lists ways and places for the client to pursue the possible activities. Way refers to the manner in which the client can most advantageously and appropriately participate in the activity—as a performer, leader, spectator, learner, or joiner. Place refers to the location where the client can most conveniently engage in the activity. The counselor prepares a number of options and verifies the way/place information about each. To make the referral presentation more efficient, this listing can divide the activities into subheadings such as volunteer activities and other activities that can lead to paid employment, social enjoyment, and self-improvement.

Referral

The leisure-counseling process concludes with referral, during which the results of the analysis are shared and discussed with the client. Counselors present activity possibilities to their counselees to serve as a basis for exploration. The referral sequence can begin with a discussion of how the clients' leisure interests, aptitudes, attitudes, and needs affect their avocational choices. The conclusions of the counselor's analysis are compared with the ideas the counselees have developed in the course of the counseling process.

Next to be presented are specific activities that counselors believe their clients should consider. Counselees are encouraged to record new thoughts resulting from the analysis process and to list the activity suggestions and information they intend to investigate. Counselors encourage clients to go personally to the places to talk to the people who would be part of the leisure activity and to see the environment for leisure pursuits. They should look at the materials the activity requires, if any, and think about the ways they can participate. As a result of these activities, the decision for leisure pursuit will be based on personal experience and informed thought. After the referral, the client is responsible for drawing conclusions and making final decisions.

The last suggested activity for counselees is to conduct a time study. Counselees who feel they have insufficient time for leisure or are unclear and unhappy about their use of time may be given instruction on how to conduct a time study by recording briefly their daily activities over a period of several weeks. This time study may be assigned any time during the counseling process. Although a time study is of no immediate assistance in one-session counseling, it can be very useful afterward. When people are aware of how their time is spent day after day, they are often moved to make beneficial changes in time allocation on their own initiative. Time studies may be employed in both individual and group counseling situations whenever a need exists.

The Leisure-Counseling Process for Groups

Leisure counseling for groups is frequently conducted in a workshop format. The leader of a workshop assists the members to work through the leisure-counseling process themselves. The members do their own analyses and learn to assist each other in examining their feelings about their current use of leisure time and in deciding whether or not to change it. The leader guides the group in the selection and implementation of new interests or of old interests they wish to reactivate. There is no one-to-one counselor/client relationship as in individual leisure counseling.

Favorable results may be obtained through workshops of varying lengths. A short, half-day workshop or a long, ten-session, three hours-a-week workshop contains similar elements, used in lesser or greater quantity. The best leader for groups is an experienced leisure counselor who is knowledgeable in individual counseling. However, a skilled group leader who uses proven leisure-counseling materials can help increase a group's awareness of leisure, the primary goal. Groups of under fifteen counselees offer the greatest opportunity for member interaction, although larger groups can operate efficiently if the leader has trained assistants.

Workshops usually begin with a presentation by the leader on the importance of leisure time, which sets a pleasant tone for the workshop. The participants are encouraged during this opening phase to discuss their expectations for the workshop and their leisure experiences. A tentative outline of the workshop is given to the members to amend and approve. Most workshop leaders administer an interest survey or questionnaire to clarify the members' leisure lives. Each member scores or analyzes another member's form. Two or more members can then discuss each other's leisure possibilities, barriers, and alternatives. The more notable of these exchanges can be reported to the group for further comment.

Numerous group exercises can be used, depending upon the length of the workshop. Members may interview each other by making up their own questions or by working with a set supplied by the leader. There can be role playing, time studies, value clarification exercises, or leisure games. The object of these aids is to make the workshop participants more aware of their leisure attitudes and aptitudes or the lack of either.

Representatives of volunteer bureaus, cultural centers, park programs, adult education, physical fitness, civic projects, travel agencies, and second careers can contribute to the group members' community knowledge. Members' knowledge may also be increased by giving them special reading and writing assignments on leisure use and misuse. Individuals are encouraged to conduct field research on their interest area. Field trips and a leisure fair are also possibilities for a longer workshop.

Workshops of all lengths would supply the group with information on leisure resources within the community and ways to take advantage of them. A leader might tailor a resource list especially for the needs of a small group. With a small group the leader might offer to meet briefly with each individual during the final phase of the workshop. Any technique may be used to make the members aware of their leisure needs and the alternatives open to them. Most valuable of all, the participants become aware of each other and the great variety of ways leisure can improve the quality of their lives.

Implications for Retirement Specialists

The leisure portion of retirement preparation programs should be a pleasant, agreeable experience for the preretirees. It will probably take place in a group setting. The members should be encouraged to voice their views on leisure and to participate in the presentation. Ideally, an experienced leisure counselor should present this portion, but the regular program leader should be able to stimulate constructive interest in the subject after studying the suggested readings listed at the end of this chapter.

The main goal of the leisure component is to make the participants aware of their leisure activity feelings now and for the future. Leisure-counseling materials and assessment instruments are available that can channel this awareness and act as a springboard for informed discussion. In addition, participants can be assigned projects in advance of the formal presentation to gather information on leisure activities within their local community. Then, during the session they can assist each other in planning for their leisure lives and implement some of their current plans.

Leisure is a vital part of peoples' lives; therefore, every person in the class is an authority on the subject. This situation makes for a lively and interesting exchange of ideas. The session will promote a greater awareness of leisure and will lessen the chances of its misuse. It will highlight an important preparation issue the preretirees previously may not have appreciated.

A combination of career and leisure counseling is valuable for pre-retirees who are planning to re-enter the work force after retiring from their present positions and who are uncertain what to do. The counseling trend toward whole-person counseling, toward examining what a person wants from life, not from work or leisure, as separate entities is very appropriate. Work is no longer expected to fulfill one's goals, and leisure time takes an increasingly larger part of the average working week. The two factors should be synthesized and considered together for well-balanced career counseling.

The process for career and leisure counseling is similar. After determining current life interests and comparing them with existing skills, it is not difficult, with the help of an experienced counselor, to select activities for making money and others for nonwork enjoyment.

Preretirees looking for career counseling should search for a career center that includes interest inventories and/or examines the use of leisure time in its counseling process. Counselors who emphasize leisure usually offer career guidance as well. By taking advantage of this dual service, preretirees can plan a fulfilling life after they leave their jobs.

Reference

Buros, D.K., ed. *The Eighth Mental Measurements Yearbook.* 2 vols. Highland Park, N.J.: Gryphon Press, 1978.

Suggested Readings

Bolles, R.N. *The Three Boxes of Life.* Berkeley, Calif.: Ten Speed Press, 1978.

> A long, well-illustrated book that contains tests, questionnaires, diagrams, and abundant valuable information about life/work planning.

Dickinson, P.A. *The Complete Retirement Planning Book.* New York: E.P. Dutton, 1976.

> This excellent guide covers five broad-based areas—health, finance, housing, law, and leisure. A practical how-to book with a wealth of well presented information.

Edwards, P.B. *Leisure Counseling Techniques: Individual and Group Counseling Step-by-Step,* 3rd ed. Los Angeles: Constructive Leisure, 1980.

> A detailed description of the individual and group leisure-counseling method and materials used successfully by a private leisure-counseling

and consulting center in Los Angeles. Written in a clear, easy-to-understand style for the learning practitioner.

Edwards, P.B. *The Leisure Counselors' Annotated Bibliography for Serving the General Public.* Los Angeles: Constructive Leisure, forthcoming.

> An annotated bibliography for leisure counselors serving the adult population with emphasis on the years 1968–1984.

Gault, J. *Free Time: Making Your Leisure Count.* New York: John Wiley & Sons, 1983.

> The first six chapters of this easy-to-read book give common sense information on the benefit of good use of leisure time and how to go about developing a satisfying leisure life. The last two chapters present a strategy for success that the author calls "Scimode," "a scientific mode of thinking about ourselves in interaction with our environment," that helps the readers take control of their time.

Kaplan, M. *Leisure: Lifestyle and Lifespan.* Philadelphia: W.B. Saunders, 1979.

> With a subtitle, "Perspectives for Gerontology," this book is a thoughtful, extensively researched philosophical and factual presentation of the relationship between leisure and the elderly in U.S. and other cultures.

Loesch, L.C., and Wheeler, P.T. *Principles of Leisure Counseling.* Minneapolis, Minn.: Educational Media Corp., 1982.

> An overview of leisure counseling and guidelines for individual, group, and developmental leisure counseling are presented. Information on available leisure-counseling assessment instruments and a good bibliography are included. The book acts as an introduction to and description of the authors' leisure-counseling model called Triangulation Leisure Counseling (TLC).

McDowell, C.F. *Leisure Counseling: Selected Lifestyle Processes.* Eugene: University of Oregon Press, 1976.

> This comprehensive book presents a good picture of different classifications and models of leisure counseling and gives a variety of exercises to help with leisure-counseling resources and publication references.

Moran, J.M. *Leisure Activities for the Mature Adult.* Minneapolis, Minn.: Burgess Publishing, 1979.

> Some activities are described in the fields of sports, exercise, and creative arts and crafts, but the main thrust of the book is background information for specialists working in recreation programs for mature

adults. This information includes the biological, psychological, and sociological aspects of aging.

Overs, R.P.; Taylor, S.; and Adkins, C. *Vocational Counseling Manual: A Complete Guide to Leisure Guidance.* Washington, D.C.: Hawkins, 1977.

> This guide covers the avocational-counseling field well, up to 1977. It gives background, theory, a counseling model, counseling instruments, case histories, and a long, excellent list of avocational activities.

12 Preretirement Issues that Affect Minorities

Fernando Torres-Gil

Retirement planning is a new profession, the growth of which signifies the concern of all individuals, regardless of age, to ensure income security for their retirement years. Retirement preparation programs have increased dramatically in recent years to meet this need and have provided the impetus for training specialists who can provide the necessary education and training. The field of retirement planning and preparation, however, has yet to serve a heterogeneous population that differs by sex, language, race, and socioeconomic status. The retirement literature concentrates exclusively on a population that is white, educated, and relatively affluent, implying that techniques and educational models used by retirement-planning specialists for that population can be just as useful for individuals who are of a different race, ethnicity, and/or language.

The purpose of this chapter is to attempt to increase the number of populations that retirement preparation programs now serve. The chapter discusses preretirement issues that affect minorities and brings to retirement specialists' attention the challenges and opportunities of reaching out to those groups. In order to suggest strategies and recommendations for developing effective methods and techniques in serving those groups, the chapter provides an overview of blacks, Hispanics, Asians, and native Americans and identifies the salient issues and factors that affect these groups' willingness and ability to use retirement preparation programs.

Facts and Issues about Minorities

Concerns of minorities are taken into account in diverse issues such as social welfare, civil rights, human services, and employment. Retirement, pension, and preretirement planning, however, normally have not been considered areas in which minorities' interests, needs, or concerns were of major importance. This conclusion may be due to assumptions that minorities are not interested in or aware of retirement-related issues because they are a relatively youthful population and, therefore, are more interested in educational and soical issues; are poor or struggling for middle-class status and thus are more concerned with issues of employment and income security; and are not employed in occupations providing pension and retirement programs that give them sufficient income to plan for retirement and to prepare for leisure activities. It may be that retirement specialists simply have not been aware of these populations and their needs and, therefore, have not developed strategies that take into account any differences due to race, ethnicity, or language. The reasons why minorities may not take advantage of retirement preparation programs are explored later.

Changes are now occurring with respect to minorities in the United States, changes that are cultural, social, and demographic and that may make various groups of minorities more amenable to retirement preparation programs. At present, however, minorities are not accustomed to planning for retirement, in part because of barriers preventing them from using retirement preparation programs and also because of their attitudes regarding retirement. In order to interest them in preparing for retirement and identifying the strategies that may work best for them, it is important to understand the characteristics relevant to retirement planning and to identify the differences that may affect how specialists approach this topic.

Demographics

Minorities comprise a heterogeneous population of four national minority groups (Cuellar et al. 1982): black Americans (with growing numbers of blacks from the Caribbean nations); Hispanics (Mexican-Americans, Puerto Ricans, Cubans, and other Latin and Central Americans); Asians (Japanese, Chinese, Southeast Asians, Koreans, and Filipinos) and Pacific Islanders (Samoans, Guamanians, and Hawaiians); and native Americans (Indians and Eskimos). These national minority groups share four characteristics that set them apart from other ethnic groups: (1) they have their own special histories; (2) their histories typically are marked by discrimination and negative stereotyping; (3) they are characterized by the institutionalization of coping structures; and (4) they are faced with a need to adjust to rapid social change (Moore 1971). The 1980 census reveals that of the total U.S. population of 226 million, blacks make up 26.5 million (11.7 percent); native Americans, 1.5 million (0.07 percent); Asian and Pacific Islanders, 3.5 million (1.5 percent); and Hispanics, 14.6 million (6.5 percent) (U.S. Department of Commerce 1983). The 65-years-and-over population is approximately 7.9 percent black, 12.4 percent white, 4.8 percent Hispanic, and 5.3 percent native American (U.S. Department of Commerce 1983). In 1980, the median age of minority persons of Spanish origin was 23.2 years; of whites, 31.3 years; of Asians, 28.6 years; of blacks, 24.9 years; and native Americans, 22.9 years (U.S. Department of Commerce 1981).

Economic Status

Minorities in general have lower incomes and higher poverty rates than whites. For example, the poverty rate in 1978 for white families (6.9 percent) was much lower than the rates for black families (27.5 percent) and families of Spanish origin (20.4 percent) (the poverty threshold for a nonfarm family of four was $6,662 in 1978) (U.S. Department of Commerce 1979b). Among persons aged 65 and over, 38 percent of blacks and 30.8 percent of persons of Spanish origin were impoverished, compared with 13 percent of whites (Watson 1983).

Health

Health plays an important part in the retirement decision process and the ability of persons to continue working into old age and enjoying their retirement years. By most measures of health condition, minorities are in greater jeopardy than whites and are more likely to be forced to retire early and to become disabled (Cantor 1976). Studies show that compared to whites, blacks and Latinos are more likely to retire involuntarily due to poor health, illness, or disability and that when retired, blacks and Latinos are more likely to report being dissatisfied with their retirement than whites (Markides 1978; Morse 1976; Newquist et al. 1979; San Diego State University 1982; U.S. Senate 1978). Life expectancy becomes an important factor in the probability that minorities will reach the eligibility age for retirement. Data show that minority life expectancy, particularly for blacks, Hispanics, and native Americans, is lower than for whites (Asians and Cubans are exceptions) and that minority men have lower life expectancies than minority women (Giles 1982; Lacayo 1979; Manton 1982; Torres-Gil et al. 1980; U.S. Department of Commerce 1979a).

Employment

The pattern of preretirement employment and the wage history determine source and amount of retirement income. Therefore, the factors that make a difference in the economics of retirement among minority elders will include the sector—public or private—in which a person works, the occupational category of the job held, and the longest time worked at a particular job (Rhodes 1982). Minorities are at a distinct disadvantage, since fewer work in the public sector—which has better pension coverage—than whites; are in lower occupational categories and therefore have lower incomes; and have a more erratic and unstable work tenure and are thus less likely to accumulate vesting rights and wage provisions necessary for receiving the maximum postretirement income from pensions and Social Security (U.S. Department of Health and Human Services 1982).

Research shows that older minority group workers experience special labor force problems including higher levels of unemployment, more frequent and involuntary labor force withdrawal, more involuntary part-time employment, and more frequent health problems (San Diego State University 1982). An examination of private pension coverage and vesting in 1979 reveals that among mature workers, blacks and Hispanics are less likely to belong to pension plans than their white counterparts and that among workers participating in pension plans, blacks and Hispanics are less likely to have vesting rights to benefits (U.S. Department of Health and Human Services 1982).

In summary, minority populations tend to have a relatively low median age and, correspondingly, fewer older persons than the white population; to have lower incomes and, therefore, a larger number who are poor; to have greater health problems and lower life expectancies and thus to be more likely to retire early; and to work in occupations considered blue collar and nonprofessional.

Barriers to Retirement Planning

The result of these factors is that barriers can be identified that make it difficult or irrelevant for some minority groups to put a priority on planning for retirement. These barriers include a greater probability that they will not be employed in jobs or occupations that give them adequate pension coverage; that health will be a problem, thus forcing them to retire earlier; that they will need to work into old age and not be able to enjoy leisure time; that low levels of education will make it difficult for them to understand or use educational programs and therefore also make them unaware of such programs; that they will not accumulate pension and vesting rights, forcing them to continue working after the normal retirement age; that they will feel they cannot afford to plan for retirement or that retirement planning is not pertinent to their situation; and that they will be exposed to the triple jeopardy of being old, poor, and a member of a racial or ethnic community subject to differential treatment in the labor market based on their minority status.

Clearly, these statements are overgeneralizations. Certain minority groups—for example, Japanese and Cubans—do not face as great a probability of these scenarios. However, to the extent that retirement-planning specialists need to be aware of the realities of retirement facing minorities, these scenarios are fairly typical.

Factors Relevant to Retirement Planning

Cultural Factors

If the described issues were the only concerns in addressing the obstacles to minorities' using retirement programs, then it would only require time, income, and upward mobility to remove those problems, and retirement programs would be as germane to minorities as they are to nonminorities. However, key cultural factors affect the relevance of retirement planning to minority groups and must be considered separate from the broader social and economic issues.

Language. The most visible differences between minorities and nonminorities lie with the large proportion of minorities that does not speak English or that prefers another language. Hispanics, of course, speak Spanish, and among Puerto Ricans, Cubans, and Mexican-Americans, there are various dialects. Asians and Pacific Islanders will speak their respective languages, be it Japanese, Korean, Chinese, or Guamanian. The majority of these populations, particularly higher-income individuals, can and does speak English. However, the growth of bilingualism and the continuing influx of refugees and immigrants ensure that large numbers of minorities will prefer to speak their ethnic language.

Social Factors. An important factor in understanding the social and cultural status of minorities lies with their historical experiences in this country and their development as ethnic groups. Each minority group has a history that is instructive in understanding their relationship with their host country. The story of black Americans and their long years of struggle against racism and discrimination and ongoing efforts to participate equally in the U.S. mainstream is well known.

The remainder of the national minority groups is different from black Americans in their relationship to the United States. Mexican-Americans, although descendents of the original Spanish and Mexican colonizers, came for economic reasons as well as to flee a revolution in Mexico. Chinese, Japanese, and Filipinos were brought in as contract labor, and when their contracts expired, they stayed in this country, only to face a series of exclusionary laws limiting their ability to buy property, to intermarry with non-Asians, and to participate fully in social and economic activities. Puerto Rico, as a territory of the United States, was granted citizenship, and its people can move freely to the mainland. Cubans and Central Americans came primarily as political refugees (Bell et al. 1976). These groups have been affected deeply by their historical experiences, making them less receptive to groups outside their ethnic communities. Their concentration in ghettos, barrios, little Tokyos, and Koreatowns illustrates this exclusiveness.

Each cohort or generation differs greatly in the level of assimilation and acculturation and, hence, differs in willingness and ability of cohort members to adopt preretirement planning as a goal. Today's elderly minority is very traditional in his or her views, has suffered the greatest, has reaped the fewest rewards, and has had the least chance to prepare for his or her retirement compared with whites. These groups and those becoming elderly in the next few years may be least likely to benefit from retirement preparation programs.

The middle-aged groups of minorities in the 1950s and 1960s were likely to benefit from better education, reduction of discrimination, and the affluence of that period and therefore now are more likely to have the income and pension coverage benefits for retirement; however, due to their relative closeness to the traditional cultures, they are almost as likely not to have planned for their retirement years. They are, to some extent, the cohort most in need of preretirement planning but will probably require extensive outreach and education to convince them to participate. The younger groups, in contrast, are more likely to benefit from the advancements of previous generations, may be less affected by cultural constraints regarding retirement planning, and have the time to begin preparing for retirement. The middle-aged and younger cohorts can become the central target audiences for preretirement planners. It is also important to identify the distinct characteristics of each cohort so we do not overgeneralize from what we know about the older minority cohort.

Attitudes. Making preretirement planning amenable to middle-aged and younger minorities will require a reversal of attitudes toward retirement—attitudes shaped both by minorities' social and economic conditions and by the continuing influence of their heritage and cultural values. Retirement, as a concept, has been prominent in our society during much of this century. However, it has not been widely accepted or relevant for many minorities. For example, the positive connotation that retirement often carries has not been meaningful for most older minority persons because of the lack of employment opportunities that would lead to a time when they could enjoy retirement. They have considered retirement to be for someone else and have not considered facing or taking retirement a possibility. For some, retirement has a negative connotation—for example, disengagement from family and friends, displacement from the labor market, and loss of important roles in decision making. Therefore, many may tend to resist the idea of retiring. For others, lower incomes, larger families, and lower levels of education ensure that they must continue working until they can no longer or are not allowed to do so.

Some researchers have raised the attitude issue with respect to a particular national minority group. In an attempt to put retirement into perspective for the Pacific and Asian elderly, Fujii (1978) suggests that misconceptions such as older Asians' maintaining a favored and honored status and the tendency to overromanticize the role of the elders must be clarified. Curley (1978) feels that for American Indians, it may be fruitless to discuss how to use their retirement time because "Indian elderly know what to do with their time " (p. 47), although retirement preparation would probably be applicable to middle-aged Indians. Dieppa (1977) found that retired Mexican-Americans have less positive attitudes toward retirement than whites. As Stanford (1978) points out, the minority elderly are not in a position of choosing whether they wish to retire because continued work is essential for their survival; therefore, the attitudes among minority groups, young and old, may indicate a negative association with retirement, and this association creates a disincentive to prepare for it.

Natural Support Networks. Although retirement is an economic concept, that fact does not diminish the social and psychological problems arising from lack of companionship and from failed health, making support systems important aids and requiring retirement specialists to understand the role such networks play for minorities (Rhodes 1982). Differences in attitudes toward retirement between minorities and nonminorities are reflected in the extensive reliance by minorities on the natural support networks that include family, church, and neighborhood groups. Studies on black, Hispanic, and Asian communities reveal that the extended family, community groups, and churches continue to play a major role as members age (Valle and Martinez 1981; Weeks and Cuellar 1981).

The family, in particular, is important. As minorities age, they expect that financial, emotional, and physical supports will be available from the family and that their major activities will center around the family. Their role is not expected to be one of leisure or to consist of individual retirement activities. This reliance on natural support networks has precluded some individuals from even considering that they will be alone or can have time to seek meaningful roles outside their ethnic group or the family, even if they eventually find themselves alone. It is important to be knowledgeable of these support networks and to use them where necessary in retirement preparation programs. As Langston (1978) states, these networks can be utilized effectively by and for the minority elderly in the retirement phase of their lives.

Public Benefit Programs

The economic, attitudinal, occupational, and cultural issues previously described are reflected in the overdependence on public benefit programs by today's cohort of older minorities. Retirement income depends on a combination of private pension income, savings, and Social Security. Minorities have little savings, with the possible exception of a home, and have been unable to acquire adequate pension coverage. Therefore, they find themselves relying extensively on Social Security benefits and Supplemental Security Income (SSI) as well as Medicare and other public welfare services. For example, blacks and Hispanics have lower rates of insured status under Social Security than whites but are more dependent on Social Security for a major part of their income (Garcia 1980).

This overdependence on income transfer programs puts minorities in double or triple jeopardy (Dowd and Bengston 1978). They are at risk if any changes occur in public benefit programs. Cutbacks in Medicare and social services will affect them directly, while policies designed to assist older persons may not benefit them at all. For example, the passage of the Age Discrimination Act and the increased mandatory age for retirement may have little significant effect on their ability to keep their jobs because of the employment and health factors that lessen opportunities to work at an older age (Arnold et al. 1978). In addition, many have difficulty getting access to public benefit programs. Minority group membership has been found to be a significant reason for under- and nonutilization of public benefits, with logistical and psychological factors acting as barriers for utilizing available benefits (Guttman 1980).

The central point in this discussion is not to demonstrate the irrelevance of retirement planning to minorities but to stress the importance of beginning to involve minorities in retirement preparation programs—in particular, the younger cohorts—precisely to avoid or minimize the circumstances in which older minorities now find themselves. If minorities are to reduce overdependence on public benefit programs as they age, they need to become more educated and aware of the importance of planning for their later years. Many minorities are poor even in their younger years and therefore will face the same obstacles as their older cohorts. This fact only reinforces the importance of developing new approaches that take the previously mentioned barriers and factors into account so that low income minorities can benefit, even if it is to a limited extent. In addition, it is important to focus on groups of minorities who are younger and economically better off—to identify them now and take advantage of changing demographics in the minority population. Research on minorities has shown that for some groups, particularly blacks, increased opportunities for employment, improved health, and better education will make retirement more relevant (Rhodes 1982; San Diego State University 1982). It is important to begin a tradition in these groups of preretirement planning, even if not all minorities can be reached immediately.

Retirement Preparation

The literature on retirement has ignored the aforementioned issues. Retirement research assumes that retirement is irrelevant for most minorities and therefore has not examined the peculiar situations that face minorities that, to some degree, make retirement appear irrelevant. This lack of research is due primarily to the definitions and methods currently used for preretirement planning. Without an understanding of why retirement has been seen as irrelevant in the past, it is difficult to understand what modifications are needed to make retirement planning more relevant, at least to some segments of the minority community. Taking two major areas commonly assumed to comprise retirement planning and education, we can examine their applicability to minorities and raise the key issues affecting them, giving insights into how retirement planning and education can become germane to those groups.

Financial Planning

Financial planning is considered to be the most important consideration of retirement planning. Financial adequacy in retirement is a direct result of financial planning during most of an individual's working life. Without a reasonably adequate income level, however, the whole issue of retirement planning is assumed to be moot. Therefore, the barriers and limitations to accumulating the necessary capital (via savings, assets, and pensions) that low-income minorities face during their working lives clearly make financial planning difficult. However, the premise that inadequate financial resources renders planning irrelevant need not be moot. To follow that logic would relegate low-income minorities to a status quo they now face: overdependence on public benefit programs for retirement income. Even for these groups, preretirement planning can be relevant. The key is to begin some planning at an early period, even if it is relatively limited compared with that of affluent groups. Alternative methods of financial planning must be developed for those low-income minority groups who have limited financial resources to invest and save.

In addition, we must emphasize that not all minorities are poor. Significant segments of the minority population, particularly in the middle-aged cohort, are in relatively good economic shape and have been able to accumulate savings, assets, and pensions. In particular, minorities have predominated some categories of occupations despite racial and discriminatory barriers. For example, blacks who have worked for the railroads and the federal Civil Service are receiving pension benefits from the Railroad Retirement Board and the Civil Service Retirement System. Blacks and Hispanics have had good fortune in finding employment with the U.S. Postal Service and have enjoyed generous salary and retirement benefits. Many blacks and Hispanics, particularly those from the World War II and Korean War generations, have made the military a career and, in many cases, have retired after twenty years, have obtained new employment, and have been able to double and even triple dip with multiple pension benefits. Minorities employed in occupations with strong unions such as the United Auto Workers and the United Mine Workers have benefited from health and pension benefits gained through collective bargaining. Retirement specialists should identify those categories of occupations where minorities are able to accumulate pensions and benefits and perhaps begin their initial efforts to reach out to those groups.

In those groups, the concepts of financial planning—spendable income in retirement, reducing expenses to increase one's net worth, estate, and wills—are relevant issues. However, it is important to keep in mind one central point: even though certain segments of minority populations are becoming affluent, particularly the young and middle aged, cultural factors will continue to affect their definitions and attitudes toward retirement and, therefore, must be incorporated in financial-planning techniques.

An important component in conducting preretirement education is the concept of the three-legged stool of retirement income (see chapter 5). This concept presupposes that in order to have adequate retirement income, an individual should have three major sources of income: Social Security, pensions (public, private, or employer), and personal assets (investments, home equity, and savings). Retirement planners, educators, and counselors should be aware of these sources not only for knowledge to lead discussions on financial planning but also to examine the issue of adequate retirement income. Minorities also have a three-legged stool of retirement income. However, at the risk of overgeneralization, it differs in significant ways from the traditional concept. The three sources include a combination of (1) working until they are physically or occupationally incapable of doing so, regardless of age; (2) relying upon the family and natural support systems to provide financial support and assistance to supplement their work income and to provide for them when they can no longer work; and (3) Social Security.

The first source, working until it is no longer possible, is a function of both having no other choice (they need the money) and their value system about nonretirement. For some, *retirement* continues to be a positive word, indicating continued involvement. Leisure, in contrast, is considered unbecoming to the older person who remains self-sufficient and who contributes to the household. The problem with standing on this leg is that minorities increasingly are victimized by the types of occupations they have had throughout their lives: manual, back-breaking, physical work (for example, agriculture, warehouse, assembly line) that may create serious health problems, and when coupled with inadequate health coverage and lack of preventive health care and proper nutrition, these jobs create a high probability for disability or forced early retirement. When that happens, or when they are simply too old to work because of physical limitations, age discrimination, or racism, that leg of the stool is pulled out from under them, eliminating a major source of income.

The second leg, the family, traditionally has been insurance for those who lose their jobs or need supplemental assistance, particularly in extended households. For many minorities, particularly Hispanics and Asians, the family continues to play the major role in providing emotional, physical, and financial support. This role is changing. The traditional extended family is declining in importance, whether it is due to assimilation and upward mobility of the younger cohorts, to geographic dispersion of family members, or to the fact that families can no longer provide income supports or have grandparents live in the same household. As traditional characteristics change, making the family less reliable, another important element of the minority three-legged stool begins to crumble.

The final leg, Social Security, is of paramount importance. Minorities, particularly blacks, are dependent on Social Security benefits, whether Old Age, Survivors, and Disability Insurance, SSI, or Medicare and Medicaid. For many, it is their sole source of assistance. With changes in Social Security—the raising of the eligibility age, more stringent disability requirements, and delays in cost-of-living increases—the impact is greater and more adverse, further jeopardizing the viability of this primary leg of their retirement income.

These ongoing changes in the minority stool of retirement income point out the importance of providing retirement preparation programs that take into account their situation. As work becomes difficult to obtain or handle, and as the family structure changes, additional legs must be introduced. Retirement-planning specialists and educators can make an important contribution by introducing new legs to the stool and by educating younger cohorts about the need to develop more modern three legs.

Health Promotion

Health promotion, health enhancement, wellness, and prevention of illnesses are increasingly popular topics in preretirement planning. The ability to minimize stress and tension, to exercise, and to maintain a healthy state of mind and body are considered essential to retirement preparation. The importance of these issues transcends race, ethnicity, and income; all persons can benefit. The difference with minorities is the extent to which they have the luxury to maintain their health. As cited earlier, minorities have greater health problems and are more likely to become disabled or to retire for health reasons. Their occupations are less amenable to progressive and generous benefits such as exercise programs and recreational facilities. Miners and agricultural workers, for example, have high incidences of tuberculosis, environment-related diseases, and back problems. Assembly line workers have high levels of alcoholism and stress caused by repetitive and monotonous activities. Many minorities have inadequate or no health coverage and must forego preventive medical care until an illness is severe. In this area, perhaps, the effects of health problems are a function of social class and income, and as long as minorities are poor and occupationally disadvantaged, they will face this obstacle. What can be done about this by preretirement planners is probably limited, aside from their being aware of the problem. The solutions fall within the scope of health-care policy and public health programs.

Implications for Retirement Specialists

This chapter has provided an overview of social, economic, health, and labor force issues that affect retirement behavior in the minority population, as well as a discussion of the cultural factors important in understanding the propensity of minorities to use preretirement-planning programs. Specific areas in preretirement programs have been presented as examples of their applicability to the unique situation of minorities.

This information is important in developing preretirement-planning techniques and programs for those populations. However, it is also important to note that the issues raised here may not be applicable in every case. Since few models exist for incorporating these issues in preretirement planning and education, retirement specialists will need to be creative and innovative in integrating the concepts into their current practices. To assist them in these endeavors, this section outlines four areas of practical suggestions for working with the minority population.

Understanding the Situation of Minorities

In developing programs and educational packages to use in serving the minority population, specialists must be aware of a variety of factors including the social and economic variations in the minority population, encompassing many relatively poor minorities who lack the fiscal resources to prepare for retirement; the labor force participation of these groups, which may deny them the opportunity to develop retirement and pension portfolios; the health and life expectancy factors, which may force some to retire earlier because of disability; and their educational levels, which may require that sessions and instructional aids reflect different levels of educational attainment.

In addition to these areas, which will differ according to the income and educational levels of the target audience, specialists must remain cognizant of the unique cultural and linguistic issues facing all minorities, albeit in different ways. The language of the particular groups, their attitudes and values toward retirement, the use of natural support networks, and the history and traditions they retain will affect how and when they can be reached and served by retirement programs. Based on those factors, several principles that must be recognized in developing ethnically and culturally sensitive techniques are that minority groups have different conceptions and definitions about retirement, planning for retirement, and use of leisure time; that each group, and subgroups within them, have social and political histories that may affect the degree to which rapport and working relationships develop between the minority participant and the trainer; that for many minorities, regardless of income level, planning for retirement is a relatively new concept; and that retirement planning remains visible for low-income minorities but requires a creative analysis of financial-planning practices.

Therefore, it is important for specialists to know their target audience. The specialist will need an accurate profile of the demographic, social, economic, and cultural characteristics of the group. If the profile is developed accurately, the specialist will understand the level of assimilation and acculturation in the group and, thus, the extent to which cultural factors must be taken into account. Cohort differences and how they affect retention of cultural and linguistic features must be recognized among and within the minority groups. Some groups of minorities are assimilated and can benefit from existing programs used by nonminorities. It is important, however, for specialists not to be misled by similarity in social and economic backgrounds: individuals may appear to be well off, sophisticated, and professional and thus like the people for whom most retirement-planning programs are designed, but in actuality, they may differ considerably according to ethnicity.

To develop an accurate picture of the target audience, retirement specialists will have to make a careful assessment through interviews, surveys, or basic research. In turn, the instructors and counselors may need to educate themselves about the characteristics of different minority groups. Courses on ethnicity and minority aging will be useful.

Reaching the Minority Community

A major element in serving minorities will be an active reaching out to minority communities. This requires first a desire and willingness to serve that population and, second, a well-conceived outreach plan. Preretirement programs may unwittingly be excluding minorities from their participant pool by either a lack of outreach or outreach to certain types of individuals perceived as fairly well off, educated, and especially receptive to those programs.

In order to reach minorities who have not been involved with these programs, it will be necessary to include any or all of the following elements. The first is active consultation with the minority community. Minority communities should be consulted on program content, format, and approach from the initiation of project planning. Specifically, consultation on the history, family system, and local language idioms and use patterns can be obtained from community leaders, organizations, and experts in those areas. The second element is development of planning meetings and advisory boards. It may be useful to set up formal planning meetings with representatives of minority groups and to establish groups such as advisory committees and task forces to ensure ongoing dialogue between minority representatives and the specialist. The third is assistance from employers, union representatives, and company officials. These groups must play a major role in encouraging minorities to take advantage of retirement preparation programs. The fourth element is use of radio and television. In every community with large numbers of minorities, radio, television stations, and print media exist that cater to those groups. The media should be identified and used. Finally, sessions and courses could be conducted in minority neighborhoods. Ethnic neighborhoods in every large metropolitan area, where minorities often prefer to live, regardless of income, offer excellent locations for preretirement sessions. Utilization of these locations will create a comfortable surrounding and will indicate a serious intent to reach out to those groups.

Minorities as Retirement Specialists

Ultimately, to understand the unique characteristics of minorities and to reach out effectively and involve them in retirement preparation programs, it will be necessary to recruit and train minorities to become educators, trainers, and specialists in the programs. Outreach programs will become more effective when minorities who possess multilingual and multicultural skills are trained as specialists. Although data are not available to indicate the degree to which minorities are currently involved in this field, it is clear that their numbers are few. Educational institutions with gerontology programs are excellent recruiting grounds for minorities who wish to become involved in this area. With proper training they can become invaluable resources in working with all persons, not just minorities.

Providing Preretirement Planning and
Education to Minorities

Various steps exist in approaching the revision and modification of methods and practices used in conducting educational and planning sessions to focus more on the retirement issues of minorities. The first step is for the instructor to be aware of the biases and stereotypes that may be inherent in their perceptions, values, and training methods as they relate to working with minorities. Specialists must be honest and open in understanding that they may not relate well to nonwhites. Communicating with minority clients will involve more than speaking their language. It will involve a sensitivity to their history, traditions, and situations.

There is also a need to examine the training programs and materials in terms of cultural bias. How can they be changed to account for variations in realities, perceptions, and conditions faced by those persons who are not the so-called typical retiree? How can materials, handouts, and teaching aids be revised to provide factual data and information about the retirement experiences of minority groups?

The curriculum content within the educational program takes on critical importance. Normally, a comprehensive curriculum will include content on pension and insurance aspects of retirement, health, leisure, employment services, housing, attitudes, and finances. In relating to lower-income groups of minorities, content also should consider the following areas. First, the importance of planning for as many as five, ten, twenty, and thirty years of retirement and developing and maintaining adequate retirement and pension benefits, even if it means saving a small amount on a regular basis, should be stressed. This plan requires a sensitive understanding of the problems and crises created when even a small amount of income is set aside. The specialist will need to emphasize the consequences that could occur in the long term that counterbalance the sacrifices in the short term. This area entails identifying alternative methods of financial planning for those groups.

Program content should include an awareness of individual rights and privileges in the United States, particularly concerning citizenship, residency status, and civil rights. Some minorities are not familiar with their legal and civil rights in the United States, and that will affect their sense of security and stability—elements necessary for planning.

Specialists need to emphasize the changes in family and social relationships that may occur over a lifetime, which may create culture shock to those who expect that the older years will follow traditional patterns and who find that, in retirement, those patterns no longer exist. Educating the client to these changes and how to cope with cultural transitions will be useful. This understanding also will include the cultural and psychological adjustments necessary in adapting an ethnic identity to the values and attitudes of their new country.

Programs should indicate the extent and use of informal and natural support networks. Informal networks that provide information, services, and support have existed in many minority communities for years, and programs need to identify and discuss these networks in reference to their utility in planning for retirement.

Minorities also must be made aware of the availability and appropriateness of public benefit programs and services, including those retirement programs developed for low-income elderly. This area would include health- and disability-related programs. In addition, the realities of getting access to these programs and the types of barriers and difficulties in acquiring benefits would be useful.

Finally, consumer education and the need to be aware of fraud, scams, and con artists are important aspects. Low-income persons are especially susceptible to exploitation, particularly in acquiring life insurance and medical policies, as well as in enrolling in programs and services that may not provide immediate benefits but that require investments over long periods of time.

Curriculum usually includes discussion of various types of retirement and volunteer activities. Specialists should suggest that retirees become involved in recreational, cultural, and sports activities, as well as in hobbies and traveling, if possible. In some cases, discussions may be held on where to move to maximize leisure time and quality of life. For low-income minorities, recreational activities may take on a totally different concept (for example, rather than visiting museums or attending operas, it may mean tending one's garden to reduce food bills and staying close to the neighborhood). Specialists will need to develop creative ways of spending leisure time and recreational activities relevant to the experiences of minority groups. Volunteer activities play another important part in preretirement planning, but for minorities, voluntary activities may mean that instead of working with the Red Cross, the individual may work with neighborhood gangs to reduce crime against the elderly.

Retirement preparation programs offer a variety of methods that present information, help people plan, and attempt to improve perceptions and attitudes toward retirement. These methods include avoiding stereotypes about the aged; recognizing the need for instructors to become facilitators; promoting self-directed learning; relating learning to existing knowledge, experience, or need; using materials only when needed; and allowing feedback. These points are relevant in working with minority groups.

In addition, the educational program should take into account the following elements: first, the setting of the program can be enhanced by providing an informal location in an ethnic neighborhood. This technique becomes culturally and symbolically important in promoting rapport and respect. Second, the relationships of minorities with the family and grandchildren are paramount. Providing day care at the program's location and allowing other family members to attend can increase participation. Third, instituting advisory committees and having minorities involved in developing the curriculum will support the feeling that the participants have a stake in the program. Fourth, minimizing formal procedures may reduce the discomfort some minorities have with bureaucratic and formal meetings. Structure is acceptable, but formal procedures may be threatening, particularly when detailed questions and information are solicited. Fifth, instructors need to develop a personal relationship with the minority learner. The teacher's personality and ability to relate is crucial to attracting and maintaining participation. A familiarity and sensitivity to cultural habits and ways of communicating are essential, but so is the sense of respect and equality brought forth through the interaction of the instructor with the participant. Finally, classes with low-socioeconomic-group minority participants often have to begin at the students' educational level. This necessitates variation in teaching style and materials used in the training session.

Conclusion

The information in this chapter is intended to make retirement preparation programs relevant to blacks, Hispanics, Asians, and native Americans by taking into account their unique racial, cultural, and ethnic realities. Specific planning issues were presented, and suggestions for incorporating them into programs, curriculum, and planning were described. Greater attention to these areas are needed, and further research and analysis of this topic will be valuable in refining and revising the suggestions presented in this chapter.

Specialists in the areas of preretirement planning and retirement preparation are faced with great challenges in serving minority populations. However, these challenges can lead to opportunities for expanding the scope of their programs and the market for their services. Minorities now comprise a significant portion of the population and, in many regions, are the majority. It is significant that despite the social and economic barriers they face, increasing numbers are becoming affluent and upwardly mobile. With the aging of these ethnic and minority populations, a new and urgent need to be prepared for the retirement years will develop. Specialists and planners have much work to do to prepare for these changes, but the positive results from doing so will be great.

References

Bell, D.; Kassachau, P.; and Zellman, G. *Delivering Services to Elderly Members of Minority Groups: A Critical Review of the Literature.* R-1862-HEW. Santa Monica, Calif.: The Rand Corporation, 1976.

Cantor, M.H. "Effect of Ethnicity on Life Styles of the Inner City Elderly." In *Community Planning for an Aging Society: Designing Services and Facilities,* edited by P. Lawton, R. Newcomer, and T. Byertz. Stroudsburg, Penn.: Dowden, Hutchinson and Ross, Inc., 1976.

Cuellar, J.; Stanford, E.P.; and Miller-Soule, D.I. *Understanding Minority Aging: Perspectives and Sources.* San Diego: University Center on Aging, San Diego State University, 1982.

Curley, L. "Retirement: An Indian Perspective." In *Retirement: Concepts and Realities of Ethnic Minority Elders,* edited by E.P. Stanford. San Diego: The Campanile Press, 1978.

Dieppa, M.D. "Retirement: A Comparative Study of Mexican-Americans and Anglos." Ph.D. dissertation, Denver University, 1977.

Dowd, J.D., and Bengston, V.L. "Aging in Minority Populations: An Examination of the Double Jeopardy Hypothesis." *Journal of Gerontology* 33 (1978):427–36.

Fujii, S. "Retirement as It Relates to the Pacific/Asian Elderly." In *Retirement: Concepts and Realities of Ethnic Minority Elders,* edited by E.P. Stanford. San Diego: The Campanile Press, 1978.

Garcia, A. "The Elderly Chicano Male and Social Security." Paper presented at the Annual Meeting of the American Gerontological Society, San Diego, November 20–25, 1980.

Giles, H.F. "Differential Life Expectancy among White and Non-White Americans: Some Explanations during Youth and Middle Age." In *Minority Aging: Sociological and Social Psychological Issues,* edited by R. Manuel. Westport, Conn.: Greenwood Press, 1982.

Guttman, D. *Perspective on Equitable Share in Public Benefits by Minority Elderly.* Executive Summary, Administration on Aging grant no. 90-A-1671. Washington, D.C.: Catholic University of America, 1980.

Lacayo, C. "Considerations of the Relative Effects of Chronological and Biological Age as the Primary Determinants for Service Delivery to the Elderly." Paper presented at the 29th Annual Conference of the National Council on the Aging, Cincinnati, Ohio, March 25–28, 1979.

Langston, E. "The Role and Value of Natural Support Systems in Retirement." In *Retirement: Concepts and Realities of Ethnic Minority Elders,* edited by E.P. Stanford. San Diego: The Campanile Press, 1978.

Manton, K. "Differential Life Expectancy: Possible Explanations during the Later Ages." In *Minority Aging: Sociological and Social Psychological Issues,* edited by R. Manuel. Westport, Conn. Greenwood Press, 1982.

Markides, K. "Reasons for Retirement and Adaptation to Retirement by Elderly Mexican Americans." In *Retirement: Concepts and Realities of Ethnic Minority Elders*, edited by E.P. Stanford. San Diego: The Campanile Press, 1978.

Moore, J. "Situational Factors Affecting Minority Aging." *The Gerontologist* 2 (1971):88–93.

Morse, D.W. "Aging in the Ghetto: Themes Expressed by Older Black Men and Women Living in a Northern Industrial City." *Industrial Gerontologist* Winter (1976):1–10.

Newquist, D.; Berger, M.; Kahn, K.; Martinez, C.; and Burton, L. *Prescription for Neglect: Experiences of Older Blacks and Mexican-Americans with the American Health Care System*. Los Angeles: Andrus Gerontology Center, University of Southern California, 1979.

Rhodes, L. "Retirement, Economics and the Minority Aged." In *Minority Aging: Sociological and Social Psychological Issues*, edited by R. Manuel. Westport, Conn.: Greenwood Press, 1982.

San Diego State University. *The Minority Retiree: An Untapped Resource.* Final Report. San Diego: University Center on Aging, 1982.

Stanford, E.P. (Ed.). *Retirement: Concepts and Realities of Ethnic Minority Elders,* San Diego: The Campanile Press, 1978.

Torres-Gil, F.; Abbott, P.; and Ragan, P. "Implications for Raising the Eligibility Age for Minority Elderly." Paper presented as testimony to the President's Commission on Pension Policy, Washington, D.C., 1980.

U.S. Department of Congress. Bureau of the Census. "Social and Economic Characteristics of the Older Population." *Current Population Reports.* Series P-23, p. 85, Washington, D.C.: U.S. Government Printing Office, 1979a.

U.S. Department of Commerce. Bureau of the Census. "Money Income and Poverty Status of Families and Persons in the United States, 1978." *Current Population Reports.* Series P-60, no. 120. Washington, D.C.: U.S. Government Printing Office, 1979b.

U.S. Department of Commerce. Bureau of the Census. "Age, Sex, Race and Spanish Origin of the Population by Regions, Divisions and States, 1980." *Supplementary Reports.* Washington, D.C.: U.S. Government Printing Office, 1981.

U.S. Department of Commerce, Bureau of the Census. *General Population Characteristics: United States Summary, 1980.* Washington, D.C.: U.S. Government Printing Office, 1983.

U.S. Department of Health and Human Services. Social Security Administration. *Private Pension Coverage and Vesting by Race and Hispanic Descent, 1979.* Prepared by Gayle Thompson Roger. Staff report 42. Washington, D.C.: U.S. Government Printing Office, 1982.

U.S. Senate. Special Committee on Aging. *Retirement, Work and Lifelong Learning.* Prepared by H.L. Sheppard. 95th Cong. 2nd sess. September 1978.

Valle, R., and Martinez, C. "Natural Networks of Elderly Latinos of Mexican Heritage: Implications for Mental Health." In *Chicano Aging and Mental Health*. U.S. Department of Health and Human Services, National Institute of Mental Health, DHHS publication no. ADM 81-952. Washington, D.C.: U.S. Government Printing Office, 1981.

Watson, W. "Selected Demographic and Social Aspects of Older Blacks: An Analysis with Policy Implications." In *Aging in Minority Groups*, edited by R.L. McNeely and J.L. Colin. Beverly Hills: Sage Publications, 1983.

Weeks, J.R., and Cuellar, J. "The Role of Family Members in the Helping Networks of Older People." *The Gerontologist* 21 (1981):388–94.

Suggested Readings

McNeely, R., and Colen, J.L., eds. *Aging in Minority Groups*. Beverly Hills, Ca.: Sage Publications, 1983.

> This is a state-of-the-art book on minority aging. It provides the most recent information about the demography of minority aging; the cultural context of aging in these groups; selected social problems including housing, crime, health, employment, and income maintenance; and guidelines for service delivery.

San Diego State University. University Center on Aging. *The Minority Retiree: An Untapped Resource*. Final Report. San Diego, Ca.: San Diego State University, 1983.

> This monograph is essentially a report on the findings of a study on the retirement experiences, attitudes, and expectations among selected racial groups in San Diego and Denver. It provides a comprehensive and analytical review of the literature on retirement and older minorities. It is an excellent reference guide for examining and selecting materials and publications on retirement expectations, retirement attitudes, retirement behavior, propensity for work among retirees, organizational participation, and policy implications.

Stanford, E.P. "Perspectives on Ethnic Elderly Retirement." *Retirement: Concepts and Realities of Ethnic Minority Elders*. University Center on Aging, San Diego State University. San Diego, Ca.: The Campanile Press, 1978.

> This is a volume of the proceedings of the Fifth National Institute on Minority Aging that devoted its theme to retirement and ethnic minority elders. It is a useful description of the views, opinions, and statements of minority researchers about the situation of elderly minority vis-à-vis retirement. The monograph includes sections on retirement concepts of ethnic minority elderly, minority elderly lifestyles, natural support systems, employment and income, and preretirement and retirement programs for ethnic minority elders.

13

Retirement Preparation Needs of Women

Marilyn R. Block

Misconceptions about Women and Retirement

Of the many widely accepted stereotypes about women, one of the most pervasive is the belief that work is not meaningful to them. Cumming and Henry (1961), the originators of the theory of disengagement, state that "retirement is not an important problem for women because . . . working seems to make little difference to them" (p. 144). This view is echoed by others who suggest that employment for women does not have the same social value as the role of homemaker. The logical extension of this belief suggests that women are faced with less of a dilemma upon retirement than men because women are relinquishing a secondary or tertiary role while men are losing a primary role. In addition, women are thought to be well rehearsed for retirement since the life cycle of a woman is thought to provide her with several retirement experiences (for example, relinquishing the role of caretaker to her children) (Donahue et al. 1960).

From the view that work is not meaningful for women comes the belief that retirement is a minor event in the lives of working women. Perhaps the best illustration of the impact of outmoded assumptions, stereotypes, and biases is the way in which researchers have dealt with the variable of work as it relates to women. Although 90 percent of all women work for pay at some point in their lives (Barnett and Baruch 1978), paid employment has not been conceptualized as central to the lives of women, who are not expected to function as economic providers or to derive self-esteem and identity from this role (Cumming and Henry 1961; Donahue et al. 1960; Palmore 1965). Since industrialization separated work and family life, women have been seen as committed primarily to the family and, thus, as out of place and unreliable at places of employment (Coser and Rokoff 1971).

Expression of these stereotypes is widespread in retirement and gerontological literature. The view is largely based on role theory, which holds that giving up a primary role is what makes retirement a crisis. Thus, the female retiree is often portrayed as maintaining an advantage over the male retiree because she is imagined as returning to her primary role of wife and mother. In fact, women at retirement age are much less likely to be married than men (Ragan 1977). Approximately 82 percent of men aged 55 to 74 years are married, compared to 67 percent of women aged 55 to 64 and 47 percent of women aged 65 to 74. Widowhood, of course, predominates among those women not married, with 42 percent of the 64-to-74-year-old women widowed.

As a result of the traditional view that women's primary role is that of homemaker, special conflicts exist for many working women who must attempt to juggle successfully their multiple roles (Coyle and Fuller 1977). Several studies (for example, Coser and Rokoff 1971; Sokolowska 1965) view the problems of working women as resulting from the conflict between the dual roles of wife and mother. One might expect female workers to be eager to retire given the strain of combining the demands of work and home obligations (Coyle and Fuller 1977). Contradictory evidence exists about retirement attitudes, however, as discussed in the following section.

Impact of Retirement for Women

Data from the few empirical studies of the meaningfulness of work and the impact of retirement for women have shown the exact opposite of the stereotypes described in the preceding section, which suggested a greater importance of work to men. In a study of retired teachers and telephone company retirees, respondents were asked to check from a list of life goals the areas in which failure would be most troublesome (Atchley 1975; 1976). Work was valued by most of the respondents regardless of sex, a finding that runs counter to the common assumption that work is a less important activity for women than for men. In addition, the retired men in this study were more likely than the retired women to become accustomed to retirement in three months or less, a finding that contradicts the conventional idea that retirement adjustment is easier for women because they can return to the housewife role.

The impact of retirement for women has been documented by other researchers. Lehr and Dreher (1970), for example, report a process of reorientation for both sexes following retirement. They indicate, however, that men do not generally experience retirement as a severe crisis, while women tend to experience problems in adjusting to their changing role.

Positive retirement adjustment is significantly related to the orderliness or continuity of one's career (Simpson et al. 1966). Since women have few opportunities for orderly careers in terms of the traditional male work pattern, disorderliness may persist in retirement.

Women are less likely than men to be positively oriented toward retirement (Jacobson 1974) and more likely than men to express apprehension and display high anxiety about the effects of retirement (Atchley 1976; Streib and Schneider 1971). Women not only have a harder time getting used to retirement but also show a greater prevalence of negative psychological characteristics compared to retired men. These conclusions are based on male-female comparisons of attitudes toward work and retirement, self-concept, psychological well-being, self-reported health, perceived income adequacy, and perceived social participation (Atchley 1976). The data were derived from 3,630 questionnaires that were completed by a random sample of retired teachers in a Midwestern state, as well as the entire population of retirees from a Midwestern telephone company. All comparisons were controlled for age, education, income adequacy, and marital status, a control that has been lacking in numerous sex comparisons. Findings indicate that retired women are more often lonely, anxious, low in self-esteem and self-stability, highly sensitive to criticism, and highly depressed (Atchley 1976). Men were found to adjust to retirement faster than women, to like retirement better, and to have fewer negative psychological symptoms (Atchley 1976).

Jacobson (1974) also presents data supporting the notion that women are less positively oriented toward retirement than men. Interviews with 145 male and 70 female semiskilled factory operatives near London elicited the information that nearly twice as many women as men (31.4 percent and 16.6 percent respectively) would be "eager to go on working beyond the pensionable age even if they were assured of an adequate income without having to work" (Jacobson 1974, p. 482).

For women, work-based social ties emerge as the chief correlate of the wish to go on working. They more frequently referred to affective (expressive) rewards such as pleasant atmosphere, congenial co-workers, and so forth. Men tended to refer to income as the major reason for liking their jobs.

It would appear that retirement does constitute a crisis for today's older women. While most older women did not train for paid employment, by the middle 1960s, more women in their forties than younger women were in the labor force. This trend has since reversed because the baby boom generation is now entering the marketplace in large numbers. In 1980, the overall labor force participation rate was 60 percent for women aged 45 to 54, 42 percent for women aged 55 to 64, and 8 percent for women aged 65 and older; at some point all will retire. Added to the increasing number of women entering and retiring from the work force is the fact that women live longer than men and so are faced, at least statistically, with a longer period of retirement. It is likely that retirement patterns for these women will reflect the shift from homemaker to work role and that women who have turned from a housewife orientation would be reluctant to return to it.

Women's Participation in Preretirement Programs

The rapid increase of female workers and, thus, female retirees over the past twenty years has not been reflected by increasing female participation in retirement preparation programs. Despite acknowledgment that such programs ease the transition from work to retirement, women have been far less likely to pursue this option than men. Several factors appear to influence involvement in retirement preparation programs.

Occupational Status and Education

Kroeger (1982) asserts that workers with higher levels of educational attainment and the broader world view that accompanies professional positions predispose individuals toward retirement planning to a greater degree than those of lesser educational and occupational achievement. Middle-aged women are far less likely than middle-aged men to have a baccalaureate degree. Women who are college graduates and who are employed in professional positions are overrepresented in low-status occupations and rarely attain executive/administrative responsibility.

The vast majority of working women are not professionals, however. Seventy-three percent of all female workers over the age of 45 are employed as clerical workers, service workers, operatives, and sales workers (U.S. Department of Labor 1980).

Readiness to Retire

Individuals who retire suddenly have far less time to formulate a strategy for successful adjustment to their new role than individuals who have anticipated retirement. Women are particularly vulnerable to sudden retirement because of the expectation that caretaking and companionship are primary responsiblities. Many women are forced to retire before they are ready because a husband or an aging parent unexpectedly falls ill. Traditional roles dictate that the wife/daughter provides care for the ailing relative.

Other women are forced to retire simply because the husband has retired. The tendency for women to marry men who are several years older results in a family configuration in which a woman anticipates additional years in the labor force at a time when her husband is relinquishing that role. Retired husbands often pressure a wife into retirement to alleviate their boredom and loneliness at home. Some retired husbands desire to relocate despite the likelihood that the working wife will have difficulty obtaining employment after a move. The working wives of retired men often have little choice but to retire several years sooner than anticipated.

Women who retire because of family obligations are unlikely to engage in retirement preparation programs because they had not foreseen retirement occurring for several years. Lack of readiness obviously precludes planning for the event.

Existence of a Social Network

Another factor that inhibits women from seeking retirement preparation education is the belief that a woman can rely on her husband during the retirement years. That this is a misconception is documented all too vividly by the vast numbers of women who are widowed, the increasing numbers who are divorced, and the disproportionate number of older women who are living in poverty as a result of their changed marital status.

Access to Programs

Perhaps the greatest deterrent to retirement preparation for women is inadequate access to preretirement programs. Institutionalized programs are not prevalent among the service industries and small businesses where most women are employed. In settings where such programs are available, they are often limited to specific categories of employees (usually predominantly men). If women should manage to avail themselves of a retirement preparation program, the material presented is usually targeted toward the male retiree, with little or no emphasis on the specific concerns of female retirees.

Role of Retirement Counselors

Despite the many hindrances to retirement preparation for women, the impact of such programs on adjustment to retirement is well documented. Much research has indicated that health and income are the two most important variables for successful retirement. A study of retirement satisfaction among professional women (Block 1981; 1982) indicates that, after health, retirement planning is the most important predictor of adjustment to retirement, exceeding income in its importance.

Retirement counselors can take several important steps to ensure that female workers participate in retirement preparation programs. First, programs should be accessible to all occupational levels within a company. Workers in all positions within an organization, from the chief executive officer to the custodial staff, should be invited to participate in some form of retirement preparation. The retirement counselor needs to be aware that the educational level of different categories of workers may require different approaches to material. The possibility of different classroom sessions for groups of workers should be considered. Although more time consuming with regard to preparation of materials and training, the program would be more meaningful. This ensures that workers at lower occupational levels (usually women) can participate in structured programs.

Second, the age at which workers are invited to participate in a retirement preparation program should be considered carefully. Traditionally, retirement preparation programs are offered to employees within five years of anticipated retirement. However, women frequently retire prior to that point because of family obligations. Retirement planning should be offered to any worker aged 40 or older. In addition to increasing the likelihood that women will be able to participate, this strategy has the additional benefit of enabling workers to plan well in advance and perhaps to make long-range financial decisions that could not be considered within the usual five-year span between program participation and retirement.

Third, the timing of retirement preparation programs should be varied. The usual pattern is to offer the program on an annual basis at a set time—for example, late afternoon. Female workers in subordinate positions (especially clerical workers) are often unable to be absent from their offices during business hours. If this is the case for the majority of workers, the retirement counselor might consider offering training sessions over the lunch hour, during the evening, or on weekends. Conversely, some women are unable to participate in programs outside of regular working hours because of family commitments. When this is the case, the retirement counselor should attempt to organize sessions during regular working hours so that subordinate workers can participate. In either case, it is incumbent upon the retirement counselor to ascertain the kinds of problems caused by different timing options instead of arbitrarily selecting a schedule.

Finally, the material to be presented must be carefully thought out. The kind of information required by female retirees encompasses areas not usually considered in retirement programs. Women have special problems—financial, health related, and social—that men do not experience. Ideally, retirement planning offers a framework that can encourage women to examine their lives to ascertain areas of strength and weakness. In addition, it should provide a structure directed toward information gathering and action.

The following section outlines a retirement planning program geared toward the needs of women.

A Model Retirement-Planning Program

Seminar I: Financial Planning

Economic insecurity is the single greatest difficulty faced by female retirees. While most retirees are not poor, most poor retirees are women. Their financial plight results from their employment patterns and their marital status. Relatively few working women exhibit the lifelong employment history of male workers. The low salaries and intermittent work patterns of women mean that retirement benefits are likely to be low. Many older women who are widowed or divorced discover that, with the loss of a spouse's retirement benefit, their own is inadequate to maintain a household. In addition, state inheritance laws may result in the loss of substantial assets accumulated during the course of a marriage.

Pension Issues. The two primary pension concerns for women regard coverage and vesting. Female workers are heavily concentrated in occupations where pensions are nonexistent. In 1980, only 35 percent of female workers had pension plan coverage.

Coverage does not ensure a retirement benefit, so it is likely that few female workers will receive pension income. In 1979, only 10 percent of women aged 65 years and older had private pension income. The Employee Retirement Income Security Act (ERISA) sets minimum years of service for an individual to participate in a pension plan before she receives a vested right to a pension.

Because most plans require a ten-year vesting period, women often find themselves at a disadvantage because they frequently do not work at a job long enough to achieve vesting. As of January 1978, the longest median job tenure for women aged 55 to 64 years was 8.5 years, about 1.5 years under the 10-year requirement for vesting.

Social Security Issues. While most female workers are covered by Social Security, their intermittent work histories yield low Social Security benefits. In 1977, half of female beneficiaries received an annual Social Security retirement benefit of $3,810 or less. Female workers should be encouraged to calculate probable benefit amounts, to recognize likely expenses after retirement, and to engage in financial planning in order to ensure a viable standard of living after retirement. They also should be encouraged to ascertain the effect of marital status on their Social Security benefit because collecting a retirement benefit based on their work history may not be as advantageous in many cases as collecting a benefit as a dependent spouse or a widow.

Estate-Planning Issues. The vast majority of husbands dies intestate—that is, without a will. With the exception of community-property states in which a wife is presumed to own half of all assets acquired during a marriage, women usually inherit property from a deceased husband. Although most couples mistakenly assume that joint ownership assures the widow of property retention, it is common for a widow to lose one-third or one-half of her husband's estate to children or other relatives. A retirement preparation program thus should alert women to the inheritance laws in their state of legal residence in order to plan for the best way of disposing of the estate regardless of which spouse dies first.

Retirement Expenses Issues. Most middle-aged adults think largely in terms of housing, energy, and food costs when they anticipate retirement expenses. Rarely do they consider catastrophic events. This is of particular concern for women for two reasons. First, unlike men, who usually have a spouse to provide support during a crisis situation, women often face crises by themselves. Thus, a man may be able to avoid certain expenses because his wife can perform some number of caretaking services that otherwise would have to be paid for. If expenses cannot be avoided, a wife's retirement benefits can help defray costs. Second, women usually have lower retirement incomes than men. If services need to be purchased by women, the impact of that expense is disproportionately large relative to total income and may result in a substandard style of living.

Seminar II: Health

Next to economic insecurity, diminished health is a major concern for retirees. The usual approach to health in retirement-planning programs involves a look at the normative aging process. However, this is of limited value to middle-aged and older women because longitudinal studies of the normative aging process have utilized male subjects almost exclusively. The following health-related issues are of particular relevance to female retirees.

Chronic and Acute Illnesses. The health-care system extant in the United States can be described as acute-responsive. This orientation emphasizes cures for conditions. Thus, the health-care system is not congruent with the health-care needs of older women who have higher rates of chronic conditions than older men.

Health-Care Costs. The major forms of health-care coverage in the United States are private health insurance policies and publicly supported programs for the aged (Medicare) and the poor (Medicaid). Although many female workers are covered by private health insurance through employer-sponsored group plans, they usually lose this protection at retirement.

Publicly supported health-care programs are inadequate in meeting the cost of health care for older women. Medicare covers, on the average, 40 percent of health-care expenses. Necessary health-care services that are not eligible for reimbursement include preventive treatment and care related to chronic conditions. Medicare does not cover long-term care in nursing homes or long-term home health care unless it is prescribed by a physician.

Medicaid is also inadequate in meeting the health-care needs of older women. Eligibility criteria and reimbursable services vary widely among the states. Even older women who are eligible for Medicaid may not be able to obtain necessary services because the range of services is not uniform among states.

The impact of existing reimbursement policies is particularly acute for older women since they are disproportionately poor. More than 50 percent of middle-aged women and nearly 75 percent of women aged 65 and older had annual incomes below $6,000 in 1979. This suggests that without reimbursement policies that account for their special health concerns, many older women will continue to be unable to obtain necessary health care.

Mental Health Issues. Twice as many women as men in the United States are diagnosed as depressed. Less clear-cut is the reason for this discrepancy. While some researchers might argue that differences in depression rates are biological, it seems more likely that women seek medical help for emotional problems more often than men and that when men and women describe similar symptoms, the diagnosing physician assumes a different problem. A certain level of depression is expected among retirees who are beginning to cope with loss. Of particular concern to the female retiree is appropriate coping mechanisms to deal with depression. Psychotropic drug use (especially Valium) continues to be widely accepted by physicians and patients, despite evidence of negative side effects and addiction.

Community Resources. Many women, upon discovering that needed services are ineligible for medical program reimbursement and unaffordable out-of-pocket, simply do without or forego other necessities. A retirement preparation program can identify programs, services, and resources in the community that benefit female retirees by ensuring awareness of community alternatives.

Seminar III: Interpersonal Relationships

Retirement preparation programs are based on the assumption that most retirees will spend their retirement years with a spouse; thus, information is almost always presented in the context of the married couple. This is a valid assumption for men, the majority of whom live with a wife until their own death. Most women, however, survive their husbands. Thus, a retirement-planning program for women does a disservice if it fails to address issues around growing old alone.

Marital Relationships after Retirement. Because women usually marry men who are older, many couples experience a retirement transition twice, once when the husband retires and again when the wife retires. A retirement preparation program should help female workers identify the positive and negative aspects a husband's retirement has had on the marital relationship and project how the woman's retirement will ameliorate or exacerbate existing problems.

Parent–Child Relationships. Female retirees often must deal with parent–child relationships from both ends of the continuum. They usually have adult children and adolescent grandchildren with whom contact is important. Also, with the steady increase in life expectancy during the century, many have aging parents who require some level of emotional and financial support. Female retirees need to consider the caretaking demands and housing alternatives imposed by their parents and the needs they expect their children to meet.

External Support Networks. This is one area in which women appear to have an advantage over men. While men traditionally maintain social contacts through employment, women do not. Thus, the support network is easily maintained beyond retirement. Although most men identify their wife as their primary confidante, most women identify a female friend. Women with narrow support networks should be encouraged to expand these before retirement in order to reduce the likelihood of isolation.

Growing Old Alone. There are five times as many widows as widowers. Most widows experience specific stages of bereavement, and most believe they are alone in their response to the loss of a husband. Retirement preparation programs should explain the impact of these stages and provide women an opportunity to anticipate the problems they will encounter at widowhood. The availability of support groups should also be identified so women are aware of this resource before a spouse's death. Finally, the legal and financial implications of widowhood should be presented so that couples can engage in appropriate planning that will reduce stress at a time when the widow needs to deal with a myriad of problems.

Seminar IV: Use of Time

The information that should be presented in this segment of a retirement preparation program is not necessarily different for men and women. This area is often neglected for women because of the assumption that a return to housework is satisfying for female retirees. Opportunities for second careers, educational pursuits, volunteer services, and leisure activities should be presented.

References

Atchley, R.C. "Adjustment to Loss of Job at Retirement." *International Journal of Aging and Human Development* 6 (1975):17–27.

Atchley, R.C. "Selected Social and Psychological Differences between Men and Women in Later Life." *Journal of Gerontology* 31 (1976):204–11.

Barnett, R.C., and Baruch, G.K. "Women in the Middle Years: A Critique of Research and Theory." *Psychology of Women Quarterly* 3 (1978): 187–97.

Block, M.R. "Effect of Work Pattern on Women's Satisfaction with Retirement." *Dissertation Abstracts* 41 (1981):888.

Block, M.R. "Professional Women: Work Pattern as a Correlate of Retirement Satisfaction. In *Women's Retirement: Policy Implications of Recent Research,* edited by M. Szinovacz. Beverly Hills: Sage Publications, 1982.

Coser, R.L., and Rokoff, G. "Women in the Occupational World: Social Disruption and Conflict." *Social Problems* 18 (1971):535–54.

Coyle, J.M., and Fuller, M.M. "Women's Work and Retirement Attitudes." Paper presented at the meeting of the Gerontological Society, San Francisco, November 1977.

Cumming, E., and Henry, W.E. *Growing Old: The Process of Disengagement.* New York: Basic Books, 1961.

Donahue, W.; Orbach, H.; and Pollak, O. "Retirement: The Emerging Social Pattern." In *Handbook of Social Gerontology,* edited by C. Tibbitts. Chicago: University of Chicago Press, 1960.

Jacobson, D. "Rejection of the Retiree Role: A Study of Female Industrial Workers in Their 50's." *Human Relations* 27 (1974):477–92.

Kroeger, N. "Preretirement Preparation: Sex Differences in Access, Sources, and Use." In *Women's Retirement: Policy Implications of Recent Research,* edited by M. Szinovacz. Beverly Hills: Sage Publications, 1982.

Lehr, U., and Dreher, G. "Determinants of Attitudes toward Retirement." In *Adjustment to Retirement: A Cross-National Study,* edited by R. Havighurst, J.M.A. Munnichs, B. Neugarten, and H. Thomae. Assen, the Netherlands: Van Gorcum and Comp., N.V., 1970.

Ragan, P.K. "Socialization for the Retirement Role: Cooling the Mark Out." Paper presented at the meeting of the American Psychological Association, San Francisco, August 1977.

Simpson, I.H.; Back, K.W.; and McKinney, J.C. "Orientation toward Work and Retirement." In *Social Aspects of Aging,* edited by Simpson and McKinney. Durham, N.C.: Duke University Press, 1966.

Sokolowska, M. "Some Reflections on the Different Attitudes of Men and Women toward Work." *International Labor Review* 92 (1965):35–50.

Streib, G.F., and Schneider, C.J. *Retirement in American Society: Impact and Process*. Ithaca, N.Y.: Cornell University Press, 1971.

U.S. Department of Labor, Bureau of Labor Statistics, unpublished data, 1980.

Suggested Readings

Numerous articles concerning different aspects of women's retirement are scattered throughout a variety of journals and magazines. Their limited accessibility and focus render many of them useless to the retirement counselor who requires a broad understanding of women's concerns with the retirement process. The following book should be required reading for all retirement counselors: M. Szinovacz, ed., *Women's Retirement: Policy Implications of Recent Research* (Beverly Hills: Sage Publications, 1982). This book constitutes the first book-length publication of research devoted to women's retirement. The chapters are divided into three sections. The first of these presents information on the employment status, work history, and life situation of older women. The second section focuses on preparing for retirement. Of special interest in this section is an article on sex differences in retirement preparation. The third section of the book explores female adjustment to retirement. The bibliography to this book contains nearly 700 entries and is, in this author's opinion, one of the most comprehensive listings of articles and books related to the retirement process.

14 Retirement and the Family

Vicki Plowman

Retirement as a Stage of Life

Retirement is a stage of life that has a major impact on the retiree, his or her spouse, and other family members. Adaptation to retirement is one of the greatest adjustments for the older family (Atchley 1977). The husband and wife, for example, undergo transitions into new roles and changing lifestyles. However, with proper planning, good health, and adequate finances, the couple has an opportunity for a close, rewarding marital relationship during the retirement years.

While retirement has the greatest impact on the husband and wife, the larger family configuration can have a major impact on the retirement of the pair. Couples in or approaching retirement today may be part of the so-called sandwich generation, caught between responsibilities to one or more aging parents and the need and/or desire to assist their adult children and grandchildren.

The Transition into Retirement: Changing Roles

When either or both spouses retire, major role changes and adjustments need to be made in their lives. No longer do they have a rigorous schedule to follow; the role of breadwinner (full or partial) has diminished; opportunities for interaction with co-workers have been cut off; and the two worlds of work life and home life have merged into one. What is facing retirees is a major increase in unstructured time at home and, most likely, a much greater involvement with their spouse. If theirs has been a good marriage, the potential for a rewarding relationship in retirement is excellent. However, couples often manage to get along for many years in a marriage because they are apart so much. When they are suddenly thrust together, tensions, resentments, and anger from the past begin to surface.

An example of this is described by a family counselor who was seeing a couple who had been married for fifty-eight years. The husband, age 85, had been retired from the liquor business for three years. He and his wife, age 82, had had an arranged marriage and had never been very fond of one another. Their marriage had lasted, in part, because the husband spent so much time at his business and because his wife often worked at the store when he was home. Since the husband's retirement, their relationship had been deteriorating. His health had been poor, and he preferred to be at home. His wife had been very active but felt guilty when she left him alone. At the insistence of their children, they went for counseling. Although older than most retirees of three years, this couple is facing difficulties that are far from unique.

To understand these and other problems that newly retired couples may encounter, this section discusses differences between husbands and wives, allocation of household tasks, socioeconomic distinctions, and the marital relationship in retirement and concludes with suggestions for successful marital adjustment.

Differences between Husbands and Wives

According to Lipman (1962), men's self-concept traditionally has emanated from two sources: occupation, where he is a worker, and family, where he is a husband and often a father. Although they are separated both geographically and temporally, the two sources are connected and interdependent because "the success of the male in his familial roles (husband and father) is defined, partially, in terms of his achievement in his occupational role (worker)" (p. 475). When a national sample of married women was asked what they considered to be the most important quality of a good husband, 42 percent selected the response "Being a good provider."

The role of women, in contrast, traditionally has centered on the internal affairs of the family as the manager of household and familial activities (Lipman 1962). When asked what they considered the most important quality of a good wife, the most frequent response of a national sample of married men was "Good homemaker, good housekeeper, etc."

A study by Dunn (1960), examining the expectations of unmarried adolescents, found that the majority of girls saw housekeeping as their major responsibility, while the boys viewed earning a living as theirs. Although these attitudes may be shifting due to the increase of women in the labor force, they are still prevalent, to varying degrees, in a large segment of society and are particularly pervasive among people over 50.

If these are the traditionally held views of the proper roles for men and women, what changes will need to occur with retirement? Lipman's study (1962) indicates that both spouses will need to undergo some changes in their roles. The men's role moves from instrumental, that of provider, to an expressive one that entails giving emotional support and having involvement in the home. The women's instrumental role of homemaker declines in importance in response to her husband's involvement in the home and moves to a more expressive, loving, and understanding role. When responding to the question about qualities of a good spouse over 65, both the men and women described by Lipman felt that love, understanding, companionship, and compatibility were the most important qualities of both husband and wife. The roles of provider and homemaker assumed less significance. Lipman found that both husbands and wives who did not alter the instrumental role concept for themselves had the lowest morale.

With these role changes may come accompanying changes in personalities. Sinnott (1977) found that with age, women seem to become more assertive, dominant, and aggressive while men seem to to become more passive, dependent, submissive, and less competitive. Other studies indicate that the husband's dependence on the wife increases at a faster rate than her dependence on him and that she may view him as overly dependent (Kelly 1981). Stinnett (1970) found that elderly men seem to derive more satisfaction than their wives from their marriage. Other research suggests that the husband is more in need of his wife as a confidante than the reverse. This may be due to the fact that elderly women appear to establish new close friendships more readily than do elderly men (Lowenthal and Robinson 1976). Thus, when close friends die or move, the wife is more likely than the husband to replace them, while he becomes more dependent on her for the confidante role (Kelly 1981). In addition, due to their declining health and, typically, being several years older than their wives, men tend to have lowered vitality, less interest in activities, and less sex drive than their wives (Blood and Wolfe 1960). Because of the age differential of couples and the lower life expectancy of men, Willing (1981) speculates that a negative self-fulfilling prophecy exists for men—one based on decline, lack of vitality, and lowered activity—whereas women, with their longer life span, prepare to become stronger in order to survive widowhood.

Allocation of Household Tasks

There has been a variety of research findings on the allocation of household tasks. Ballweg (1967) found that although the retired husband did not share tasks with his wife to a greater extent than when he was working, he was more likely to assume full responsibility for select masculine tasks such as repairs, yardwork, taking out the garbage, and so forth. This in no way infringed on the wife's territory; it enabled her to relinquish tasks she disliked.

In a study by Lipman (1962), participation in household activities was considered a role for retired men by most male and female respondents. According to the wives, three-quarters of the husbands did the shopping themselves or helped with the shopping, while over half cleared the breakfast table, wiped the dishes, and picked up and put away the clothes. When asked what their husbands did when they did housework, 41 percent of wives replied that their husbands helped. When asked how they felt about helping with the housework, most of the men said they did not mind getting involved. Responses included "I enjoy doing these things, it lightens my wife's load." "I'm glad to help. It gives me something to do." "I don't like to do these things, but I have to do something to keep busy" (p. 481). According to Lipman, "This acquisition of household duties after retirement adds a new dimension of common interests for the husband and wife, solidifies emotional bonds, and is therefore functionally related both to the aged male's emphasis on expressive roles and his marital adjustment" (pp. 481–482).

In Lipman's study (1962) the level of the husband's participation in household tasks was consistently associated with higher morale for both husbands and wives than in households where the husband did not participate. In addition, Keith and Brubaker (1979) found that correlations between household involvement and well-being in old age tended to be positive and that "both spouses need to realize that involvement in household roles eases the transition from work to retirement for some persons and that these roles may be important to self-esteem in later life" (p. 501).

Lower morale occurs for both husband and wife when they have rigid role expectations concerning allocation of household tasks (Kerckhoff 1966c). Upon retirement they both tend to see the husband's increased household involvement as negative, but the husband, even with his feelings about housework being demeaning and a woman's work, still tends to spend more time in household activities. This leads to conflict based on the husband's feelings of guilt and the wife's annoyance at having her exclusive domain invaded (Atchley 1976).

Socioeconomic Differences

Kerckhoff (1966a) found some major distinctions in how different socioeconomic groups view family relationships and retirement. In his first study dealing with family relationships, he identified three groups: the nuclear family, the extended family, and the modified extended family.

The nuclear family tends to be white collar, to have high levels of education, to have grown up in urban areas, to have been geographically mobile, and to have small families. The parents in nuclear families do not necessarily expect to live near their adult children or to receive mutual aid and affection. They see change as potentially positive and see no conflict between their values and their children's social and/or geographic mobility. In addition, the couple expects to share household tasks with each other.

In contrast, the extended family tends to be blue collar, to have low levels of education, to have grown up in a rural setting, to have moved very little, and to have large families. The parents in extended families expect to live near their adult children and expect considerable mutual assistance and devotion. In addition, they do not see change as worthwhile and view their children's mobility as conflicting with family values. Their views on household tasks are stereotypic, with strict segregation for male and female roles.

The third group, the modified extended family, is between both groups in all cases except that they expect mutual assistance and affection in relation to their children but not proximity of households. In Kerckhoff's (1966) study, approximately 60 percent of the families fell into this category, and 20 percent were in each of the other two categories.

In his second study, Kerckhoff (1966b) looked at the expectations and reactions to retirement of a group of men pre- and postretirement, and their wives according to their socioeconomic levels. He divided them into three groups: upper, middle, and lower levels. The upper-level group was composed of people who were professionals and managers and their wives. This group did not welcome retirement although they had planned for it. When they reached retirement, they found it to be a favorable experience. The middle-level group was made up of white-collar workers and craftsmen and their wives. They welcomed retirement, did some planning, and had relatively good experiences in retirement. The lower-level group included unskilled and service workers and their wives. They were passive and/or negative toward retirement, made few plans, and had more unsatisfactory experiences when they retired.

We can make a number of observations and implications from these studies. First, retirees who are part of the nuclear family group are more likely to be satisfied with their children's behavior and attitudes toward them; that is, they will not have unrealistic expectations. They are unlikely to be disappointed if their children have little contact with them either because the children have moved away or are involved in their own lives. Second, with both husband and wife at home after retirement, their mutual involvement with household tasks will tend to be a positive factor. Third, since this group is most likely to be composed of upper- or middle-level workers prior to retirement, they are most likely to have the best adjustment to it. This is related, in part, to better health (because they have been in less physically demanding jobs), their earlier life experiences and activities, and a higher degree of financial security. Although they may not welcome retirement because they have enjoyed working and do not like the accompanying loss of income, they tend to make plans and find that it is a favorable experience.

The group that is most likely to have a difficult adjustment to retirement is the lower-level retirees and their wives who are part of the extended family group. They are more likely to be disappointed if their children move away or have little contact with them. As mentioned earlier, they have rigid role expectations that are likely to result in decreased morale and lowered self-esteem as well as stress and conflict in the marital relationship. In addition, they have experienced less job satisfaction during their lives and may be in poorer health due to the physical demands of their previous work. This group also has less income and anticipates financial insecurity in retirement. They typically do not look forward to retirement (although they usually are not sorry to leave their jobs) and make few plans.

Adjustment to Retirement

Married couples and never-married people generally make a better adjustment to retirement than those who are divorced, separated, or widowed, who are more likely to have low morale (Larson 1978). Other major factors associated with poor adjustment to retirement are poor health, inadequate income, low social status, and involuntary retirement. When health and income are a problem, there are many strains on the marriage and disappointments regarding the supposed golden years of retirement. People who retire involuntarily usually do so because of illness or because of job loss (which is more common in today's troubled economy).

In addition, marital relationships in retirement reflect the couple's earlier involvement. If adjustments have not been made to earlier experiences such as the empty-nest syndrome or widowhood and work has been the substitute, then retirement may require a double adjustment (Atchley 1976). Heyman and Jeffers (1968) found that wives who were sorry their husbands had retired were working class, had husbands who were in poor health, and/or had had unhappy marriages prior to retirement.

The retiree's wife faces a number of potential problems. These include a decrease in personal freedom, less privacy, too much togetherness, difficulty in coordinating activities and space (if the couple moves to smaller quarters), too many demands on her time, and disruption of previously established patterns of daytime activities such as lunches with friends, sport, and educational activities. Keating and Cole (1980) found that middle-class wives tended to look outside their marriage for many of their friendship and intimacy needs, while men preferred to meet those needs within the marriage. In addition, women favored group activities, while men preferred individual activities. Prior to retirement, women planned activities and contact with family and friends to meet their personal needs. After retirement, wives made plans according to what they believed were their husband's needs, although there was no evidence that retired men wanted an expanded social network or replacements for their work friendships. When wives continued their old patterns, they often felt uneasy or guilty whether or not their perceptions about their husband's needs were accurate. In spite of these problems, the women in Keating and Cole's study felt that showing their spouse a life outside of work was rewarding and gave them a new purpose in life. It is interesting that the men in the study were unaware of their wife's supportive role.

Bradford and Bradford (1979) describe two extreme reactions of retired husbands to changing roles within the household. In both instances, the issue of control is primary. One group of husbands overacted and "tried to regain a turf by dispossessing their wives from theirs. They endeavored to take command of the house and order their wives like servants" (Bradford and Bradford 1979, p. 27). These husbands felt that with their experience running things in the business world, they could better manage a household than their wives. The other extreme was made up of husbands who underacted: "Unable to cope with retirement successfully, they remained unhappy. They stayed at home, expecting or demanding their wive's total time and attention" (Bradford and Bradford 1979, pp. 27-28). The result of either extreme is, of course, stress, tension, and an unhappy marriage.

Medley (1977) describes three types of marriages in the retirement years: the husband–wife, the parent–child, and the associates. The husband–wife relationship stresses the intimate, shared nature of their relationship. In this relationship, the "interpersonal interaction with one's spouse is the most rewarding aspect of marital life" (pp. 9-10). The parent–child relationship is one in which one spouse assumes the nurturant, protective, and dominant role while the other spouse behaves in a dependent and submissive manner. This is more likely to occur when one spouse becomes ill or assumes a sick role. The third type, the associates, describes a marital relationship based on friendship, but "they find the most rewarding moments outside the intimacy of the husband–wife relationship." They are "apt to be quite efficient at the 'business' of managing marital and family life" (p. 10).

As mentioned earlier, illness can put severe strain on a marriage. In some instances, however, where couples are able to assist and support each other through various illnesses, they become mutually dependent and closer to one another. In cases of severe illness and disability, unequal dependence and increased conflict of interest will occur. In several studies of the interpersonal consequences of heart attacks, Kelly (1981) describes the following scenario:

> After treatment, the victim (usually the husband) returns to the home feeling worried, depressed, and helpless. He becomes irritable, demanding, and impatient with his wife. Being deeply concerned to promote his recovery and to avoid another attack, the wife becomes overly protective, seeking to limit his activities and enforce his adherence to what she understands to be the required medical regimen. Her protectiveness heightens the husband's irritability, and this creates a severe internal con-

flict for her. She feels guilty that she may not be doing enough, angry that her help is not appreciated, and afraid to criticize or create open conflict. [pp. 292–293]

For the dependent person, the basic dynamics of this unequal dependency relationship are the negative feelings about the situation and ambivalence about the assistance that is needed and the compliance expected from the spouse. For the helper, the dynamics are the complexity of fulfilling responsibilities to the dependent person while having one's sacrifices acknowledged and the difficulty in satisfying one's own basic needs during this period. Couples often need professional counseling to help them through such crises.

A recently retired couple, Bea and Irving, described to the author some of their experiences that related to illness. Irving retired because of a heart condition. When he first began to stay at home, Bea was very nervous about his condition. In retrospect, she humorously described her behavior: "I used to follow him all around the house. I was afraid to let him go out by himself. If he did go out, I was sure he'd never come back. When he had a long nap or slept late in the morning, I'd watch closely to make sure he was still breathing." Irving's health has improved and they both can laugh about the experience, but it was a frightening time for both of them as well as an annoying time for Irving who had to deal with Bea's overprotectiveness. Several months later Bea broke her shoulder and was virtually helpless. Irving took over all responsibilities in the home. As she recovered, they adjusted their household roles to what each was able to do. Their mutual support had strengthened their relationship.

One relatively new and increasingly frequent problem arises when both husband and wife are in the labor force and when they need to make decisions regarding the timing of their individual retirements. The issue of meshing retirement plans has become more prevalent as the number of married women in the work force has increased (Foner and Schwab 1981). Because men are usually several years older than their wives, they often plan to retire earlier. In the past, this has not been a problem because women usually shaped their retirement plans around their husbands (Streib and Schneider, 1971); however, as women became more involved in their work careers and also want to qualify for their own pensions and Social Security, they may remain in the work force after their husbands have retired. In 1974, 46 percent of wives of retired men aged 63 to 69 had already received or were likely to receive their own benefits, and almost one-third of the wives whose husbands had retired between 65 and 69 years had not retired (Fox 1979).

A number of potential problems exist for couples when the husband retires earlier than the wife. Typically, the women in dual-worker families have the major household responsibilities. A study by Bennetts (1979) found that only 4 percent of the men, but 44 percent of the women, put in more than three and one-half hours a day on household chores on weekdays. On weekends, 82 percent of the women and 53 percent of the men spent over three and one-half hours on housework. While it can be expected that men will assume a greater role in household tasks, it is unlikely that they will take over the major responsibilities. According to Foner and Schwab (1981, p. 72), "Whereas these women may have accepted a double burden when their husbands were working, they are likely to resent their husbands' not taking more household jobs after retirement." This is likely to result in increased tensions in the relationship.

Suggestions for Successful Marital Adjustment

In preretirement life, husbands and wives usually spend evenings, weekends, and vacations together. The rest of their time is spent at work, at home, or in the community doing separate things. When the two are together, they have individual experiences to share with one another. Then suddenly, unless there has been a gradual phasing in to retirement, the husband and wife may find themselves together at home twenty-four hours every day. A trip or a move planned shortly after retirement provides a temporary diversion, but eventually they must face and deal with the twenty-four-hour day of togetherness.

Good communication between the partners is most important if they are to adjust successfully to retirement. Ideally, couples should begin to examine their individual expectations for retirement well in advance of the event. They should explore jointly the following questions: How do you want to spend your days? What plans do you want to make for your leisure time? Which activities do you want to do separately, which together? What roles do you need to change or modify? How would you like to divide household tasks? Who will be responsible for which tasks? Questions like these will help the partners focus on their individual needs and understand the needs of their spouse. Discussions should be ongoing because continual adjustments will have to be made as the couple experiences retirement. If people have had a good marriage prior to retirement, they are likely to have a good one afterward. Traits that contribute to a positive relationship in retirement are good coping skills, willingness to compromise, and genuinely caring about one's mate.

Retirement is an important time for the husband and wife to learn each other's special skills—namely, the wife's teaching the husband about cooking, cleaning, shopping, and managing the household and the husband's teaching the wife simple repairs, managing the financial affairs of the family, and so on. Both should be totally informed about all aspects of their life and also know how to take over the other's role if necessary. Illness of one or both of the partners at some time during their retirement is probable, as is the death of one before the other, so it is critical to prepare while both individuals are well and able to assist each other.

Willing (1981) has written about togetherness, which he sees as potentially stifling if it means a collapse of one personality into another. He defines this kind of togetherness as "surrender on one side or as total domination on the other" (p. 149). People in these circumstances often merge because of a feeling of mortality, fear of being alone, and a need for something enduring. According to Willing, "Two people grasping each other so tightly do not support, they smother. In all relationships, some space is necessary" (p. 150). Such a relationship often causes ambivalent feelings of rebellion and guilt in the submissive partner. Willing describes a woman caught in such a situation:

> I knew Jack was lonely and didn't have anything to do; so I felt guilty about leaving him at home alone when I went off to my discussion group. I even felt guilty about feeling a sense of relief at being out of the house and away from him for a while. . . . Then I told myself that I had a right to go to the meeting by myself and that it was good for me and him to get away from each other occasionally. I told myself that finding something to do was his problem, not mine. . . . I couldn't be the answer to his loneliness, even if we spent 24 hours a day together. [pp. 151-152]

The most important lesson to be learned from this example is that no one person can be everything to another. Couples must love and support each other and be flexible and understanding, but each must maintain his or her sense of identity and personal worth.

The Sandwich Generation

People approaching retirement age may be part of what is referred to as the sandwich generation because of their position as the second generation in today's four-generation family. They tend to be age 55 to 65 (wives may be several years younger), have adult children between 25 and 45, and have one or more aging parent. At a time in their lives when they are looking forward to increased leisure and an opportunity to enjoy retirement, they are confronted with unanticipated responsibilities and stresses from their parents and children. In addition, people of retirement age are faced with their own aging, adjustment to new roles, decreased income, and possible illness and widowhood.

Adult Children

Most retirement-age family units do not include adult children. Only 14 percent of units where the head of the household is aged 55 to 64 have children aged 25 to 34 living in the home (U.S. Bureau of the Census 1981). However, because of the troubled economy, high unemployment, shortage of affordable housing, and the instability of many marriages, an increasing number of adult children are turning to their parents for assistance. This may take the form of financial help, child care, or a move back into the parents' home, which is usually a temporary but nonetheless stressful situation.

Relationships between parents and their returning children are strained because of changes in space and privacy, issues of control, expectations of behavior, and tensions brought about by small children. Both parents and their adult children may feel frustrated and put upon. A situation was described of a household where the daughter moved back home to save money for law school. This caused considerable stress on the family. On the one hand, her parents felt that since they were supporting her, she should be answerable for her actions. She, on the other hand, resented their behavior and felt as if she were being treated like a child (U.S. News and World Report 1982).

The high divorce rate has resulted in added responsibilities for the sandwich generation. Approximately 40 percent of all marriages now end in divorce (Furstenberg 1981). Divorced men tend to turn to their parents for child care while divorced women often require financial assistance as well as child care and may return to their parents' home while they work or return to school. This is likely to result in increased stress in the home. For example, a 32-year-old secretary who moved in with her parents after a marital breakup says that "Mom tries to make every decision for me, which undermines my authority with my children" (U.S. News and World Report, p. 71, 1982). In contrast, a divorce that results in an increased involvement between grandparents and grandchildren may have very positive results for both, with greater affection and contact ensuing throughout the years (Furstenberg 1981).

In situations where two or three generations must live together, it is critical that guidelines be established even if the arrangement is temporary. Communication must be open, expectations clear, and resentments not allowed to grow. Because the adult children are moving into their parents' home, they must be adaptable and sensitive to the stresses placed on their parents. The parents, in turn, must recognize the pressures on their children that resulted in the move. In addition, all members must learn to respect each other's needs for privacy.

Most relationships between retirees and their adult children, however, are less extreme than sharing a household. The major loyalty of the sandwich generation is to their children even though they also provide help and support to their aging parents. The patterns established years before of giving monetary support to their children persist into retirement (Streib 1965). Upper- and middle-class families, in particular, provide financial assistance to their children and grandchildren. In addition, both middle- and lower-class families provide assistance to their children in the form of services such as shopping, transportation, child care, and advice (Miller 1981).

While many grandparents enjoy children, older women often resent the imposition on their time and energy. In an interview in the *New York Times* (Brody 1981), Dr. Bernard Cohler, a behavioral scientist at the University of Chicago, noted, "This [imposition] is often the strongest source of resentment on the part of Grandmother, who has finished with child caring and now has her own life to live" (p. B-18). These women like to see their children and grandchildren but on their own terms. In addition to baby-sitting, grown daughters often turn to their mothers for counseling, affection, companionship, and physical resources without regard for their mother's needs for privacy and time. Problems of interdependence are more common with working-class families than with middle- and upper-class families. The working-class families tend to be geographically less mobile, to have fewer resources, and to expect more interdependence among generations.

The majority of retirees and their children, however, prefers a relationship that stresses autonomy and privacy. High morale is associated with relative independence of the two generations. Studies have indicated that couples with the highest morale had the lowest level of mutual support activities with their children. In addition, couples who made few demands on their children regarding proximity of households or mutual aid and affection had higher morale.

Studies described by Foner and Schwab (1981) suggest that visits with children may have a negative rather than positive effect on male retirees. This occurs because power relationships within the family change with retirement and men have to relinquish some control to their adult children, however subtly. A visit with their children may only point out these shifts in power to the retiree.

Aging Parents

The second part of the sandwich for the second generation is their relationship with their aging parents. It is likely that this generation will have at least one aging parent who is widowed, female, and does not share a household with her children. To understand this relationship better, it is helpful to examine some statistics. Most studies have found that over 80 percent of older people who have ever married are parents of living children and that those children either are now or may well soon become members of the sandwich generation. In addition, about one out of ten older people has a sandwiched child who is over 65 (Atchley 1977). These parents and their children prefer, whenever possible, to live in their own homes but near one another. However, Mindell (1979) found that the number of single elderly people age 75 years and older who live in multigenerational households was a significant 20 to 25 percent. This percentage is considerably higher than the 5 percent of elderly residing in institutions. When the two oldest generations do live together, their residence is usually the parents', and the younger member is an unmarried woman (Troll 1982). According to the *Current Population Report* (U.S. Bureau of the Census 1981), 10 percent of families whose head of household was between 55 and 64 years of age include a family member over 65 (8 percent being female and 2 percent male).

Numerous other statistics address the likelihood of retirement-age persons having aging parents. According to a study done by Murray (1973), approximately 25 percent of 58-to-59-year-olds have one surviving parent, and 10 percent of those between 58 and 63 have both parents living. A married couple approaching or in retirement potentially can have four very old parents between them. With more and more people reaching older ages, especially the over-75 age group, which is the fastest growing segment of our population (NCOA 1978), it is likely that there will be an increasing number of retirees with aging parents.

Still other statistics show probabilities concerning the sex and marital status of the aging parent. Older generations have more women (69 men for every 100 women over 65; 58 men for every 100 women over 75) and more who are widows (23 percent of men and 69 percent of women over 75 were widowed) (NCOA 1978). Older men also tend to be married more than older women (at age 75, 7 out of 10 men are still married, while fewer than 1 out of 4 women are married) (NCOA 1978). This is due to the fact that many more men tend to remarry and that they marry younger women. Thus, older men are more likely to have a spouse to look after them, while older women tend to be alone.

Those aging parents who do not live with their adult children tend to have close contact with them. The second generation is most likely to provide services such as escorting their parent to medical appointments, shopping, performing household tasks, and sharing leisure time and to provide financial assistance when needed (although a greater proportion of financial assistance is given to the third generation) (Miller 1981). In addition, a considerable amount of emotional support is provided. It is interesting to note that older parents usually want more emotional closeness with children, while their children would prefer to assist them with tasks (Troll 1982).

There are many stresses on the sandwich generation in their relationships with their aging parents—for example, the parents' increasing emotional and physical dependence on their children, decisions regarding the degree of involvement by the children in the lives of their parents, the burden on the children of increasing financial and household responsibilities, and the rekindling of unresolved conflicts. The stresses become particularly acute when an accident or sudden illness befalls an aged parent and institutionalization becomes a possibility.

These stresses can be handled best when the adult children have reached a developmental stage called "filial maturity," which is a personal sense of adult maturity where children can accept their parents as people who may need or give support in a relationship of mutual aid (Blenker 1965). The filial role involves being depended on and dependable with regard to the parent. In addition, adult children need to find out what community resources are available to assist them and their aging parents, and they also need information about the aging process—what is normal and what is not. In times of crisis, both individual and group counseling can be very helpful. When difficulties in dealing with elderly parents come at a time when adult children are retiring, the problems are compounded.

The major responsibilities of the sandwich generation tend to fall on the woman. She has traditionally been the caregiver for both children and elderly parents. Men typically contribute financially to satisfy their obligations to their parents, whereas women often have been expected to sacrifice their goals and to provide personal care to ill and dependent family members (Hess and Waring 1978). With the increasing number of women in the labor force, their participation as caregivers is diminishing. Today's second-generation woman finds herself in a difficult bind where internalized social expectations concerning filial behavior compete with her career goals and her other roles as wife and mother (Brody 1979). It is quite possible that many women will not be willing to withdraw from the labor force in order to minister to elderly family members or to provide child care to grandchildren. Also, many women may choose to postpone retirement even if their husband has already retired.

Implications for Retirement Specialists

The quality of life in retirement is tied closely to positive family relationships. As described in this chapter, these relationships are complex, changeable, and often require considerable adjustment of family members. What can retirement specialists do to help prepare preretirees for successful adaptation during this critical time?

Perhaps the most important requirement for success is the involvement of the spouse or significant others in the total retirement-planning process.

Since retirement affects the marital relationship most directly, it is critical that both members be involved. On occasion, it also may be appropriate for adult children to participate in a part of the planning process.

In addition, it is useful for preretirees and their spouses to be knowledgeable about research on the family in retirement. This information will provide a context in which preretirees can examine their family relationships. Retirement specialists can develop various activities such as fantasy and experiential exercises, personal inventories, questionnaires, and discussion guides to help preretirees focus on their particular retirement expectations and coping styles that relate to family relationships. When such explorations are done in a group, members can act as resources for one another. Equipped with the latest research findings on family relationships in retirement and guidelines to make use of this information, retirement specialists will be able to add an invaluable component to their educational programs.

References

Atchley, R.C. "Selected Social and Psychological Differences between Men and Women in Later Life." *Journal of Gerontology* 31 (1976):204–11.

Atchley, R.C. *The Social Forces in Later Life*. Belmont, Calif.: Wadsworth Publishing Co., 1977.

Ballweg, J.A. "Resolution of Conjugal Role Adjustment after Retirement." *Journal of Marriage and the Family* 29 (1967):277-81.

Bennetts, L. "When Homemaking Becomes Job No. 2." *The New York Times*, July 14, 1979, p. 8.

Blenker, M. "Social Work and Family Relationships in Later Life, with Some Thoughts on Filial Maturity." In *Social Structure and the Family: Generational Relations*, edited by E. Shanas and G. Streib. Englewood Cliffs, N.J.: Prentice-Hall, 1965.

Blood, R.O. Jr., and Wolfe, D.M. *Husbands and Wives: The Dynamics of Married Living*. New York: Free Press, 1960.

Bradford, L.P., and Bradford, M.I. *Retirement*. Chicago: Nelson-Hall, 1979.

Brody, E.M. "Aging Parents and Aging Children." In *Aging Parents*, edited by P.K. Ragan. Los Angeles: University of Southern California Press, 1979.

Brody, J.E. "From the Other Side of the Generation Gap." *The New York Times*, October 5, 1981.

Dunn, M.S. "Marriage Role Expectations of Adolescents." *Marriage and Family Living* 22 (1960):99–111.

Foner, A., and Schwab, K. *Aging and Retirement*. Belmont, Calif.: Wadsworth Publishing Co., 1981.

Fox, A. "Earnings Replacement Rates of Retired Couples: Findings from the Retirement History Study." *Social Security Bulletin* 2 (1979):17–39.

Furstenberg, F.F. Jr. "Remarriage and Intergenerational Relations." In *Aging, Stability and Change in the Family*, edited by R.W. Fogel, E. Hatfield, S.B. Kiesler and E. Shanas. New York: Academic Press, 1981.

Hess, B.B., and Waring, J.M. "Changing Patterns of Aging and Family Bonds in Later Life." *The Family Coordinator* 27 (1978):303–14.

Heyman, D.K., and Jeffers, F.C. "Wives and Retirement." *Journal of Gerontology* 23 (1968):488–96.

Keating, N.C., and Cole, P. "What Do I Do with Him 24 Hours a Day? Changes in the Housewife Role after Retirement." *The Gerontologist* 20 (1980):84–89.

Keith, P.M., and Brubaker, T.H. "Male Household Roles in Later Life: A Look at Masculinity and Marital Relationships." *The Family Coordinator* 28 (1979):501.

Kelly, H.H. "Marriage Relationships and Aging." In *Aging, Stability and Change in the Family*, edited by R.W. Fogel, E. Hatfield, Sara Kiesler, and E. Shanas. New York: Academic Press, 1981.

Kerckhoff, A.C. "Norm-Value Clusters and the Strain toward Consistency among Older Married Couples", (a) "Husband-Wife Expectations and Reactions to Retirement," (b) "Family Patterns and Morale in Retirement." (c) In *Social Aspects of Aging*, edited by I.A. Simpson and J.C. McKinney. Durham, N.C.: Duke University Press, 1966.

Larson, R. "Thirty Years of Research on the Subjective Well-Being of Older Americans." *Journal of Gerontology* 33 (1978):109–25.

Lipman, A. "Role Conceptions of Couples in Retirement." In *Aging around the World: Social and Psychological Aspects of Aging*, edited by C. Tibbitts and W. Donahue. New York: Columbia University Press, 1962.

Lowenthal, M.F., and Robinson, B. "Social Networks and Isolation." In *Handbook of Aging and the Social Sciences*, edited by R.H. Binstock and E. Shanas. New York: Van Nostrand Reinhold, 1976.

Medley, M.M. "Marital Adjustment in the Post-Retirement Years." *The Family Coordinator* 26 (1977):5–11.

Miller, D.A. "The 'Sandwich' Generation: Adult Children of the Aging." *Social Work* 26 (1981):419–23.

Mindell, C. Multigenerational Family Households: Recent Trends and Implications for the Future." *The Gerontologist* 19 (1979):456–63.

Murray, J. "Family Structure in the Preretirement Years." *Social Security Bulletin* 36 (1973):25–45.

National Council on the Aging (NCOA). *Fact Book on Aging: A Profile of America's Older Population*. Washington, D.C., 1978.

Sinnott, J.D. "Sex-Role Inconsistency, Biology, and Successful Aging." *The Gerontologist* 17 (1977):459–63.

Stinnett, N.; Collins, J.; and Montgomery, J.E. "Marital Need Satisfaction of Older Husbands and Wives." *Journal of Marriage and the Family* 32 (1970):428–33.

Streib, G.F. "Intergenerational Relationships: Perspectives of the Two Generations on the Older Parent." *Journal of Marriage and the Family* 27 (1965):469–76.

Streib, G.F., and Schneider, C.J. *Retirement in American Society: Impact and Process*. Ithaca, N.Y.: Cornell University Press, 1971.

Troll, L.E. "Family Life in Middle and Old Age: The Generation Gap." *Annals of the American Academy of Political and Social Sciences* 38 (1982):38–46.

U.S. Bureau of the Census. *Current Population Report*. Series P-20, no. 371. Washington, D.C.: U.S. Government Printing Office, 1981. "When the 'Empty Nest' Fills up Again." *U.S. News & World Report*, October 1982, pp. 70–72.

Willing, J.Z. *The Reality of Retirement*. New York: William Morrow & Co., 1981.

Suggested Readings

Foner, A. and Schwab, K. *Aging and Retirement*. Belmont, Ca.: Wadsworth Press, 1981.

> Gives an excellent background on older people and retirement issues on a personal as well as societal level. The chapter on family, community, and society, in particular, addresses relationships between spouses and between retirees and their adult children. Each chapter concludes with discussion questions.

Ragan, P.K. ed. *Aging Parents*. Los Angeles: University of Southern California Press, 1979.

> Contains many excellent chapters on older people and their families. This anthology covers the relationships of middle-aged adults and their aging parents, intergenerational families, problems of widowhood, issues for the middle generation, and reactivated conflicts with aging parents.

15 Using Audiovisuals in Retirement Preparation Programs

Mildred Allyn

Purpose of Audiovisuals

The usefulness of audiovisuals as educational tools is well documented. In all stages of learning, educators are incorporating some form of audiovisual material into the curriculum. In almost every field one can locate an abundance of films, videocassettes, slide/tape programs, filmstrips, and audiotapes. Audiovisual materials are prevalent in the broad field of gerontology and somewhat less prevalent in the area of preretirement planning. While there is not an abundance of material in the field of retirement preparation, new and better audiovisuals are being produced each year. The problem is to locate these materials and to determine if they are appropriate for the particular program and audience to be addressed. The purpose of this chapter is to aid the program planner in locating and using these audiovisuals.

It is important to remember that audiovisual materials are only a part of the communication and learning experience. As Davis (1979) points out:

> [T]here are limitations in media tools. They communicate some, but not all that the instructor feels is necessary. Or they communicate a great deal more than is needed. . . . The point is, they do not replace the instructor; they merely aid (p. 57).

Audiovisual materials provide ways of sharing or communicating. Audiences will use the visual communication or message with reference to their life experience. Their resultant action, if any, will reflect their personal response. This response will be as varied within the audience as the number of persons watching the film. Each person will accept the part of the film that fits what he or she already knows or can respond to immediately and can reject what is unfamiliar. Obviously, no single film will be acceptable to every member of the audience.

Locating Audiovisuals

In addition to commercial distributors, university and college film libraries and public libraries are usually good sources of films and videocassettes.

Others are government agencies on aging, labor unions, churches, and other nonprofit institutional groups. Ask to have your name added to mailing lists of film distributors so you will be aware of new titles. Keeping in touch with others who have used similar materials or who are sponsoring seminars or workshops on retirement will assist you also.

Kinds of Audiovisuals

Most materials are available in either 16-mm film or in videocassette (3/4 in.). To date, there appears to be very little available on slide/tape or on filmstrips in the area of preretirement planning. Videocassette formats are becoming increasingly popular as more and more video players are purchased, plus the fact that they are usually less expensive to purchase than 16-mm films. However, since 16-mm sound film projectors are less expensive to purchase than the videocassette-recording equipment, most programs may still be obtained on 16-mm film.

Slide and filmstrip programs are simple to use, and equipment is readily available. An advantage of this type of audiovisual is that with very little effort, either can be produced to fit individual programs. This is also true of transparencies using an overhead projector.

Preview privileges are possible if purchase is being considered. Sixteen-millimeter films are easily rented, but in some cases video programs are for purchase only. Costs vary according to running time, color or black and white, date of release, and type of format. Rental prices may vary also from one distributor to the next.

Selecting the Proper Audiovisual

It is essential that any audiovisual material under consideration be previewed by the person who is planning to use it. Previewers should keep the following points in mind:

Is the audiovisual suitable for the intelligence level, experience, and age of the audience? The highly trained professional person is going to respond in a different manner than an unskilled blue-collar worker. People who live in various locales—for instance, urban versus rural areas, cold versus warm climates, and so forth—will have varied needs. The audience must be able to relate and respond to what they are seeing.

Is the technical quality satisfactory? We are visually oriented people, accustomed to watching good technical quality on our television screens and in movie theaters. To have to watch a poorly made audiovisual—out of focus, blurred, poorly edited, with erratic sound, or boring—is something no one will do.

Is the material presented worth the expense involved? The price of 16-mm films is continually increasing. A half-hour film costs approximately $400 to purchase and $25 to $50 for a three-day rental. Videocassettes cost about the same from some distributors and a little less from others. Slides and filmstrips are usually for purchase only and cost from $50 to $100 according to running time. If an audiovisual will be used many times over the years, it is obviously worthwhile to purchase a print. There are a few films for free loan, which are in demand and must be reserved well ahead of time.

Are there guides for use with audiovisuals? Many programs come with study guides that are very useful both for introducing the program and for discussion questions. It is a good idea to determine whether or not guides are available before final selection is made.

Does the audiovisual relate the message correctly and in an interesting manner? Is it factual and timely? Is the presentation of the information simple to follow? Will it hold the attention of the audience?

Audiovisuals for Retirement Planning

The following is a listing of selected audiovisual titles that are appropriate for preretirement-planning programs:

Alternative to Retirement: Lifetime Living (30 min/1980/video). This discusses some of the misconceptions about retirement, problems that retirees must deal with, and re-employment after retirement. Lansing Community College, Center for Aging Education, 419 N. Capital Ave., Lansing, MI 48901.

Be Well: The Later Years (A series) (24 min each/1983/16 mm). These provide information from authorities who devote their time to helping others live healthy lives and from well older people. Hosted by Milton Berle, the films are up-beat and informative. The titles are "Health," "Nutrition," "Physical Fitness," and "Stress." Churchill Films, 662 North Robertson Blvd., Los Angeles, CA 90069.

But Not for Lunch (25 min/1977/16 mm). This is a dramatic film that discusses the difficulty in adjusting to retirement, all of which leads the husband to meddle in the wife's affairs. LLL Films, 2232 Welsch Industrial Court, St. Louis, MO 63141.

Come Alive! (A series) (30 min each/1981/video). These videos address career and life planning as a journey of personal growth that may be repeated many times throughout life. Discussion of career fields and changing job market is featured, along with early retirement, more leisure hours, and mid-career changes. Great Plains National Instructional Television Library, Box 80699, Lincoln, NE 69501.

Growing Older: A Time for Growth (15 min/1981/16 mm or video). This shows how vocational training can benefit the elderly and society in general by teaching older Americans new job skills, allowing job changes or new careers. National Audiovisual Center, General Services Administration, Order Section/RR, Washington, D.C. 20409.

Her Social Security (29 min/1977/video). This video discusses the Social Security system from a woman's perspective and finds women at a disadvantage. University of Michigan, Media Resources Center, 416 Fourth St., Ann Arbor, MI 48109.

Jobs for Older Workers: Green Thumb, The Starting Point (30 min/ 1980/video). This traces the history of the Green Thumb program from its inception in the 1940s to the present. Green Thumb was originally a program to find work for older farm workers. Contact Green Thumb, Inc., Washington, D.C., or a local office.

No Gold Watch (28 min/1979/video). This video reports the retirement experiences of older blacks and Hispanics in the Los Angeles area. Contact the School of Gerontology, Andrus Gerontology Center, University of Southern California, University Park/MC-0191, Los Angeles, CA 90089.

Plug Us In (20 min/1981/16 mm). This focuses on problems faced by older Americans who go to job interviews, many of them for the first time in decades, and gives assistance in this area. Manpower Education Institute, 127 E. 35th St., New York, NY 10016.

Pre-retirement Planning: It Makes a Difference (15 min/1981/16 mm or video). This discusses planning for financial, emotional, and geographical considerations of retirement. It shows the experiences of retirees who had the foresight to plan ahead. National Audiovisual Center, General Services Administration, Order Section/RR, Washington, D.C. 20409.

Prime Time Series (28 min each/1978/16 mm). Titles in this series are "Coping with Change," "Learning to Enjoy," "Inner Strengths," and "Interdependent Relationships." All deal with issues and problems faced by retired persons and focus on vignettes of those who have adjusted well to these changes. Free loan, Modern Talking Picture Service, 5000 Park Street North, St. Petersburg, FL 33709, or local branch offices.

So What if it Rains? (17 min/1979/16 mm). This film gives guidelines for financial planning for preretirees. Four vignettes show ways in which people have planned for the future, protecting their income against inflation. Filmakers Library, Inc., 133 East 58th St., New York, NY 10022.

Social Security: Change and Exchange (15 min/1981/16 mm or video). Hard-hitting questions about the Social Security program are answered by a former Social Security Administration official. Discussion provides insight into this system, which is continually undergoing evaluation and change. National Audiovisual Center, General Services Administration, Order Section/RR, Washington, D.C. 20409.

SSI Can Make the Difference (20 min/1977/16 mm). Case studies provide a wide range of information about SSI. It includes information about eligibility requirements, reviews, and the right to appeal. National Audiovisual Center, General Services Administration, Order Section/RR, Washington, D.C. 20409.

They Used to Call 'Em Trailers (17 min/1978/16 mm). This documentary portrays life-styles of older retired Americans living in mobile homes. It discusses issues of retirement. Free loan from De Anza Corporation, 1971 Wilshire Blvd., Beverly Hills, CA 90210.

Turned Loose (28 min/1978/16 mm). This film looks at the experience of losing a job either through retirement or by being laid off. It is one of a series of films from "Begin With Goodbye." Mass Media Ministries, 2116 N. Charles St., Baltimore, MD 21218.

A Week Full of Saturdays (19 min/1978/16 mm). In three separate situations, people share their thoughts about real experiences on retirement planning. A study guide is included. Filmakers Library, Inc., 133 East 58th St., New York, NY 10022.

The Wellness Revolution (27 min/1980/16 mm). This film discusses the importance of wellness, which is described as a blending of physical and mental well-being each person can achieve. A good, up-beat film on nutrition, exercise, and mental and physical health. Free loan, Modern Talking Picture Services, 5000 Park St. North, St. Petersburg, FL 33709, or local branches. May be purchased from Sunset Films, 625 Market St., San Francisco, CA 94105.

Work and Retirement (20 min/1980/video). This discusses the shift to urging people to work longer rather than to retire early. It poses questions of quality of life in retirement, the effect of inflation on the work/retirement decision, the future of older people, and the society in which they will live. University of Michigan, Media Resources Center, 416 Fourth St., Ann Arbor, MI 48109.

A Working Program (23 min/1981/16 mm). This film shows older Americans rejoining the labor force nationwide, benefiting themselves and their community. It stresses the fact that the opportunity to return to work restores older persons' self-worth, dignity, and independence. Victoria Films, 1604 Washington Plaza, Reston, VA 22090.

Incorporating the Audiovisual into Your Program

Once the audiovisual has been selected, the instructor must keep in mind several things about using it in a particular session. For example, the introduction to the audiovisual given by the instructor is very important. It should not only set the stage but also help the audience understand why it was chosen. Important points made by the film can be mentioned at this time. While almost all audiovisuals will trigger discussion of some sort, a certain amount of thought should be given to appropriate questions so that the overall discussion following the screening can be beneficial to most of the audience. If no guides are provided, the instructor should have some kind of questions in mind to start a discussion.

Another concern is properly working equipment. Everyone has experienced the frustration of the nonworking projector, the cord that will not reach, and so forth. One should be familiar with the equipment to be used prior to the start of the session. Allow time to try the equipment out before beginning. The items needed are an extension cord, an extra light bulb, a take-up reel, and a table or stand of proper height.

Implications for Retirement Specialists

The most important consideration in using audiovisuals is to determine whether or not they will enhance the learning experience. Will they supplement the already recognized importance of the lecture and the written material? Will they reach the particular audience?

After the instructor has decided to use an audiovisual, the next step is to locate the proper one. In the selection process, previewing is of utmost importance. The instructor will not want simply to take the word of another or rely on the written description.

Several types of audiovisuals are available to the user. Determining factors are the availability of equipment, cost, and the possibility of developing one's own product.

The way in which the audiovisual is used in the session is important. It is necessary to introduce the audiovisual properly: present the reasons why it is being shown, and prepare for thoughtful discussion following the screening. Consideration should be given to properly working equipment and the room arrangement.

In conclusion, those who develop educational programs must consider the objectives and expected outcomes, the nature of the learners, their motivation to learn, their capacity to learn, the instructional message, the content and context for learning, the instructors' sources, and whether or not each of these will be enhanced by the use of audiovisuals (Hartford and Lambert 1978).

References

Davis, R.H. "Understanding Media as Instructional Aids in Gerontology." *Educational Gerontology* 4 (1979):57–65.

Hartford, M., and Lambert, E. "The Effective Use of Media for Improved Gerontological Education/Training." Unpublished paper, Los Angeles: University of Southern California, 1978.

Suggested Readings

Allyn, M.W. *About Aging: A Catalog of Films*, 4th ed. Lexington, Mass.: Lexington Books, D.C. Heath and Co., 1979, and supplement, 1981.

> An annotated listing of over 600 titles and numerous distributors, updated every two years. No evaluations. Includes 16-mm films and videocassettes.

Blackaby, L.; Georgakas, D.; and Margolis, B. *In Focus*. New York, N.Y.: Cine Information, 1980.

> An extremely informative guide to locating and using audiovisuals. It is a basic how-to manual, listing numerous resources, including periodicals (a good place to find reviews and evaluations), and information on equipment and locale.

Brown, J.W., ed. *Educational Media Yearbook*. New York: R.R. Bowker Co., 1978.

> An annual publication, giving information on resources and training programs.

Hirschfield, I., and Lambert, T. *Audiovisual Aids: Uses and Resources in Gerontology*. Los Angeles: Andrus Gerontology Center, University of Southern California, 1977.

> Theoretical and practical guidelines for selecting and using audiovisuals. Evaluations included.

Kelly, M.M. *Building a Basic Film Library*. Denton: North Texas State University, 1980.

> A practical guide for purchasing 16-mm films to start a film library. Includes costs, distributors, and other useful information. Write to Center for Studies in Aging, North Texas State University, P.O. Box 13438, NT Station, Denton, TX 76203.

Sahara, P. *Media Resources in Gerontology*. Ann Arbor: Institute of Gerontology, University of Michigan, 1977.

> An annotated listing of titles and distributors including 16-mm films, videocassettes, slide/tape and filmstrips. No evaluations. For more information, write to the Institute of Gerontology, University of Michigan, 520 E. Liberty St., Ann Arbor, MI 48109.

16 Resources and Networks for the Preretirement Planner

Carol Segrave Humple

Roles of the Preretirement Planner

The roles of a preretirement planner are trainer, counselor, marketer, and manager of an unwieldy amount of information. The task of meeting the responsibilities of these roles is extremely demanding. As a trainer, the preretirement planner needs knowledge of theories of adult education and must deal with needs analysis, program design and development, facilitation, administration, and evaluation. As a counselor, the preretirement planner frequently is asked questions that would be addressed more appropriately by attorneys, career counselors, family counselors, financial planners, gerontologists, realtors, and physicians. As a marketer, the preretirement planner must sell management and the preretiree on the value of his or her services. As a manager of information, the preretirement planner must sort and sift information that often seems limitless. The act of balancing these multiple and varied roles is not easy.

A common response of preretirement planners to the multifaceted nature of their profession has been to approach their task from one of two opposite extremes. The first extreme has been to expend great amounts of physical, mental, and emotional energy on becoming an expert on all issues and answers related to topics in the field and on the effective presentation of these topics. This extreme more often than not nominates the pretirement planner for the Jack-of-all-trades—master-of-none award and leaves him or her with little, if any, sense of personal or professional satisfaction. The second extreme is merely to throw up one's hands in despair and to hide behind a select group of experts on the subject matter pertinent to preretirement education, a stack of handouts, and a series of audiovisuals. This extreme does leave the preretirement planner with physical and mental energy intact, but as with the first extreme, it does not give a great deal of personal or professional satisfaction. There is a more manageable and more satisfying approach to be taken. This approach is one in which the preretirement planner sees the key to professional effectiveness and satisfaction as being the collection of a rich library of resources and the building of an extensive support network.

The resource library and support network are necessary for two reasons. First, the command of the subject matter, methods, and materials in this field is a lifelong learning process. Mastery cannot come in six months or twenty-four months. The field is too broad and too volatile. Therefore, the training and continuing education of a preretirement planner must be very much a self-learning project, and the personal resource library is the foundation of that learning project. Second, this professional development process cannot be completed alone. The preretirement planner must build a network of organizations and individuals on a national, state, and local level to provide support. This support network can enrich, reinforce, and perfect the four roles of the preretirement planner.

The following section lists suggested materials for the preretirement planners' resource library and potential opportunities for national, state, and local networking. These materials offer an opportunity to build a solid professional foundation and to enrich the developmental process of the preretirement planner.

The Resource Library

The resource library should be made up of a set of books that deals with the basic concepts of each of the subject areas of preretirement education programs and with the process of presentation. Subscriptions to several magazines and newsletters should also be included as well as a modest library of audiovisuals (see chapter 15).

Books

The books listed here will give a good introduction to the topic areas of preretirement planning. Each looks at retirement and the issues pertinent to retirement planning at a slightly different angle. They will provide excellent background, factual information, and further suggested resources for your reference.

Aging

Comfort, A. *A Good Age*. New York: Simon & Schuster, 1976.

> A vigorous, honest, direct, and well-written attack on the myths and stereotypes of aging that abound in U.S. society. Should be required reading for Americans of any age, but particularly for those professionals working with older adults.

Davis, R.H. *Prospects and Issues*. Lexington, Mass.: Lexington Books, D.C. Heath and Company, 1981.

> A basic textbook in gerontology with sections on an introduction to gerontology, aging and society, health care, social policy issues, and education. Contains an excellent bibliography.

Bibliography

Pre-Retirement Resource Bibliography. Cambridge, Mass.: International Society of Preretirement Planners, 1981, 2400 South Downing Ave., Westchester, IL 60153

> A bibliography of books and articles on retirement planning and education, retirement planning in industry, retirement planning programs, aging and retirement, retirement, postretirement, retirement communities, and preparation for retirement. Excellent for reference and research.

Death

Colgrave, M.; Bloomfield, H.; and McWilliams, P. *How to Survive the Loss of a Love.* New York: Bantam, 1976.

> A unique guide to overcoming grief and unhappiness. Defines loss, broken into specific stages, and details a step-by-step guide to emotional healing. Designed to assist in the survival of all emotional hurts and losses, it can be most helpful to those coping with the losses of pre- and postretirement.

Kubler-Ross, E. *Questions and Answers on Death and Dying.* New York: Macmillan, 1974.

> Now a classic in the field of death and dying education and counseling. Attitudes toward death, the fear of death, and the five-stage process of dealing with death and dying are discussed in sympathetic and tender detail. Interviews with the dying and their families are included and provide moving insight into this reality of life.

Lopata, H.Z., and Brehm, H.P. *Widowhood.* New York: Praeger, 1979.

> A classic work on widowhood. Presents societal factors in lifespan disruptions and alternatives. Topics discussed are bereavement, aloneness, short- and long-range needs, support systems, life-style development, and life-style restructuring.

Shahan, L. *Living Alone and Liking It!* New York: Harper & Row, 1981.

> Defines living alone as a life-style without limits. Teaches excellent techniques for the newly widowed, separated, or divorced, including meeting personal needs without dependence and discovering the fact that life on one's own can be full, free, and exciting.

Family Relationships

Dodson, F. *How to Grandparent.* New York: Harper & Row, 1981.

> A guide to contemporary grandparenting and the need to understand the changing times and their effect on grandparents, children, and grandchildren. The need for good communication among members of

the new extended family is discussed in detail. Other topics include discipline, ages and stages, working mothers, divorce, single children, gifts, visits, long distance relationships, and desensitizing adult children from the problems of grandparents.

Lenz, E. *Once My Child . . . Now My Friend.* New York: Warner Books, 1981.

> A sensitive guide to coping with the crisis between parents and their children who are now adults. Case histories and personal experience are used to show how parents can deal with feelings of failure and guilt and with conflicts related to sex, money, interracial relationships, grandparenting, and elderly parents.

Silverstone, B., and Hyman, H. *You and Your Aging Parent*, 2nd ed. New York: Pantheon, 1982.

> An updated and expanded edition that includes the latest facts on financial and medical assistance available to those over 65, extensive coverage of community services that offer alternatives to nursing-home care, complete listing of state and local agencies, and suggested solutions to ways families can work together more effectively in dealing with the problems of aging relatives.

Financial Planning

Hallman, V.G., and Rosenbloom, J.S. *Personal Financial Planning*, 3rd ed. New York: McGraw-Hill, 1982.

> Provides a comprehensive framework whereby persons plan their total financial affairs. The essential concept underlying the book is that personal financial affairs can be planned as a whole. Considerable attention is given to the estate-planning process, Social Security, employer-provided retirement plans, and the investment decisions persons approaching retirement need to make.

Jorgensen, J. *The Graying of America.* New York: Dial Press, 1980.

> A readable, knowledgeable analysis of the nation's pension plans that examines Social Security; inflation; the baby boom generation; limited advantages of IRAs, Keoghs, and ERISA; tax laws, and weak pension legislation.

Porter, S. *Sylvia Porter's New Money Book for the 80's.* New York: Doubleday and Company, Inc., 1979.

> An easy-to-read encyclopedia of money matters that deals with every sphere of personal and family finance. An excellent basic reference book on financial-planning matters.

Rostvold, G.N. *Economic and Financial Survival in the 1980's.* Corona Del Mar, Calif.: Urbanomics Publications, 1979.

> A game plan to coping with surviving and understanding the economic picture of the 1980s. A well-written exploration of inflation, investment strategies, credit, home buying, and personal money management.

Rostvold, G.N. *How to Stretch Your Dollars to Cope with the Inflation of the 1980's.* Corona Del Mar, Calif.: Urbanomics Publications, 1981.

> A financial workbook to assist in the development of a personal money management program for the 1980s. It enables the reader to bring together information on personal spending, saving, investing, credit, and money management habits.

General Reading

Biegel, L. *The Best Years Catalogue.* New York: G.P. Putnam's Sons, 1978.

> A comprehensive handbook for living life over 50. A source book of information on guidance services, publications, and bureaus that provide for older people and directions for taking advantage of such services.

Downs, H., and Roll, R.J. *The Best Years Book.* New York: Delacorte Press, 1981.

> An authoritative guide to planning for a vital, productive, and fulfilling retirement. It identifies the issues and options presented by retirement and suggests strategies for making well-thought-out advance plans.

Tenebaum, F. *Over 55 Is Not Illegal.* Boston: Houghton Mifflin, 1979.

> A resource book for active older adults. Provides comprehensive information on institutions, organizations, and agencies. Offers advice on work, education, volunteer opportunities, and keys to life satisfaction in retirement.

Uris, A. *Over 50, The Definitive Guide to Retirement.* Radnor, Penn.: Chilton Book Company, 1979.

> A thorough, definitive encylcopedia of preretirement issues. Topics include retirement transition from office to limbo, pension and Social Security expectations, health and leisure planning, and women in retirement.

Weaver, P. *Strategies for the Second Half of Life.* New York: Franklin Watts, 1980.

> Offers an uncompromising challenge to the preretiree to make the second half of life unequivocally the better half. This theme energetically

pervades discussions of second careers, health, financial planning, relationships, leisure planning, sex, and death.

Health

Bailey, C. *Fit or Fat*. Boston: Houghton Mifflin, 1978.

> A fitness book that puts together the results of the most recent research on diet, exercise, and health maintenance. A readable, sensible, and balanced approach to getting started on fitness. Written in good humor, this is a real inspiration to the fit, near fit, and unfit.

DeVries, H.A. *Vigor Regained*. Englewood Cliffs, N.J.: Prentice-Hall, 1974.

> Outlines a simple, proven home program for restoring fitness and vitality in the later years. This program is based on the results of an extensive year-long research project on fitness restoration conducted by Dr. DeVries at Leisure World, Laguna Hills, California.

Farquhar, J.W. *The American Way of Life Need Not be Hazardous to Your Health*. New York: W.W. Norton, 1978.

> Argues the case that 90 percent of strokes and premature heart attacks can be prevented. Based on the Stanford Medical School Health Maintenance Plan, it offers an informative and active plan for the reduction of stress and cessation of smoking and the development of a safe and sound exercise and nutrition program.

Luce, G. *Your Second Life*. New York: Dell, 1979.

> A sensitively written and insightful book designed to help the years of maturity and later life become what they are capable of being. It shatters myths and suggests new attitudes toward age, longevity, self-image, intimacy, sexuality, dreams, sleep, healing, and death.

Pelletier, K.R. *Mind as Healer, Mind as Slayer*. New York: Delta, 1977.

> Defines the role of stress in the four major types of illnesses: cardiovascular disease, cancer, arthritis, and respiratory disease. The sources of stress are surveyed, guidelines for stress evaluation are offered, profiles of disease-prone personalities are presented, and preventive techniques are suggested.

Pelletier, K.R. *Longevity Fulfilling Our Biological Potential*. New York: Delacorte Press, 1981.

> The basic principles of holistic medicine and stress reduction are applied to human longevity. Chapters explore the most recent research on the link between longevity and immune systems, aging of cells, regeneration, exercise, diet, and mental attitudes. Famous centenarian communities in South America and the Middle East are examined.

Pritikin, N. *The Pritikin Program for Diet and Exercise.* New York: Grosset and Dunlap, 1979.

> Promotes a diet and health program that has an impressive record of results. The program claims to enable people of all ages to live a longer, healthier life—a life in which they feel younger and are less affected by the ravages of degenerative diseases that are prevalent among many members of the older generation.

Housing

Dickinson, P.A. *Retirement Edens Outside the Sunbelt.* New York: E.P. Dutton, 1980.

> A careful study of retirement housing options outside the sunbelt areas. A look at the option of staying put and how to design a housing situation to meet retirement needs in present home environments. Other topics include the cost of living, climate, medical facilities, nursing homes, cultural life, and recreation possibilities in the areas listed.

Dickinson, P.A. *Sunbelt Retirement.* New York: E.P. Dutton, 1983.

> A comprehensive guide to successful retirement in each of the thirteen sunbelt states. Each state, including over 500 cities and towns, is evaluated individually to give practical answers to questions of cost, climate, health care, and life-style.

Irwin, R. *The $125,000 Decision.* New York: McGraw-Hill, 1981.

> A unique and personal treatment of all the legal, financial, and even psychological questions about selling your home, pocketing your tax-free bonanza, and choosing retirement housing. Written in plain, nontechnical terms, often in the form of a question-and-answer dialogue between a retirement-bound couple and a friendly advisor.

Legal

Kess, S., and Westlin, B. *Estate Planning Guide.* Chicago: Commerce Clearinghouse, 1982.

> Reflects on the major estate and gift taxes brought about by the Economic Tax Act of 1981. Designed to aid the estate owner and his or her advisors in formulating a successful estate plan. The book analyzes planning techniques and principles, discusses the importance of wills, and includes special planning for executives, professionals, partners, owners of interest in closed corporations, sole proprietors, and single women. Provides numerous charts, graphs, checklists, and tables.

Wishard, W.R. *Rights of the Elderly and Retired.* San Francisco: Cragmont Publications, 1978.

A unique and comprehensive guide to the legal rights and legal issues that may come into question in retirement. Some of the content areas are retirement benefits (public and private), health and medical services, housing, employment, age discrimination and consumer rights, and protection. A valuable list of national and state legal services and organizations and state and regional offices on aging is included.

Leisure

Roe, R. *Leisure Alternatives Catalog*. New York: Dell Publications, 1979.

An exhaustive collection of leisure alternatives for all ages. A review of hobbies, arts, sports, wilderness challenges, education, sources of high adventure, and insights into leisure theory and practices.

Ross, M.H. *Creative Loafing: A Shoestring Guide to New Leisure Fun.* San Diego: Communication Creativity Books, 1978.

A source book that embraces all types of leisure activities from bird-watching to clownology. A book about having fun, saving money, conquering boredom, and reawakening to the richness of life.

Second Careers

Bolles, R. *The Three Boxes*. Berkeley, Calif.: Ten Speed Press, 1978.

An introduction to life/work planning. The three boxes of life analyzed are education, work, and retirement. Effective tools that can be used to blend learning, achieving, and playing during these stages of life are described.

Bolles, R. *What Color Is Your Parachute?* Berkeley, Calif.: Ten Speed Press, 1979.

A practical step-by-step guide for the career-changer or job hunter, whether he or she is 17 or 70 plus. Presents a combination of exercises for self-discovery, resources for consultation, and an extensive bibliography.

College Board Publications. *40 Million Americans in Career Transition: The Need for Information*. Princeton, N.J., 1981.

Especially helpful to adult education professionals, this publication identifies career and educational information needs, reasons for seeking career change, as well as personal and demographic characteristics of adults involved in the transition of life roles.

Jacobson, B. *Young Programs for Older Workers*. Work in America Series. New York: Van Nostrand Reinhold, 1980.

A review of the many progressive personnel policies that have recently been designed and developed for older workers: part-time employment, phased retirement, second career training, training and counseling programs for re-entry women, job redesign, retraining, and preretirement counseling and planning. An excellent interpretation of today's legal, technical, and attitudinal changes that are helping older workers re-enter the work force.

Lathrop, R. *Who's Hiring Who?* Berkeley, Calif.: Ten Speed Press, 1977.

A fresh and accurate analysis of the so-called job market and an invaluable guide to job seekers. A useful tool to job seekers of all levels and ages. A no-nonsense approach to skills and abilities exploration, résumé, writing, interviewing techniques, and guidelines to entry into the hidden job market.

Sex

Butler, R.N., and Lewis, M. *Sex after Sixty: A Guide for Men and Women in Their Later Years*. New York: Harper & Row, 1976.

An informative, authoritative, and sensitive book on the sexual lives of men and women over 60. A study of the sexual difficulties that can arise at this time of life, but with much more emphasis on the how-to of building a warm and mutually satisfying sexual relationship in the later years. A useful book to persons of any age who are trying to understand sexuality in the later years.

Peterson, J.A., and Payne, B. *Love in the Later Years*. Chicago: Follet, 1975.

A pioneering effort to help the older adult become aware of his or her potential in any loving relationship. Among the topics covered are marriage and life in the later years, retirement marriage, emerging innovations in life-styles, the economics of later marriage, and planning for the future.

Weg, R.B. *Sexuality in the Later Years*. New York: Academic Press, 1983.

This book pulls together evidence from the anthropological, psychological, social, and physiological disciplines, presenting a coherent picture of sexual roles and behavior in the later years. It makes a comprehensive contribution toward an increased awareness of sexuality in the later years and is an important addition to the small but growing list of works in the field. Sexuality is frequently a forgotten issue in the typical curriculum of retirement-planning programs. Should lack of current and valid information be the source of this situation, this book impressively fills in that gap.

Training

Craig, R.L. *Training and Development Handbook*. New York: McGraw-Hill, 1976.

Featuring the work of fifty-nine top specialists, an authoritative survey of the most important body of knowledge in the field of employee development and training. A basic nuts-and-bolts guide to staff selection, facilities, equipment, methods of role playing, game simulation, and computer-assisted instruction. Areas of interest to preretirement planners are job enrichment and redesign, training for special groups, needs assessment, literature searching and surveillance, and using external programs and training package.

Knowles, M.S. *Self-Directed Learning: A Guide for Learners and Teachers*. Chicago: Follet, 1981.

A resource for the self-directed learner, whether student or trainer. Trainers will find this a guide for helping students take more responsibility for their learning. Presented are many techniques for designing a learning climate of mutual trust with well-defined learner/facilitator roles, including diagnosing needs and evaluating programs.

Knox, A.B. *Adult Development and Learning*. San Francisco: Jossey-Bass, 1978.

A handbook that describes the circumstances under which adults learn most effectively, the learning abilities that decline or increase with age, and how development and learning are affected by family roles, social activities, education, occupation, personality characteristics, and health. A classic text in the field of adult education that presents a wide range of information and shows how it can be practically applied by educators and helping professionals.

Peterson, D.A. *Facilitating Education for Older Learners*. San Francisco: Jossey-Bass, 1983.

This book is directed toward people who are currently involved in interacting with older adults in a learning setting. It is a must in the library of retirement-planning professionals. This book brings together relevant research and experience concerning problems that confront instructors and program planners and identifies the implications and applications of that research. It is designed to help teachers and program planners understand the educational needs, wants, and characteristics of older learners so they can develop appealing, valuable, and efficient instruction.

Transition

Bradford, L.P., and Bradford, M.I. *Retirement: Coping with Emotional Upheavals*. Chicago: Nelson-Hall, 1979.

Discusses four rarely touched upon problem areas in retirement: unexpected shocks in retirement, losses and displacements, the need for a planned transition, and marital adjustments. Based on the personal experience of the authors, strategies are suggested to encourage self-acceptance, better communication, and mutual support in retirement.

Bridges, W. *Transitions*. Reading, Mass.: Addison-Wesley, 1980.

> A valuable contribution to the field of adult development. A decep-
> tively simple yet creative and most insightful analysis of the uniform
> process of change experienced by adults in transition. Strategies for
> coping with the difficult, painful, and confusing times in adult life are
> outlined. An invaluable tool for understanding and coping with the
> retirement transition process.

Women in Retirement

Jacobs, R. *Life after Youth: Female, Forty—What Next?* Scranton, Penn.:
Harper & Row, 1979.

> A sensible, sympathetic and informed look at the older women of
> today—their past, present, and future. The author suggests exciting,
> new, liberating roles for women in their later years and offers ways to
> translate past experiences as wives and mothers into new roles as in-
> novative contributors to society.

Seskin, J. *More Than Mere Survival: Conversations with Women over 65*.
New York: Newsweek Books, 1980.

> Twenty-two women between the ages of 66 and 97 reveal how much joy,
> interest, and pleasure they find in their lives—and how they found it.
> Despite physical disabilities, economic hardship, or the loss of family
> and friends, each has preserved her zest for living, self-confidence, and
> sense of humor. Each continues to live actively and productively.

Szinovacz, M. *Women's Retirement: Policy Implications of Recent Research*. Beverly Hills: Sage Publications, 1982.

> Despite increasing interest in retirement issues, women's retirement has
> been widely neglected by social scientists. This book attempts to fill in
> the desperate need for relevant information on women's needs in and
> response to retirement. The author admits the research is exploratory.
> However, this by no means invalidates its welcome contribution to the
> data base of the retirement planner. The book consists of three parts:
> part one concerns itself with the impact of work history and employ-
> ment status on the life situation of the older women. Part two ad-
> dresses attitudes toward retirement and retirement preparation among
> women. Part three is devoted to analyses that deal more specifically
> with the determinants and consequences of retirement for women.

Troll, L.E. *Looking Ahead: A Woman's Guide to the Problems and Joys
of Growing Older*. Englewood Cliffs, N.J.: Spectrum, Prentice-Hall,
1977.

> A pioneering work that reviews a variety of aspects of aging as they ap-
> ply to women. A collection of some of the first thinking on the issues
> of the sociology of aging of women, retirement, parent-child relation-
> ships, friendships, education, marriage, and widowhood.

Community Service Directories

Community service directories are a valuable tool to locate a variety of services in local communities. Some of these services include free health screening and transportation services, home health care, housing information, legal aid, and employment services.

Area Agency on Aging Senior Services Directory

> This is a complete guide to community services available to the older adult within the confines of the agency's territory. These include alcohol and drug abuse, education, employment training, financial assistance, health, housing, legal, recreation, and transportation services. Request a personal copy from the local Area Agency on Aging office.

Norback, C., and Norback, P. *The Older American's Handbook.* New York: Van Nostrand Reinhold, 1977.

> This handbook provides a complete listing of local agencies that can provide information on medical and nursing care, recreation, employment, legal services, food, mental health, in-house services, and counseling for older Americans.

To Find the Way to Services in Your Community

> This free publication will assist you in working your way toward the federal, state, and social services organizations you may need support from. It is available free from the U.S. Department of Health and Human Services Publications Department, Washington, D.C. 20201.

Retirement Publications

Many of the following publications will prove to be very useful tools in the development and updating of preretirement programs. They are published monthly or bimonthly and provide current information on issues pertinent to retirement planning and retirement life. Write to several or to all of these publications to request a free copy and subscription information. You will then be able to choose the one or two publications that will prove most useful to you.

Periodicals

Aging. Published monthly by the Administration on Aging (AoA), an agency of the U.S. Department of Health and Human Services, Superintendent of Documents, U.S. Government Printing Office, Washington, D.C. 20204.

Dynamic Years. Published bimonthly by Action for Independent Maturity (AIM), 1909 K St., N.W., Washington, D.C. 20049. A subscription is included with membership in AIM.

50 Plus. Published monthly by Retirement Living Publishing Company, 99 Garden Street, Marion, OH 43302.

Generations. Journal published quarterly by the Western Gerontological Society, 785 Market Street. Suite 1114, San Francisco, CA 94103.

The Gerontologist. Journal published bimonthly by the Gerontological Society of America, 1835 K St., N.W., Washington, D.C. 20006.

Modern Maturity. Published bimonthly by the American Association of Retired Persons (AARP), 215 Long Beach Blvd., Long Beach, CA 90801. A subscription is included with membership in AARP.

Money. Published monthly by Time, Inc., Rockefeller Center, New York, NY 10020.

Retirement Planning: A Journal of the International Society of Preretirement Planners. Journal published quarterly by the International Society of Preretirement Planners, 2400 South Downing Ave., Westchester, IL, 60153

Newsletters

AARP News Bulletin. Published monthly by the American Association of Retired Persons, 1909 K St., N.W., Washington, D.C. 20049.

RAI Insights. A newsletter for Human Resource Executives and Retirement Counselors. Published quarterly by RAI, 919 Third Ave., New York, NY 10022.

Newspapers

The Network. Published quarterly by the Gray Panthers, 3700 Chestnut St., Philadelphia, PA 19014.

Subject Guide

Current Literature on Aging. Published quarterly by the National Council on the Aging, Inc., 1600 Maryland Ave., S.W., West Wing 100, Washington, D.C. 20024.

Networking

Networking is the process of being in active communication with people you know, have known, and should know for the purpose of gathering the information and referrals you need to achieve your professional goals. A list follows of national, state, and local organizations and institutions with which the preretirement planner should be affiliated. These organizations and institutions provide marvelous opportunities for networking. The closeness of your affiliation depends upon your specific information and support needs for your professional development and that of your program.

Professional Organizations and Associations

The organizations presented are well worth investigating as resources. Their publications, newsletters, and regional and national conferences can be very useful in updating and expanding a program. Many of these organizations also offer beginner and advanced train-the-trainer programs.

> American Association of Adult and Continuing Education
> 810 18th St., N.W., Washington, D.C. 20006

> American Society for Training and Development
> 600 Maryland Ave., S.W., Suite 305, Washington, D.C. 20024

> Gerontological Society of America
> 1835 K St., N.W., Washington, D.C. 20026

> International Society of Preretirement Planners
> 2400 South Downing Ave., Westchester, IL 60153

> Western Gerontological Society
> 785 Market St., Suite 1114, San Francisco, CA 94103

Retirement Associations and Organizations:
Private, Nonprofit, and Profit

The following retirement associations and organizations offer a variety of membership benefits. Contact these organizations for further information on membership fees, benefits, and services.

Action for Independent Maturity (AIM)
1909 K St., N.W., Washington, D.C. 20049

> A division of the AARP. Membership is open to anyone between the ages of 50 and 65. This organization offers supplemental life and health insurance, prescription drug discounts, and group travel. Membership includes a subscription to *Dynamic Years* magazine.

American Association of Retired Persons (AARP)
1909 K St., N.W., Washington, D.C. 20049
or
P.O. Box 2400, 215 Long Beach Blvd., Long Beach, CA 90801

> Membership is open to anyone 55 and over. Dues are nominal. National membership includes a subscription to *Modern Maturity* magazine, opportunities for discount prescription drugs, supplemental life and health insurance, and group travel. There are 2,500 local chapters that provide support groups for older adults as well as continuing education programs.

Gray Panthers
3700 Chestnut St., Philadelphia, PA 19014

> This is a dynamic national group. Membership is open to persons of all ages. Members are committed to promoting the concept that older adults are a great national resource and to making this message known nationally.

Older Women's League
3800 Harrison St., Oakland, CA 94611

> A national organization defined as a political advocacy organization. Some of the issues in the forefront are Social Security cuts, medical care for older women, and pension programs.

National Council on the Aging, Inc.
1828 L St., N.W., Washington, D.C. 20036

> This organization has an extensive list of free and low-cost publications on retirement and aging issues.

Senior Sports International
5670 Wilshire Blvd., #360, Los Angeles, CA 90036

> This organization sponsors the annual Senior Olympics and many regional Senior Olympic events. It is an excellent organization for participants who are interested in working toward their full physical potential in retirement.

Government Agencies and Committees

Agencies on Aging

Administraiton on Aging (AoA)
U.S. Department of Health and Human Services
Washington, D.C. 20201

This federal agency acts as a referral service and a clearinghouse of information on many areas of interest and concern to older Americans, such as employment and volunteer opportunities, retirement housing, senior centers, transportation, nutrition programs, and additional federal programs for older adults.

The State Offices on Aging are the state arms of AoA. They serve as a referral and resource clearinghouse on the state level. Pose your questions on state programs and services for the older adult to the Office on Aging at your state capitol.

The Area Agencies on Aging are the local extension of the State Offices on Aging. There are more than 500 agencies. They also provide referral services and information related to the concerns of the older adult. Information on the Area Agencies on Aging closest to you can be obtained by contacting your state Office on Aging.

Many counties also have Offices on Aging. They will provide you with printed information on services offered to older adults in your county. If your county has such an office, it will be listed in the white pages of your phone book under the county listing.

Other federal organizations include:

ACTION
806 Connecticut Ave., N.W., Washington, D.C. 20525

ACTION funds and administers community services agencies for people over 60: Foster Grandparents, Retired Senior Volunteer Program (RSVP), and Senior Companions.

National Institute on Aging
900 Rockville Pike, Bethesda, MD 20014

This is one of the National Institutes of Health. This institute focuses on research in the areas of biological, medical, and behavioral aspects of aging. Write them if you are interested in receiving copies of their published research on these aspects of the aging process.

The following committees are concerned with bills, issues, government programs, and other policy matters of vital concern to older Americans. It is advisable to keep these committees informed about the concerns and needs of your local older adult community and to have them inform you of their efforts. Write and request that you be added to their mailing list.

U.S. House of Representatives, Select Committee on Aging,
House Office Building, Room 712, Washington, D.C. 20515

U.S. Senate, Special Committee on Aging
Dirksen Senate Office Building, Room G-233
Washington, D.C. 20510

Community Networks

Communities may well prove to be one of the richest sources for the pre-retirement planner to develop a network. A phone call to or a personal conversation with one of many organizations listed should prove very helpful. Not only will questions be answered, but also many new ideas and options will be opened.

Banks. Your local bank is a resource of factual information as you develop and update the financial-planning component of your program. The customer relations department can direct you to the right person for advice on investments and trusts. Many banks offer free pamphlets and books on retirement planning and general financial planning.

Bookstores. The manager of your local bookstore can direct you to any number of readings on topics pertinent to retirement—fitness, transition, financial planning, work options, or leisure options. What is not in stock he or she can order for you. It is a good idea to request that your bookstore keep you informed about new titles on topics related to retirement-planning interests.

Churches and Synagogues. Your local church or synagogue can be a resource to you in several ways. Many offer adult education classes with or without a religious orientation. They offer excellent opportunities for your participants to develop volunteer careers. Many also offer a counseling service should your participants be in need of counseling at any time before or after retirement.

Educational Institutions. The educational institutions in your community will be most valuable sources for continuing education and networking opportunities for both you and your participants, especially if your local university or college has a center, institution, or program of gerontology. Such programs frequently include courses, seminars, or workshops in the field of preretirement education. Familiarize yourself with the course offerings, faculty, and library facilities at such centers. If your local educational institution does not have some sort of gerontology program, investigate department offerings in fields related to the subject matter of preretirement education: education, training, psychology, financial planning, and counseling. Identify your educational needs to faculty members and librarians. They will be most willing to assist you.

Other Community Education Sources

The community organizations listed offer continuing adult education programs that may be of interest to you or your participants. Phone them and request a list of their course offerings. Watch your local newspaper and your mailbox for flyers. In addition to resources discussed in the following sections, be sure to check into cultural centers such as community theater, art museum, or opera company; the YMCA, YWCA, YMHA, YWHA; and the Red Cross.

In many ways television is a valuable learning tool. The TV series *Over Easy* should be on the required viewing list for preretirement planners. In most cities throughout the country, it is broadcast daily. It focuses on the issues and personalities that are making a difference in the lives of present, pre-, and postretirees.

Elderhostel. Elderhostel is a network of over 400 colleges, universities, independent schools, and other educational institutions in fifty states, Canada, the United Kingdom, Denmark, Sweden, Finland, and Norway that offers special low-cost, short-term, residential academic programs for older adults. Contact Elderhostel, 1000 Boylston St., Suite 200, Boston, MA 02116.

Hospitals. Your local hospital is another source for continuing education for yourself or your participants. Many offer free or reduced-tuition classes in nutrition, stress management, and other areas of health maintenance. Volunteer opportunities are readily available. Look into low-cost health-care programs as well as free health fairs or screenings.

Legal Aid Society. The Legal Aid Society provides a broad range of free legal services to the older adult through their Senior Legal Advocacy Program. These services include legal representation, advocacy for groups, advice, and information.

Libraries. Most libraries have become much more than a collection of reading materials. Many offer a variety of adult classes and lectures. Your library will be a great help to you in finding information about sources such as periodicals, films, reference books, and other libraries. The library also offers many volunteer opportunities. It is perhaps your most useful community resource. Get to know the librarian well. Let him or her know your professional information needs.

Police Department. The police department in many communities provides educational opportunities. They offer classes in personal and home safety. They are the resource to begin with if you are interested in forming a group to fight crime against the elderly or crime in the community as a whole. The police department also has many opportunities for volunteers.

Senior Center. Local senior centers are rich in information, lectures, classes, and volunteer opportunities. Get to know the director. Identify your needs and the needs of your participants to this individual. At most centers, you will be able to gather information on Social Security, group travel, health fairs, and many other topics. Lectures frequently cover topics such as estate planning, taxes, personal safety, and financial planning. Classes for future retirees are offered on any number of crafts and hobbies. Volunteer opportunities are most often related to seniors helping seniors such as filing tax returns, locating housing, and meeting transportation needs.

Social Security Office. The local office of the Social Security Administration is your contact for any questions you may have regarding Social Security, Medicare-Medicaid benefits, disability, and work restrictions after retirement. Local offices are listed in the white pages of your phone directory under Social Security Administration.

Topic Specialists in the Community. It is critical to develop a network of local specialists in each of the topic areas of your program. You would be wise also to build a network among training and development specialists and counselors. These experts will support you in your professional development as a preretirement planner. These experts can assist you in the research, design, presentation, and enrichment of your program. You may need to work with several experts in a particular field until you can identify the one that best meets your needs and the needs of your participants and the one with whom you can have a good working relationship. Set up a network of persons with whom you can be comfortable and in whom you can place your trust. Keep close to this network by phone or lunch meetings. This network should be made up of the following professionals:

Career development counselor

Family counselor/psychologist

Financial planner

Gerontologist

Lawyer

Librarian

Physician

Realtor or realtor associate

Representative from Social Security Administration

Senior center director

Successful retirees

Volunteer Organizations. The National Office of the National Center for Voluntary Action has a clearinghouse of information on opportunities for volunteering. The local Center for Voluntary Action is listed in the white pages of your phone book under Volunteer Action Center or Volunteer Bureau, or write to National Center for Voluntary Action, 1216 16th St., N.W., Washington, D.C. 20036.

ACTION is a federal agency that offers many volunteer opportunities for older adults. It unites the following federal organizations: VISTA (Volunteers in Service to America), Peace Corps, RSVP (Retired Senior Volunteer Program), SCORE (Service Corps of Retired Executives), Foster Grandparents Program, and Senior Companion Program. For further information, write to ACTION Recruiting Office, Action, Washington, D.C. 20525.

Personal Network

Inform all relatives, friends, and acquaintances who read newspapers, magazines, journals, and books that you are a preretirement planner. Identify your particular informational needs to them, and ask them to clip, copy, take notes on, and pass on any materials they think might be useful to you. Attend professional conferences, seminars, and workshops. View and listen to meaningful television and radio programs.

Conclusion

Unfortunately, no institute of preretirement planning exists that offers all the answers and that grants a reassuring set of credentials. As a result, many preretirement planners feel somewhat alone and abandoned. This negative aspect of the field is easily neutralized by the opportunity this situation offers for creativity, freedom, and a sense of the pioneer spirit as the preretirement planner pursues professional development. Anxiety is assuaged once the preretirement planner makes the decision to develop a resource library and to establish a support network.

17 Retirement Preparation: An Expanding Field

Helen Dennis

The concept of retirement is relatively new. An 1828 dictionary by Noah Webster did not include the term *retirement* as it is currently used. However, during the past fifteen years, there has been a significant increase in the acceptance of retirement as a well-known term, concept, and institution. The following facts address its growing recognition and support: over 25 million people are currently retired; retirement preparation programs have proliferated; 5,000 persons have been trained as group leaders (Reich 1977); and retirement-planning services are offered by management-consulting firms, financial-planning institutions, banks, independent consultants, community colleges, and profit-making organizations.

Retirement and Society

Retirement as we know it today is a creation of the industrial society (Atchley 1976). This society brought about many changes that set the scene for the evolution of retirement and provided the conditions for retirement to exist as a social institution in the United States. According to Atchley, there are four such conditions:

1. People must live long enough to accumulate a defined number of years of employment. In the industrial society, more people survived to old age because of a decline in infant mortality that resulted from the success in combating childhood diseases. In addition, adult mortality rates declined due, in part, to medical advances, improved nutrition, and sanitation. As a result, there was a rapid growth in the population because more people were living longer.

2. The economy must produce adequate surpluses to support non-workers. A marked increase in the availability of economic surpluses allowed the resources to be diverted to those no longer participating in the labor force. Increased surpluses resulted from greater production of goods and services. One factor responsible for this change was the use of new forms of energy.

3. Part of the economic surplus must be directed to support retired persons. The U.S. government and employers regulated the distribution of these surpluses through pensions and insurance. Various systems emerged—

state pension plans, state old age insurance programs, the federal Social Security program, and employer pension systems. At the same time, the growing interest and political influence of the elderly promoted the use of these mechanisms to alleviate poverty in old age.

4. Individuals in society must accept the notion that an adult can live with dignity without paid employment. In the height of Calvanistic Protestantism, activities that were not work-related were considered sinful. With the rise of secularism, work became less preeminent in society's value system, which in turn, permitted individuals to give up their work ethic and accept retirement without guilt. As a result, retirement emerged as an earned right, particularly with the development of contributory pension and insurance systems.

Meaning of Retirement

It is difficult to find a single definition of the word *retirement*. Semanticists, government officials, and social scientists differ in their views of the subject. The following definitions provide a range of meanings.

Webster (1965) defines retirement as a withdrawal from one's position or occupation, which essentially means giving up work. Another well-accepted definition includes the "giving up of work" but adds "in old age." Joseph Califano, former secretary of Health, Education, and Welfare, suggests eliminating the "old age" part of the definition and substituting a more realistic definition: retirement is a reward for a certain period of work (U.S. Congress 1978).

Atchley (1976) believes that receipt of a pension is a necessary feature of retirement. He views retirement as "a condition in which an individual is forced or allowed to retire and is employed less than full-time and in which his income is derived in part from a retirement pension earned through years of service as a job holder" (p. 1). Using this definition, a part-time worker receiving a pension is considered retired. Kaplan (1979) defines a retiree as an individual who withdraws, temporarily or permanently, from an activity, interest, or commitment. This definition recognizes that retirement can be temporary but does not include the notion of partial retirement (Parker 1982).

Retirement can be viewed in several other contexts. According to Robert Benedict, former commissioner of the Administration on Aging "retirement as we know it may be obsolete" (p. 9); it should no longer be viewed as the cessation of work. Retirement is more of "a *process* by which we all prepare ourselves for living in the later years" (U.S. Congress 1978, p. 11). Retirement is an event when an individual separates from the job. The event is frequently accompanied by a retirement ceremony. It is a social role that has rights and duties (Atchley 1976). However, some view retirement as a roleless role with no vital function to perform (Donahue et al. 1960). Finally, retirement is a phase of life that begins with the retirement event and ends when the individual becomes dependent and/or institutionalized and unable to carry out retirement roles (Atchley 1976).

The concept of retirement seems simple, but it is deceiving. The diverse meanings and implications of retirement affect the continued development of the field of retirement preparation and the type of training and education that retirement students and specialists seek in preparing themselves to provide effective retirement services to middle-aged and older adults.

The field of retirement preparation addresses aspects of the role, phases, and events of retirement. In the broadest sense, it is a specialty in which planners, educators, and counselors assist individuals to prepare for their later years. To many retirement specialists, adequate preparation is achieved when preretirees increase their awareness and understanding of retirement issues, when they develop a retirement plan, implement that plan, and/or have a positive attitude toward retirement. One or more of these objectives can be achieved with a multidisciplinary knowledge base that includes education, gerontology, psychology, sociology, physiology, and economics. The emphasis of retirement-planning programs may vary according to the specialist's discipline orientation, view of retirement, and perceived or real needs of preretirees.

Current Roles of the Retirement Specialist

Although retirement preparation may be approached from many disciplines, definitions, and objectives, the role of the retirement specialist has evolved with some consistency. The functions are extensive, whether as a corporate employee, a consultant to several organizations, or a counselor working with an individual client.

The diverse roles require the retirement specialist to have specific knowledge and skills to develop, conduct, and evaluate retirement preparation programs. The specialist should have knowledge in the following content areas: demographics of the elderly, the normal aging process, adult development, principles of adult education, program planning and evaluation, topics in preretirement education, and resources. Skills areas should include group process, communication, public speaking, administration, organization, program planning, and instruction for adults. The roles and functions described in the following sections may occur selectively, sequentially, and/or simultaneously.

Educator

One of the primary roles of the retirement specialist is that of an educator. This function consists of conducting an assessment of participant needs, developing a program curriculum that reflects those needs, providing instruction to middle-aged and older adults, and evaluating the program. The educators should know the principles of adult learning (*andragogy*); understand elements of program development in terms of objectives, methods, and outcomes; and be able to conduct a needs assessment, to teach using effective methodologies, and to evaluate the program.

Facilitator

As a facilitator, the retirement specialist leads discussions and moves the group toward the goals that are outlined for the program. Specialists should have an understanding of group dynamics, skills in facilitation, and a clear sense of their role in relationship to the preretirees.

Counselor

The retirement specialist is sensitive to personal and interpersonal issues that arise in the group. Problems related to death, sexual relationships, marriage, aging parents, role crises, and alcoholism may be expressed overtly or covertly within a preretirement session. Appropriate response to these types of issues requires the retirement specialist to have an accurate self-perception of competence and an ability to discriminate which issues should be referred to a licensed clinician. Good communication skills in both listening and responding to groups and individuals are important for this role.

Motivator

The retirement specialist, as a motivator, invites individuals to participate in retirement planning, encourages internal support for the program, and motivates participants to act (if that is a program objective). To be an effective motivator, the specialist should be able to describe the program accurately and effectively, to present its significance to the sponsor and the preretiree, and to understand reasons for cooperation or resistance from clients or colleagues.

Administrator

The retirement specialist, as an administrator, has many facets. The specialist is responsible for the logistics of the program or seminar, which requires skills in organization, planning, staffing, supervision, and communication. The administrator usually develops a budget and works within it, which requires additional planning and fiscal capabilities. In some cases, retirement specialists spend only 10 to 20 percent of their time on retirement preparation; the major portion of their time is consumed by benefit or personnel responsibilities. In these instances, specialists need skills in time management to maximize their efforts in retirement preparation.

Resource

It is unlikely that the retirement specialist will have the information necessary to respond to all questions. Therefore, the specialist should be aware of resources and be able to suggest ways to get access to them. Needed services might focus on employment, health, counseling, or financial needs. The retirement specialist should also be aware of retirement-planning literature as a resource, including books, periodicals, and newsletters.

Salesperson

As a salesperson, the retirement specialist must sell the concept of retirement planning and the specific program to senior management to ensure adequate financial and human resources to implement the program. It is imperative for the specialist to understand the politics and the significant players in the organization. This can be accomplished by learning about the organization from a network of colleagues and publications such as newsletters and annual reports. Attending various corporate committee and management meetings will provide additional insights into the working relationships of key decision makers.

Issues and Trends

Several issues have emerged that require an examination of professional aspects of the field. Three have been selected for discussion: program evaluation, professional certification, and competition and cooperation.

Program Evaluation

Determining the purpose and objectives of retirement preparation programs has been an ongoing challenge. The issue is of great significance because without objectives, evaluation becomes impossible. Objectives can be thought of from the perspective of the institution (employer) and the participant (preretiree). Essentially, objectives address the outcomes of a program and should be stated in behavioral terms so they can be measured or observed. A guide to the formation of objectives is recommended. Begin the objective with the following statement: at the end of the program, participants will be able to. . . . Thus, at the end of the program, participants will be able, for example, to write a financial plan, to implement an exercise program, or to discuss retirement plans with a spouse. The same procedure can be used for institutions. For example, at the end of the program, ABC Corporation can expect 15 percent of the participants to commit to phased retirement, or 20 percent of the preretirees will elect to retire in one year.

After objectives have been determined and the program addressing these objectives has been completed, evaluation is possible by measuring the extent to which the objectives were met. In an era of shrinking resources and greater accountability, evaluation will continue to be of importance to sponsors and funders of retirement preparation programs.

Professional Certification

A second issue deals with certification of retirement specialists. For several years, professional retirement and gerontology organizations have discussed establishing a minimum standard for those practicing or providing retirement services. To date, standards have been suggested, but these are only recommendations for sponsors who want to base their decisions to hire retirement specialists according to consistent criteria (Dennis 1982).

Certification will require a consensus on the elements of effective retirement-planning programs and the knowledge, skills, and abilities required to provide retirement services. One of the important unanswered questions is Who or what organization would make the certification decision? Other important questions include Whose needs are being met through certification? Is certification a mechanism to keep new specialists out of the field? Is it a protection for sponsors and preretirees? Until these fundamental questions are answered and a consensus is reached on the elements of effective programming and specialist qualifications, certification is unlikely to occur in the near future.

Competition and Cooperation

The last issue involves competition and cooperation among retirement specialists. Specialists are usually seeking improved and new materials, methods, and content for their programs. The issue focuses on the extent to which sharing occurs among professionals. If the retirement planner is a private consultant with a new or unique program, he or she may be unwilling to share information for fear of losing the competitive edge. Retirement-consulting and financial-planning organizations may have developed extensive programs that cost large sums of money to produce the best programs. They, thus, may be reluctant to share program information. Retirement specialists, who have personnel or pension responsibilities within a corporate setting may have less to lose in sharing their program since their function does not depend exclusively on seeking out independent clients.

However, a new trend is developing among corporate financial institutions—primarily, banks and savings and loans. Many of these institutions are expanding their internal preretirement programs to the general community, using their programs as a public service and business development tool. Thus, competition exists here also. Although retirement services are provided in a competitive environment, there are indications that retirement specialists and their institutions are interested in continued growth and development. They are eager to attend and participate in professional organizations, courses, conferences, and discussion groups, as well as to publish articles that provide new insights into this growing field.

Implications for Retirement Specialists

If the field of retirement preparation is to reflect the growing needs of preretirees in U.S. society, traditional programs that assume that all adults move out of the labor force to a nonwork existence must be critically examined. Several trends that have emerged have shifted attention from aging and retirement to aging and work. First, although early retirements are continuing, there is some indication that the rate may be decreasing. Second, people are living longer, resulting in more years to assume a vital and productive role in society. Third, many workers have been affected by inflation and need additional revenue for an adequate retirement income. Fourth, multiple careers are becoming more prevalent. Fifth, the U.S. Government has passed legislation raising the mandatory retirement age to 70 years and has passed Social Security legislation that will increase the age to receive full retirement benefits. These trends are likely to encourage continued employment and to delay labor force exits.

What does this mean for the retirement specialist? Middle-aged and older workers are likely to approach retirement in new ways. Retirement may not be full time or permanent; it may be partial or phased where the individual works part time—part week, month, or year—and devotes the remainder of his or her time to activities independent from the primary employer. Retirement may be the withdrawal from one position and the acceptance of a new one. It may be a period of preparing for a new career or searching for part-time employment. Support for part-time employment rather than total retirement was found in a Louis Harris poll (1981) that indicated 79 percent of workers aged 55 to 64 years preferred part-time paid work after retiring. The same preference was expressed by 75 percent of the total labor force sample.

Programs must be designed to respond to the emerging needs of this population. Retirement specialists frequently report that all of their participants intend to take full and permanent retirement. This is not disputed. However, what would occur if the notice or invitation to the seminar included, as part of its curriculum, a component on career development, improvement of job-seeking skills, and a listing of employment opportunities? It is likely that such an announcement would attract participants interested in partial retirement and employment. If new programs and services are going to be developed, additional knowledge will be required of the specialist: elements of career development including interest and ability tests and psychometrics; job-seeking skills of résumè writing and interviewing; and knowledge of growth areas of employment—in particular, career opportunities for older persons.

The role of the retirement specialist can expand to respond to inquiries and needs of employer institutions. Employers have multiple concerns about their aging work force: labor force projections and needs, benefits packages, health-care costs, cost implications of phased retirement and part-time work, recruitment strategies, retraining of older workers, rehiring of retirees, and age discrimination. The retirement specialist, currently the only expert on aging recognized and accepted in the work place, has the opportunity to become knowledgeable and skilled in these described areas, which collectively may be termed *industrial gerontology.*

According to Sprague, industrial gerontology is the "study of employment and retirement problems of middle-aged and older workers. It deals with the employment problem relating to age . . . and continues with retirement." It is a "new applied social science subdiscipline" (Sheppard 1970, p. v).

The retirement specialist will be in a position to respond to institutional age-related needs with additional education, training, and experience. Several universities are offering courses, certificates, and internships that relate to industrial gerontology. The curriculum for such programs includes the aging process, policy issues, economics of retirement, retirement planning, managing the older worker, aging and the law, and compensation/benefits for an aging work force. Curricula at schools of business administration offer an important context for an industrial gerontology specialization, which may encourage individuals to pursue certificates or degrees in both business and gerontology. These two disciplines may be combined to address the aging, employment, retirement, and management issues in relationship to an aging work force.

The primary challenge for the retirement specialist is to provide a service to middle-aged and older persons that enables them to master their later years in work or retirement with the greatest fulfillment. A second challenge is to provide a service that influences the work environment to utilize older workers most effectively, meeting the needs of the older person and the organization. Building on the existing knowledge, experience, and position of retirement specialists in U.S. society, these expanded programs and roles are timely, exciting, and greatly needed to ensure adequate preparation for the future.

References

Atchley, R.C. *The Sociology of Retirement.* New York: John Wiley & Sons, 1976.

Dennis, H. "Criteria for Judging a Preretirement Program." *Generations,* Summer (1982):62.

Donahue, W.T.; Orbach, H.; and Pollak, D. "Retirement: The Emerging Social Pattern." In *Handbook of Social Gerontology,* edited by C. Tibbitts. Chicago: University of Chicago Press, 1960.

Harris, L. *Aging in the Eighties: America in Transition.* Washington, D.C.: National Council on the Aging, 1981.

Kaplan, M. *Leisure: Lifestyle and Lifespan.* Philadelphia, Penn.: Saunders, 1979.

Parker, S. *Work and Retirement.* Boston: George Allen and Unwin, 1982.

Reich, M. "Group Preretirement Education Programs: Whither the Proliferation?" *Industrial Gerontology,* Winter (1977):29–43.

Sheppard, H.L., ed. *Toward an Industrial Gerontology.* Cambridge, Mass.: Schenkman Publishing Co., 1970.

U.S. Congress. House. *Preparing for Retirement: Crisis or Challenge?* Hearing before the Subcommittee on Retirement Income and Employment of the Select Committee on Aging. Washington, D.C.: U.S. Government Printing Office, 1978.

Webster's Seventh New Collegiate Dictionary. Springfield, Mass.: G. & C. Merriam Co., 1965.

Suggested Reading

Fischer, D.H. *Growing Old in America.* New York: Oxford University Press, 1979.

> This book presents a social history of aging in the United States. Major historical changes include the exaltation of age, the revolution in age relationships, the youth cult, and old age as a social problem. The history of retirement in the United States is woven throughout the text.

McClusky, N.G., and Borgatta, E.F. *Aging and Retirement: Prospects, Planning, and Policy.* Beverly Hills: Sage Publications, 1981.

> Multiple aspects of aging and retirement are presented, focusing on demography and economics of aging, aging and retirement planning, and personnel and federal policies. This book presents a good introduction to retirement and retirement planning.

Index

Administration on Aging (AoA), 15
Aging: and cancer, 12; and cardiovascular disease, 12; characteristics
of, in U.S., 7–28; and education,
21–22; and life expectancy, 22–23;
and health-care costs, 13–15; and
health status, 9–10; and hospital
stays, 10; and hypertension, 12–13;
and marital status, 19–21; and mobility, 10; and morbidity, 11; and
mortality, 13; and nursing home
stays, 10; and physician and dental
visits, 11; population, 7–8, 23–24;
and poverty, 17; process, 1–5
Allyn, Mildred, 159–65
American Association for the Advancement of Science, 22
American Institute of Research, 4
Audiovisuals, for retirement preparation programs, 159–64; incorpora-
tion of, 163–64; kinds of, 160;
locating, 159–60; purpose of, 159;
and retirement specialists, 164;
selection of, 160–61; titles, 161–63.
See also Retirement preparation;
Retirement programs

Birren, James E., 1–5
Block, Marilyn R., 129–40
Bureau of Census, 21, 22, 23

Consumer price index (CPI), 13, 45, 46
Cost-of-living adjustments (COLAs),
45, 46, 47
Counseling, leisure, 97–107; analysis
of individual, 101–2; assessment of
individual, 100–1; barriers to satisfying leisure, 98; books offering,
174; definition, 97; facts regarding,
98–99; group, 103–4; individual,
99–103; interview of individual, 100;
misuse of time, 97–98; referral of
individual, 102–3; and retirement
specialists, 104–5; vs. therapy, 99
Counseling, preretirement, 89–107;
approaches to, 89; and identity,
90–91; and marriage and family,

92–93; methodologies, 90; objectives, 90–92; and retirement
considerations, 92–94; and retirement specialists, 94–95; and social
loss, 91–92; and widowhood, 93–94.
See also Counseling, leisure
Counselors, retirement. *See* Retirement
specialists

Dennis, Helen, 189–98

Education, 4, 21–22; for financial
planning, 35–37; for minorities,
123–25; preretirement, 89; sources
for, 184–86; for women, 132. *See
also* Financial planning; Preretirement planner
Edwards, Patsy B., 97–107
"Eldering," 4
Employee Retirement Income Security
Act (ERISA), 47, 48, 135. *See also*
Financial planning, Pension plans
Employee Stock Option Plans (ESOPs),
48. *See also* Financial planning;
Pension plans
Employment: books on second careers,
174–75; labor force, 17–18; and
minorities, 111–12; policies, 18–19.
See also Employment options; Pension plans
Employment options: compressed work
week, 54–55; flexitime, 53–54; job
redesign, 57; job sharing, 55; job
transfers, 57–58; phased retirement,
55–56; and retirement specialists,
58; returning retirees, 56; role of,
53. *See also* Employment
Estate planning, 39, 135–36. *See also*
Financial planning; Pension plans

Family, retirement and, 92–93, 141–57;
adjustments for, 146–48; adult children, 151–52; aging parents, 152–54;
books on, 169–70; household tasks,
143–44; husbands and wives, 142–
43; and retirement specialists, 154–
55; sandwich generation, 150–54;

About the Contributors

Mildred Allyn is administrative assistant to the director of the Leonard Davis School of Gerontology, Andrus Gerontology Center, University of Southern California. She is editor of *About Aging: A Catalog of Films,* a resource of audiovisuals available in the field of aging that is now in its fifth edition. As a media consultant, she has reviewed films for professional journals in gerontology.

James E. Birren, Ph.D., is executive director of the Andrus Gerontology Center, dean of the Leonard Davis School, and professor of psychology at the University of Southern California. His research and teaching have focused on adult development and aging and aspects of human behavior in relation to age, such as perception, memory, intellectual functions, creativity, and wisdom.

Marilyn R. Block, Ph.D., has served as director of the National Policy Center on Women and Aging, University of Maryland, College Park, since its inception in 1980. Her research interests focus on employment and retirement concerns of protected workers, women, and minorities. Currently, she provides technical assistance in these and related areas to private industry, trade associations, and government agencies.

Patsy B. Edwards, M.S.Ed., founded Constructive Leisure in 1968, a privately owned leisure and career guidance service. She has written books and articles, conducted workshops and classes, appeared on radio and television, and consulted with individuals, businesses, and organizations on the varied facets of the use and abuse of leisure time.

Dorothy Fleisher, D.S.W., is an associate clinical professor in the School of Social Work, University of Southern California. Prior to holding this position, she was a policy analyst with the National Policy Center on Employment and Retirement at the Andrus Gerontology Center, University of Southern California, where she conducted research on older workers' interest in alternative work options. Her current interests include industrial social work and program evaluation.

Margaret E. Hartford, Ph.D., is professor emeritus of gerontology and social work at the Leonard Davis School of Gerontology and School of Social Work, both at the University of Southern California. Her teaching and writing focus on curriculum development in gerontology and social work, group theory and group work practice, postretirement and independence in aging, and retirement planning and adjustment. Her workbook, *Making the Best of the Rest of Your Life,* is designed for pre- and postretirees.

Carol Segrave Humple, M.Ed., is president of Retirement Designs of Irvine, California, and director of professional development and publications for the International Society of Preretirement Planners. Her professional interests are directed toward retirement planning and older worker management and training issues. She is co-author of *Management and the Older Workforce: Policies and Programs* and *Computing Your Tomorrow,* a retirement-planning self-study workbook.

Mary Jackson, M.P.H., is a program evaluator, statistician, and computer programmer at the Andrus Gerontology Center, University of Southern California. Her recent work is concentrated on statistical design and program evaluation in the area of employment and retirement.

Phoebe S. Liebig, Ph.D., is planning director and a policy analyst of the Andrus Gerontology Center, University of Southern California. For the past four years she has been engaged in research on retirement policies, especially in the areas of Social Security and state pension systems. She worked with the House Select Committee on Aging and is associated with the National Policy Center on Employment and Retirement at the Andrus Center.

David A. Peterson, Ph.D., is professor and director of the Leonard Davis School of Gerontology, Andrus Gerontology Center, University of Southern California, where he administers undergraduate and graduate degree programs in gerontology. He was director of training at the University of Michigan's Institute of Gerontology and director of the Gerontology Program and Center on Aging at the University of Nebraska at Omaha. His research and publications deal with the planning and conduct of gerontology instruction and the education of older people.

James A. Peterson, Ph.D., professor emeritus of sociology, is the director of the Emeriti Center at the University of Southern California. His latest books are *Widow and Widowhood: A Creative Approach* and *Aging and Life: An Introduction to Gerontology* (with Arthur Schwartz and Cherie Snyder). He is the director of the Journey's End Foundation at the Andrus Center, which has produced two films, "Journey's End" and "Grieving: Suddenly Alone."

Vicki Plowman, M.S.G., is a program developer at the Leonard Davis School, Andrus Gerontology Center, University of Southern California.

She is presently working on a project, Managing an Aging Workforce, which will provide training for managers of older workers. Prior to holding this position, she counseled multigenerational families at a family service agency.

Gordon P. Ramsey, B.S., is a tax partner in the Los Angeles office of Coopers & Lybrand, an international public accounting firm. He has national responsibility for the firm's practice in retirement-planning seminars and is the author of texts, monographs, and articles on financial planning and employee benefits subjects. He is a frequent speaker and lecturer for professional organizations and academic institutions.

Robert M. Tager, M.D., is a neurologist and health educator with a practice in Santa Cruz, California. He is an adjunct associate professor of gerontology at the Leonard Davis School of Gerontology, Andrus Gerontology Center, University of Southern California. He has been lecturing in the fields of stress management, health promotion, and various topics in aging for the past ten years and has written a number of publications in related areas.

Fernando Torres-Gil, Ph.D., is an assistant professor of gerontology and public administration at the Leonard Davis School of Gerontology and a research associate with the Research Institute, Andrus Gerontology Center, both at the University of Southern California. His research interests focus on social policy and aging, minority aging, and long-term care. His publications include a book on the *Politics of Aging among Elder Hispanics.*

Ruth B. Weg, Ph.D., is associate professor of biology and gerontology at the Leonard Davis School of Gerontology, Andrus Gerontology Center, University of Southern California. She is author of *The Aged: Who, Where, How Well; Nutrition in the Later Years* and writer and editor of *Sexuality in the Later Years: Roles and Behavior.* Her research interests are in nutrition, health promotion, sex differences in illness/health behavior and mortality, the middle and later years, and sex roles and behavior.

About the Editor

Helen Dennis, M.A., is a project director and lecturer at the Leonard Davis School of Gerontology, Andrus Gerontology Center, University of Southern California. She teaches a course on retirement planning and has developed and directs a training program on aging for managers of older workers. She is currently a member of the national board of the International Society of Preretirement Planners and president of the Southern California chapter.